Product Market Structure and Labor Market Discrimination

Product Market Structure and Labor Market Discrimination

Edited by
John S. Heywood
and
James H. Peoples

State University of New York Press

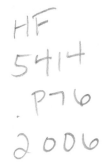

Published by
State University of New York Press, Albany

© 2006 State University of New York

For information, address State University of New York Press,
194 Washington Avenue, Suite 305, Albany, NY 12210-2384

Production by Kelli Williams
Marketing by Michael Campochiaro

Library of Congress Cataloging-in-Publication Data

Product market structure and labor market discrimination / edited by John S.
Heywood and James H. Peoples.
          p. cm.
Includes bibliographical references and index.
ISBN 0-7914-6623-X (hardcover : alk. paper)
1. Social marketing.   2. Discimination in employment.   I. Heywood, John S.,
1957–   II. Peoples, James.

HF5414.P76 2005
331.1—dc22

                                                                              2005006556

10 9 8 7 6 5 4 3 2 1

Contents

Tables

Foreword

Competition may be an American economic force, even a venerated social icon. But it is always under threat from monopoly power. Perhaps a quarter of U.S. markets have significant market power, and in many major industries, the market power is severe.

Market power has long been known to harm efficiency, innovation, fairness, freedom of choice, and even the democratic process itself. More recently it has been seen as a distortion working against fairness for women, African Americans, and other minorities in the markets for labor. It can reduce both the chances to get jobs and the rates of pay for the jobs that are gotten.

This book is a major contribution to studying those labor market impacts. It explores the issues from a wide variety of technical angles, of specific job groups, of gender and ethnic groups, and of countries around the world. The authors are eminently qualified, the writing is clear and crisp, and the conclusions are developed with great skill and objectivity. Moreover, the editors have designed a format that is logical and effective. And their introduction conveys the book's content lucidly.

This book sets a high scholarly standard. I trust that you will find it a pleasure to read and a fine source of technique and information.

Professor William G. Shepherd
University of Massachusetts

Preface

Most books require the efforts of people not listed on the cover page or table of contents. This volume is no exception. We owe great appreciation to our families for providing us supportive home environments and our colleagues and students at the University of Wisconsin–Milwaukee (UWM) for providing challenging work environments. Specific thanks are expressed to Richard Meadows, William Holahan and Sunwoong Kim at UWM for their support of our research efforts in general and this project in particular. We are especially pleased that this volume joins together colleagues with whom we have worked in the past, new colleagues with whom we have enjoyed working for the first time, and former students who are now colleagues in their own rights.

John Heywood gives special thanks to Susan Donohue who does her job so well that coming to work Monday mornings is always a pleasure. James Peoples gratefully acknowledges the long-term support and encouragement of the Ford Foundation.

Chapter 1

The Influence of Market Structure on Labor Market Discrimination

John S. Heywood and James H. Peoples

The motivation for this book comes from many years of involvement in an often acrimonious debate over the influence of increased product market competition on labor market outcomes. This debate is often phrased as whether product competition reduces labor market discrimination. The formal suggestion that it does reduce discrimination nears its fiftieth birthday as Nobel Prize winner Gary Becker (1957) first proposed what is often referred to as the "neoclassical" theory of discrimination. The essence of that proposal is that prejudice is costly. The desire to replace a more efficient worker with a less efficient worker because of preferences over gender, race, ethnicity, or religion reduces the profit that would otherwise be earned. Thus, asks Becker, which firms are in a position to "afford" these costs? As competition forces the economic rate of return to zero and only those firms with positive economic profit can afford discrimination, the firms in a position to act on their prejudice are those in monopolistic product markets enjoying monopolistic rates of return.

This relatively straightforward logic is subject to a rather long series of important caveats. Owners with prejudice may gain utility from discrimination and may be willing to pay for it in any market structure not just those associated with positive economic profit. Indeed, they may experience economic losses but value the utility they receive sufficiently to compensate for those losses. Yet, the more common story is one in which the managers who run the firm have prejudice, and owners, separated from operations of the firm, care only about profits. In this case, Becker's prediction depends on sufficiently severe agency problems that managers' discriminatory behavior cannot be controlled by owners or eliminated through the corporate takeover mechanism. In addition, the exact

1

impact of the prejudice on wages and employment depends dramatically on the underlying labor supply and demand elasticities at the product market, or industrial, level. Perhaps most importantly, the source of prejudice may be outside the direct authority of the firm. Customers or workers may be prejudiced and willing to pay more for a product sold by a particular type of person or be willing to work for less to have those same people as coworkers. In this case, there is no particular reason to anticipate that competition will fully eliminate the resulting discrimination, discrimination that can be in the profit interest of the firm. A full list of these and other caveats are found in Heywood (1998) but the point is that sophisticated observers have never assumed that increased competition will, in all cases and in all times, eliminate discrimination.

This view has often been lost in the sometimes loud cries of both supporters and opponents of Becker's original proposition. For instance Epstein (1992, 9) writes in strong support claiming: "Competitive markets with free entry offer better and more certain protection against invidious discrimination than *any* anti-discrimination law." In opposition, Coleman (2002) dismisses the Becker proposition as a largely unsubstantiated belief in "the magic of the market-place." In contrast to these rather hardened positions, the authors of this volume come to the subject with the desire to provide the detailed empirical work that delineates both the scope and limitations of the proposition that product market competition reduces workplace discrimination.

As will be emphasized, testing for the role of competition in reducing discrimination remains an area of vital interest. One of the most recent areas of testing focuses on international trade as an element of product market competition. Globalization has often been blamed for generating greater inequality within the U.S. labor force. Yet, Black and Brainerd (2004) emphasize that the true story is more complex and that while inequality across skill groups has increased due to foreign trade pressure, that same trade pressure has reduced the ability of U.S. firms to engage in gender discrimination. In nearly parallel findings from outside the United States, Hazarika and Otero (2004) show that foreign trade has dramatically increased product market competition in Mexico and that as a consequence of this increase, gender discrimination has been reduced in that country. Thus, despite nearly fifty years of being a "textbook" theory, the proposition that product market competition reduces discrimination remains under active debate.

Yet, while many of the chapters in this volume address this fundamental proposition head-on, we have tried to expand on the relationships examined previously in the literature. We hope to present a broader definition of the dimensions of the product market and trace some of these dimensions through to their potential influence on labor market treatment. Thus, chapters 2–5 can be viewed as efforts to examine the relationship between product market competition and discrimination in roughly the same vein as has been followed since Becker. Chapters 6–9 represent an effort to pick up new threads by focusing on dimensions of the product market beyond simply a measure of monopolization.

One of the valuable contributions of this collection is to expand not only to other dimensions of the product market but also to provide additional investigations from countries beyond the United States. Thus, the investigations of Germany, the United Kingdom, and Hong Kong are respectively among the first inquiries using data from those countries to explore the Becker proposition. There is no reason to think that the theory behind that proposition holds any less outside the United States. Indeed, other countries stand as additional laboratories for testing the proposition, laboratories that differ in labor market regulations, product market characteristics, and ethnic and racial makeup.

In the end, the collecting of the chapters in this volume has provided us all an opportunity to take stock of one of the potentially more important consequences of product market structure. If dimensions of the product market influence treatment in the labor market, the practical effort of detecting and punishing discrimination can be directed more effectively. Part of the profile in searching for and confirming discriminatory behavior may emerge as specific dimensions of product market structure. If to any extent the chapters in this collection can point to such dimensions, we will consider it to have been a highly successful enterprise.

We now turn to brief highlights of the chapters but emphasize that this but touches the surface. We encourage the reader to continue to the chapters to dig beneath that surface for a more complete sense of the findings, their limitations, their prescriptions, and their suggestions for future research. What follows is designed only to whet the appetite.

In chapter 2 Agesa and Monaco use a new approach to examine the influence of product market competition on racial earnings differentials. They note that the standard empirical approach estimates earnings equations looking for an effect of product market concentration on the coefficient associated with minority racial status. While many (but not all) of these studies find larger racial earnings differentials in monopolistic market structures, they also suggest that the association between market structure and racial earnings differentials may be limited to nonunion workers. They emphasize that unions standardize wages severely limiting the effect of many worker characteristics, including race, on earnings.

Agesa and Monaco argue that in addition to union status, the extent to which market structure influences racial earnings may be limited to workers with lower skill levels and earning potential. This argument returns to the notion that discrimination represents a reduction in the demand for minority workers (Becker). On the one hand, a reduction in demand will be translated into a larger earnings decline for those minority workers with a less elastic supply schedule and one might anticipate that the more highly skilled have a less elastic supply schedule. On the other hand, Agesa and Monaco suggest that the effect of a discriminatory decline in demand is more likely to be offset in the market for the highly skilled. This offset occurs on both sides of the ledger. First, the relative supply of highly skilled blacks is small, helping to maintain earnings similar to those of highly skilled whites. Second, there may be an offsetting demand for firms, and especially prominent firms with market power, to hire highly skilled black workers. This offsetting demand may be the result of public pressure and scrutiny directed toward these very visible positions and additional governmental attention by equal opportunity authorities (Shepherd, 1969).

Constructing data from Current Population Survey files, Agesa and Monaco divide their population sample by union status and estimate quantile regressions to examine the effect of competition on racial wage differentials at different places in the earnings distribution. The findings reinforce some old insights and provide some new insights. Within the union sample, market structure is not significantly associated with racial earnings differentials at any of the quantiles examined. There is also some evidence that the size of the racial earnings differential within the union sample declines in the upper end of the earnings distribution. Within the nonunion sample, less concentrated market structure is significantly associated with lower racial earnings differentials among those in the middle and bottom of the wage distribution. In contrast, there appears to be little or no influence from market structure at the high end of the earnings distribution but it is among high wage workers that nonunion racial earnings differentials are smaller.[1] These latter findings support this study's general hypothesis that competition may help shrink racial earnings differentials but is likely to do so among nonunion workers in the middle and bottom of the skills and earnings hierarchy.

In chapter 3 Belfield and Heywood examine a large representative survey from the United Kingdom. This survey includes linked employer and employee data. Thus, detailed individual wage equation estimates that control for specific worker characteristics and human capital can be married to extensive characteristics of the specific firm for which they work. This is an important innovation in the work examining the Becker proposition as much of the previous work has assumed that matching aggregate industry data on market structure to individual workers is sufficient. Yet, to the extent that there are differences in market structure across firms within the same industry this could be a misleading aggregation that might bias previous studies away from finding results that actually exist. An illustration of such a difference can be generated by dramatic asymmetries in market shares of firms within the same industry. Thus, we would not expect the latitude to express prejudice to be the same between a dominant firm and a firm in that same industry that is part of a competitive fringe. Moreover, the definition of the relevant product market from the point of view of the firm, as given in the survey, may be much more relevant than a matched governmental measure of industrial concentration at an industrial level that may be overly narrow or broad in terms of both the product and geographical market definition.

Belfield and Heywood examine gender earnings differentials in the United Kingdom, finding that within the set of establishments that identify themselves as being in a highly competitive product market the gender differential is approximately .12 log dollars per hour in favor of men. This contrast with the differential within the set of establishments that identify themselves as being in a less competitive product market where the gender differential is approximately .18 or half again larger than among the highly competitive establishments. Separating these estimates by union status brings a dramatic difference. Within the union sector, the highly competitive and less competitive establishments report more nearly similar gender differentials. Within the nonunion sector, the gender differential among the establishments in less competitive markets is more than twice that among the establishments in the more competitive markets.

The authors go on to examine the determinants of financial performance of the UK establishments in the survey. In particular, they find that those establishments with a large share of women workers tend to be more profitable all else equal. This is taken as evidence that women workers are "on sale," a direct implication of the Becker hypothesis. Thus, firms willing to avoid prejudice and hire those discriminated against by others will benefit from doing so. It is in this sense that Posner (1998, 716) claims that "the least prejudiced sellers will come to dominate the market." The evidence on establishment performance and gender composition is then divided by market structure with mixed results. In some specifications the influence of gender composition on performance is greater among those establishments in less competitive structures but this is not uniform. Thus, to the extent that the neoclassical theory would predict that the greatest gains to hiring more women would come from those firms in the least competitive markets, there is not convincing support.

In chapter 4 Jirjahn and Stephan exploit matched employer and employee data from Germany. Recognizing that output-based pay such as piece rates are unusually common in Germany (Jirjahn, 2001), they focus on the relationship between the use of such pay, market competition, and the gender earnings differential. Following past work on the determinants of using output pay, the authors confirm that when German industries are more competitive, their employees are more likely to receive output pay.[2] This follows earlier theoretical work arguing that heightened competition forces firms to rely on compensation methods that more closely tie a worker's earnings to their productivity. In a second stage estimation, individual earnings equations are estimated separately for both men and women. The estimation reveals that women receive a larger positive increase in their earnings from working under an output-based pay scheme than do men. Confirming increased earnings from such schemes is relatively common across estimations from many countries, reflecting, at least in part, the increased effort of workers in response to the incentives inherent in output pay. The fact that women receive a larger increase in Germany means that the gender differential among those earning output pay is smaller than that for those not on such pay. In turn, the authors argue, the fact that increased competition is associated with greater use of output pay implies that increased competition is associated with reduced gender earnings differentials

In addition to this indirect effect through output-based pay, the authors search for a simultaneous direct effect of competition on the gender differential. In their individual earnings equations by gender, the authors include a fixed effect for every employer in their sample. These fixed effects by gender are then subtracted from each other to provide a gender differential fixed effect for every employer. This represents the gender differential at each employer not explained by the regressors in the individual-level estimates. This gender differential fixed effect becomes a dependent variable in a third stage employer-level regression. Among the explanatory variables are two measures of product market competition: the domestic concentration ratio and a measure of international competition to which the employer is subject. The signs of each measure suggest a direct effect for competition but only the measure of international competition is statistically significant. When establishments are subject to greater international competition, there is a reduction in the gender earnings differential that is a direct effect and happens simultaneously with the influence competition has indirectly through increasing the use of output pay.

Several additional points on the German case are worth making. First, it provides an interesting case study for examining the role of collective bargaining on gender differentials as the level of the bargaining. The authors find that for men bargaining at the firm level tends to increase the earnings by a larger amount than bargaining at the industry level but that this is reversed for women. Second, none of the authors' estimates suggest that the combination of the direct and indirect effects of competition eliminate the gender earnings differential, which remains around 15 percent, even when controlling for the influence of output pay and the establishment fixed effects. Finally, it is interesting to note that the share of women within the establishment is an important determinant of the gender differential fixed effect. The gender differential within the firm is larger as the share of women grows.

In chapter 5 Heywood and Wei present empirical results from Hong Kong. They use data they collected in the months immediately prior to the return of Hong Kong to China in the summer of 1997. They use a sample of establishments to investigate the determinants of gender composition. The authors make the case that Hong Kong is a unique laboratory as it is frequently identified as the single most competitive and unregulated labor market in the world. Importantly, the data was collected during a period in which there were no formal prohibitions on gender discrimination. Thus, they provide a snapshot available in few U.S. studies, one in which the pattern of gender hiring is not influenced by governmental policies.

In setting the stage the authors point out Hong Kong's unique success despite the absence of prohibitions on gender discrimination. Female earnings are, on average, 84 percent of male earnings, a ratio higher than that in the United States, the United Kingdom, and Canada. Nonetheless, the majority of the gender earnings gap in Hong Kong cannot be explained by typical controls. Moreover, there has been a strong tendency for women to be concentrated in particular types of occupations and industries.

The authors use the share of female workers in an establishment as a dependent variable in a series of log-odds estimations. Despite using nearly two dozen relevant controls, the role of market structure emerges very strongly. Those establishments that dominate their product market are projected to have a female share of employees that is as much as 13 percentage points lower than those establishments in more competitive product markets. This is an enormous difference given that the average female share of employment is 44 percent and that the estimate holds constant many statistically significant controls such as industry and occupation, the age of the establishment, and the tenure of the workers, as well as others.

The authors bring the reader up to date on the institutional changes in Hong Kong, including the establishment of an equal opportunities commission empowered with legislation prohibiting gender discrimination. The results of the establishment estimations might inform the actions of the commission, encouraging it to concentrate detection and enforcement resources in those product markets dominated by a few firms. Finally, the authors are careful to point out that their data do not allow estimation of typical individual-level earnings equations and that the role of product market structure in determining earnings and gender earnings differentials in Hong Kong remains for future research.

While each of the previous chapters involve measuring the extent of product market competition across industries on an economy-wide basis, the next set of chapters move beyond that single dimension of the product market.

In chapter 6 Peoples and Talley examine the effect of privatization on racial earnings differentials in the public sector. Most research examining the effect of competition on racial earnings disparities focus on wage patterns in the private sector. The lack of research on public sector disparities seems warranted since the environment in this sector is less supportive of earnings discrimination. For instance, public sector employers traditionally faced both strict enforcement of Equal Employment Opportunity Commission guidelines and a highly organized workforce. Indeed, the adherence to equal opportunity guidelines may be a reason why the public service sector is a major source of high wage jobs for minorities. Nonetheless, racial earnings differential might still arise across employers in the public sector. Indeed, the existing empirical evidence suggests that while racial earnings differentials are smaller in the public sector than in the private sector, they are not zero (Heywood, 1989).

While a large percentage of blacks reside in southern localities that are rural, nonunion, and pay relatively low public sector wages, a large percentage of blacks also reside in large, heavily unionized metropolitan areas paying relatively high public sector wages. These residency patterns take on importance when estimating the consequences of the increasing tendency to privatize local public services. Peoples and Talley use Sam Peltzman's political economy model to identify the effect of privatization on black–white earnings differentials. They hypothesize that privatization occurs mainly in large high wage metropolitan areas where a disproportionate share of blacks reside and where public sector racial earnings differentials may be smaller. Given both the threat of competitive privatization and these racial residency patterns, Peoples and Talley argue that privatization maybe associated with smaller racial earnings differentials.

The mean earnings in this study show smaller racial earnings differentials for the privatized versus the nonprivatized municipalities. Black municipal workers residing in privatized localities that pay high public wages explains the small racial earnings premiums. Multivariate estimation results indicate that differences in the characteristics of local public sector workers across privatized and nonprivatized localities help explain the smaller racial earnings differentials in these localities. Despite this, in three of the four public services with a significant negative racial differential, privatization continues to emerge with a large and positive interaction with race indicating a narrowing of the local public sector racial earnings differential. These smaller public sector racial differentials in locations that have privatized closely resemble the racial earnings differentials reported for private businesses providing the same public service. The authors suggest that a pro-competitive policy such as privatization may contribute as much to lower racial earnings differentials in the public sector as increased structural competition does in a private sector market.

The succeeding chapter by Baldwin focuses on customer prejudice toward the disabled, arguing that the nature of product market remains an important determinant. Customer prejudice was one of the original sources of discrimination cited by Becker. Examining discrimination of the disabled presents special research challenges such as distinguishing health-related limitations on productivity from the effects of discrimination. Yet, the heterogeneity of the disabled provides a unique opportunity to test alternative theories of discrimination. Specifically, the heterogeneity allows distinguishing disabilities that are more or less observable. These distinctions, in part, allow Baldwin to test for the influence of disability-related discrimination by customers.

Baldwin also identifies whether workers' job responsibilities require direct contact with customers. Having customer contact is an obvious necessary condition for the prejudice of customers to influence the employment conditions of the disabled. Making this assessment allows estimating the probability that disabled workers attain jobs that might involve visibly serving prejudiced customers. While those with visible disabilities are less likely to be in jobs requiring customer contact, Baldwin finds large disability wage discounts for men in jobs that require greater customer contact than in those that do not require such contact. Moreover, the more visible the impairment, the greater are the earnings loss for those in jobs requiring customer contact. These findings combine to support the notion that prejudice is the source of discriminatory earnings patterns and that this prejudice emanates, at least in part, from customers.

Identifying consumer prejudice as a determinant of earnings and employment for disabled workers is important because it indicates that antidiscrimination legislation aimed at employers may have limited success eliminating labor market disparities faced by the disabled. This follows because if customers are the source of prejudice, discriminatory behavior by the employer can be important for maximizing profit. Indeed, Baldwin reports that even as earnings disparities have eroded following the antidiscrimination laws, disabled men still face substantial, and even growing, employment discrimination. Competitive market structure with many firms allows those customers that do not have prejudice to purchase from nondiscriminatory employers; while a monopolistic firm will be discriminatory if most, or perhaps even many, customers have prejudice.

The chapter by Husbands Fealing and Peoples examines whether pro-competitive policies in network industries reduce racial employment disparities. The advantage of examining network industries is that businesses in these industries experienced both government policies, encouraging stepped-up competition and antidiscrimination legislation and enforcement. Hence, this study is able to compare the effectiveness of both government equal opportunity intervention and product market changes on racial employment disparities.

During the civil rights era antidiscrimination legislation and enforcement targeted racial employment disparities in several network industries. The success of these policies could be influenced by the industry market structure. William Shepherd (1969) argues that national monopolies are most likely to adhere to equal employment guidelines because they are secure enough to take such measures. This chapter reports evidence supporting Shepherd's argument. During the civil rights era, the most impressive employment gains by minorities occurred in the monopolistic telecommunications industry. Less impressive minority employment gains occurred in rail, airlines, and public utilities. The least impressive minority employment gains during the civil rights era were in trucking. These employment trends prompt the questions, Would pro-competitive deregulation further contribute to minority employment gains in telecommunications, rail, airlines, and public utilities, and would any minority employment gains arise in trucking? Husbands Fealing and Peoples contend that deregulation should help the telecommunications industry at least sustain its impressive minority employment record. The inherently competitive trucking industry, though, presents the best opportunity for postderegulation employment gains by minorities given this industry's low barriers to entry and the elastic labor supply schedule faced by truck drivers.

The authors' statistical evidence shows a complete erosion of employment disparities among black and white union drivers following deregulation. Occupational employment results for the five network industries reveal that minority employment gains made immediately after the implementation of civil rights era affirmative action policies were sustained following economic deregulation even as some of those policies became less binding. Husbands Fealing and Peoples interpret these employment findings as suggesting that pro-competitive policies such as deregulation are most likely to discourage employment discrimination in industries with low barriers to entry and highly elastic labor supply.

In chapter 9 Heywood and O'Halloran argue that the method of payment influences the racial pattern of earnings. They present a model that shows workers receiving performance-related pay tend to have smaller racial earnings gaps than those paid time rates. They argue that this follows because prejudice is harder to translate into differential earnings treatment in the face of objective evidence presented by a piece rate or commission-based pay plan. Moreover, the probability of detecting such differential earnings is greater when objective evidence (say, the evidence on sales associated with commissions) does not support those differences. In short, the cost to discrimination becomes greater when pay is tightly tied to objective measures of performance suggesting that less discrimination should be observed.

Heywood and O'Halloran review the evidence from the economics of personnel, predicting the determinants of productivity-based payment schemes. The review isolates that jobs associated with a narrow range of tasks and jobs with little teamwork most often involve productivity, or performance, pay. Importantly, the review isolates the important role played by product market competition. Often, when markets are highly competitive, firms attempt to better link pay and productivity, and previous research confirms a strong positive link between product market competition and the use of performance pay. Hence, the authors suggest an alternative mechanism through which product market competition and earnings discrimination may be linked. Increased competition brings greater reliance on payment methods that more closely link pay and performance, and the presence of this link serves to reduce earnings differentials.

Using panel data from the National Longitudinal Survey, the authors reveal a robust relationship between racial earnings differentials and the method of pay. They show that racial earnings differentials are consistently lower among those workers paid by piece rates or commissions than among those paid time rates. This picture is confirmed by the finding that the additional earnings associated with performance pay are actually larger for racial minorities than for whites. In other words, minorities have more to gain from performance pay, in part because they are associated with reduced racial earnings differentials. Interestingly, the authors also show that the earnings differential is the very highest among those who are paid bonuses based on a supervisor's rating. This is the very opposite of objective performance pay. It is pay determined by subjective evaluation. Both this finding on bonuses and the more general finding on performance pay suggest the importance of objective measures of productivity as part of the pay process in reducing earnings differentials. The authors' findings persist in panel estimates and after correcting for sample selection.

Importantly, the influence of payment methods on racial differentials is not matched by an analogous influence on gender earnings differentials. On the one hand, this may suggest that gender differentials have other roots that are not altered by a more objective payment scheme. On the other hand, the authors tend to favor the view that women are disproportionately attracted to jobs with individual performance pay because they involve less teamwork. Women balancing home and work value a job in which there is less teamwork (duties that must be done together with other workers at a place of employment) as it provides greater flexibility. According to this view, the authors suggest it is possible that the continued large negative gender differential among women paid performance pay may represent, to some unknown degree, a compensating differential associated with value of this flexibility.

The early chapters help provide bounds for the estimates of the influence of product market competition on reducing racial and gender discrimination. The estimates do not suggest that competition is magic and will always completely eliminate discrimination. Most of the studies show significant gender and race differentials even under reasonably competitive product market structures. Yet, neither do the estimates suggest that competition is powerless. Competition is associated with reduced racial earnings differentials in the middle and bottom of the nonunion U.S. wage distribution. It is associated with smaller estimated gender earnings differentials in both the United Kingdom and Germany. It is associated with more nearly equitable employment distributions for women in Hong Kong.

The later chapters expand the types of discrimination examined and the dimensions of product market structure considered. Again, the new dimensions examined appear influential. When the product market means that customers have contact with workers, those workers who have a highly visible disability will suffer greater earnings penalties for their disability. When production allows individual output to be determined and rewarded, racial earnings differentials are lower.

Notes

1. Indeed, it is interesting to note that if one includes the interaction term of race and market structure (only weakly significant at the 10 percent level), the estimated racial earnings differential at the 90th percentile of the earnings distribution among firms with market power is essentially zero.

2. Brown and Heywood (2003) provide a recent review of the international evidence on the association between output-based pay and market structure.

References

Becker, Gary S. *The Economics of Discrimination*. Chicago: University of Chicago Press, 1957.

Black, Sandra E., and Elizabeth Brainerd. "Importing Equality? The Impact of Globalization on Gender Discrimination." *Industrial and Labor Relations Review* 57 (2004): 540–59.

Brown, Michelle, and John S. Heywood. "The Determinants of Incentive Schemes: Australian Panel Data." *Australian Bulletin of Labour* 29 (2003): 218–35.

Coleman, Major G. "Contesting the Magic of the Market-place: Black Employment and Business Concentration in the Urban Context." *Urban Studies* 39 (2002): 1793–1818.

Epstein, Richard A. *Forbidden Grounds: The Case against Employment Discrimination Laws*. Cambridge, MA: Harvard University Press, 1992.

Hazarika, Gautam, and Rafael Otero. "Foreign Trade and the Gender Earnings Differential in Urban Mexico." *Journal of Economic Integration* 19 (2004): 353–73.

Heywood, John S. "Regulated Industries and Measures of Earnings Discrimination." In *Regulatory Reform and Labor Markets*, ed. James H. Peoples, 287–324. Boston: Kluwer Academic Publishers, 1998.

———. "Wage Discrimination by Race and Gender in the Public and Private Sectors." *Economic Letters* 29 (1989): 99–102.

Jirjahn, Uwe. "The German Experience with Performance Pay." In *Paying for Performance: An International Comparison*, ed. Michelle Brown and John S. Heywood, 148–78. Armonk, NY: M. E. Sharpe Publishers, 2002.

Posner, Richard A. *Economic Analysis of Law*. 5th ed. New York: Aspen Publishers, 1998.

Shepherd, William G. "Market Power and Racial Discrimination in White Collar Employment." *Antitrust Bulletin* 14 (1969): 141–61.

Chapter 2

Market Power and Racial Earnings
A Quantile Regression Approach

Jacqueline Agesa and Kristen Monaco

Introduction

Neoclassical theories of labor market discrimination suggest that profit in noncompetitive industries gives employers the latitude to engage in discrimination (Becker, 1957). Thus, discrimination is at least partly driven by market structure, and the intense pressure to reduce cost in fiercely competitive industries reduces employers' latitude to engage in discrimination. Recent presentations of Becker's theory stress that the effect of market structure–driven employer discrimination differs by skill level (Heywood, 1998; Heywood and Peoples, 1994). In noncompetitive industries if there is an abundance of low-skill workers (resulting in labor supply that is perfectly elastic), discrimination will result in the underrepresentation of black employees while having little or no effect on the racial wage gap. However, in noncompetitive industries with highly skilled workers, with inelastic labor supply, discrimination increases the racial earnings gaps, while having little or no effect on employment levels by race.

Agesa and Monaco (2004) provide a recent multiple-industry empirical test of the market structure–employment discrimination relationship for high- and low-skill workers. They find support for the skill-based hypothesis: noncompetitive market structure reduces black employment among low-skill workers but has no influence on black employment among high-skill workers.

The skill-based model also suggests an analogous hypothesis regarding the effect of market structure on earnings discrimination. In particular, the model predicts that market structure–driven discrimination creates greater racial earnings disparity for high-skill workers relative to low-skill workers. This prediction, however, deserves further scrutiny. Despite years of affirmative action programs, high-skill blacks remain relatively scarce in the labor market.[1] The limited supply of high-skill blacks combined with those programs may put upward pressure on earnings for this group, suggesting that employer discrimination in noncompetitive markets may not result in the larger racial wage disparity among the high skilled.

This chapter examines the impact of market structure on earnings discrimination in U.S. manufacturing industries. We initially use ordinary least squares (OLS) to estimate separate wage equations for union and nonunion workers, allowing the impact of noncompetitive market structure on racial earnings to differ by union status. We then estimate the same models using quantile regression allowing the measurement of the black–white wage gap at various points over the distribution of earnings and skill levels. We find no evidence of market structure–driven discrimination for union workers (confirmed by Belfield and Heywood for the United Kingdom in chapter 3 of this volume). This supports the notion that standardized union earnings protect black workers from market structure–driven discrimination (Freeman, 1980; Peoples, 1994). Additionally, we find no evidence of market driven discrimination for high-skill blacks while confirming such an effect for low- and medium-skill blacks. These findings imply that union membership and advanced education and training provide black workers protection against market structure–driven earnings discrimination.

Prior Findings and Theory

The research on market structure and discrimination reflects early interest in agency problems and the ability of managers to engage in discretionary behavior (Williamson, 1963). The basic notion is that profit in noncompetitive industries gives employers the latitude for increased discretionary spending, resulting in excessive expenditure on workplace amenities (Edwards, 1977; Hannan, 1979; Hannan and Mavinga, 1979) and the payment of supracompetitive wages to workers (Peoples, 1998). Becker's early work (1957) provides a theory of labor market discrimination that applies this logic in explaining discrimination as a result of employers' increased latitude for discretionary spending in noncompetitive markets.

Past studies test the relationship between market structure and racial earnings discrimination by either examining the effects of a dramatic change in market structure in an industry (such as deregulation or privatization) on racial wages (Agesa and Brown, 1998; Heywood, 1998; Husbands, 1998; Peoples and Saunders, 1993; Peoples and Talley, 2001; Rose, 1987) or by examining the effect of market concentration on racial earnings across many industries (Agesa and Hamilton, 2004; Fuji and Trapani, 1978; Heywood, 1987; Johnson, 1978; Peoples, 1994). Single industry analyses find strong support for Becker's hypothesis, while evidence from multiple industry analyses has been mixed.

The single industry approach to examining the relationship was initiated by Nancy Rose (1987). Although the primary purpose of her analysis was to examine the effect of deregulation on earnings in the motor carrier industry, she presents evidence that increased competition of deregulation reduced the racial wage gap of drivers in the formerly profitable for-hire sector of the trucking industry. Peoples and Saunders (1993) expand this work by examining the relationship between deregulation and the wage differential separately for union and nonunion truck drivers. They find significant evidence that deregulation reduced the black–white wage gap for both union and nonunion drivers. The findings of Agesa and Brown (1998) find additional support for this notion. The sum of this work provides convincing evidence that the increased product market competition of deregulation decreased the racial earnings gap in the previously lucrative for-hire sector of the motor carrier industry.

Additional studies examine the racial earnings effect of other previously regulated industries. For the telecommunications industry, Peoples and Robinson (1996) examine the influence of the increased competition of AT&T divestiture on earnings and employment by race and gender. Findings of a clear racial wage effect of enhanced competition is not a forgone conclusion given that AT&T was subject to a court mandated Equal Employment and Opportunity Commission consent decree before divestiture. Their findings suggest that although employment patterns for underrepresented groups remained unchanged following divestiture, earnings disparity for minority males and white females decreased. However, decreased earnings disparity was also found for a control group of similarly skilled workers in other industries.

Heywood (1998) examines the effect of deregulation (in airlines, trucking, rail, and telecommunications) on racial earnings relative to industries that remain regulated. He finds a clear pattern of decreased earnings differentials associated with deregulation for all previously regulated industries except airlines. Because airline carriers competed on the basis of nonprice factors prior to regulatory reform, while engaging in rigorous price competition following deregulation, he argues that airline deregulation does not produce the marked difference in racial earnings of other industries.

With the exception of the airline industry, single industry studies find evidence that enhanced competition reduces racial earnings discrimination, however, multiple-industry analyses of the relationship have met with mixed success. Johnson (1978) finds that market concentration did not influence the racial earnings gap in the communications, the utilities, and the transportation industries. Fuji and Trapani (1978) find no evidence that market concentration significantly influences earnings discrimination in manufacturing industries. A shortcoming of both of these studies is the lack of industry detail. In both analyses, industry categories are broad, two-digit Standard Industrial Classification (SIC), which may conceal the variance from more precisely defined industries.

Heywood (1987), like Johnson, utilizes the Panel Study of Income Dynamics but his analysis follows 1980, when new, narrow, three-digit SIC industry definitions were included. Additionally, Heywood includes market concentration in the estimation of earnings, with a dummy variable for workers who are black and the interaction of race and market concentration as independent variables (along with other interactions). Such a specification allows the measurement of the differential impact of market concentration on earnings of black and white workers. The inclusion of such race–market structure interactions has been the standard in much of subsequent work on the relationship (Agesa and Hamilton, 2004; Peoples, 1994; Peoples and Saunders, 1993).

Peoples (1994) uses the Current Population Survey (CPS) to examine the relationship with an emphasis on the impact of unionization. As unions standardize wages, the relationship between market structure and earnings discrimination may be partly determined by both union density and union status. He finds no significant effect of market structure on the racial wage gap for union workers and a modest, but consistently significant, impact for nonunion workers. His findings illustrate the importance of controlling for unionization when estimating market structure's effect on the racial wage gap. Indeed, recent work that does not control for union status finds little or no evidence of a relationship between market structure and earnings discrimination (Agesa, Agesa, and Hoover, 2001; Agesa and Hamilton, 2004). However, the absence of unionization controls is particularly problematic given Peoples' findings.

In their analysis of employment discrimination in the trucking industry, Heywood and Peoples (1994) provide a theoretical model suggesting that the skill level of industry workers determines if discrimination results in the underrepresentation of blacks and increased racial earnings disparities. Consider two extremes. In a noncompetitive industry, if workers have low skills and so elastic supply to the industry, discrimination results in the underrepresentation of blacks while having no affect on the racial wage gap in the industry. The opposite is true for high-skill workers who have more inelastic supply to the industry. In a noncompetitive industry, if there is a limited number of highly trained workers for high-skilled jobs such that labor supply is perfectly inelastic, discrimination would result in increased earnings gaps, while having no effect on employment levels. Heywood and Peoples provide empirical evidence to support their theory with a case study of truck drivers (a relatively low-skill occupation with elastic labor suppy), finding that the increased competition from deregulation of the for-hire segment of trucking increased the prevalence of black drivers.

The preceding argument suggests that market structure–driven discrimination results in larger racial earnings disparities for high-skill workers relative to their low-skill counterparts. However, the overall level of labor supply of high- and low-skill workers is pivotal in determining the magnitude of racial earnings gaps in the markets for high- and low-skill labor. Suppose an industry is noncompetitive but there are a limited number of blacks with the required training and expertise necessary for high-skill jobs. While discrimination reduces demand for black workers, the limited supply of high-skill blacks moderates the influence of the reduction on racial earnings gaps. Indeed, the reduction in demand may even be smaller if equal employment protection is greater for those high-skilled occupations in which blacks have been traditionally underrepresented. Under this scenario, one might actually expect market structure–driven discrimination to result in greater racial earnings disparities for low-skill workers for which black labor supply is abundant than for their high-skill counterparts. Ultimately this is an empirical issue.

Data

To test the above hypotheses, we use data from the Outgoing Rotation Groups (ORG) files of the Current Population Survey from 1991 to 1996. As workers are observed twice in CPS ORG files, we omit the second observation for each individual. We limit our analysis to working-age white and black males employed full time in the manufacturing industries. We also remove "white-collar" occupations (managerial, professional, and sales) from our sample. This leaves us with a sample of 55,301 workers. We match the individual's three-digit Census industry code with industry-level data on the capital-labor ratio and plant size taken from the *1992 Census of Manufacturers*. Additionally, union density was computed from the CPS ORG. Industries are divided into competitive and noncompetitive classifications based on whether the four-firm concentration ratio is less than 65 (competitive) or 65 or greater (monopoly).[2] Descriptive statistics are presented in Table 2.1.

Table 2.1 Descriptive Statistics of Workers in Manufacturing Industries, 1991–1996

	Monopoly				Competitive			
	Union		Nonunion		Union		Nonunion	
	White	Black	White	Black	White	Black	White	Black
Number of Observations	984	138	1,477	175	13,051	1,806	4,054	3,616
Real Hourly Wage	$16.24	$14.96	$15.84	$12.59	$14.12	$12.60	$11.82	$9.83
Personal Characteristics								
Married	73.68%	65.94%	72.81%	65.74%	73.21%	60.02%	61.52%	48.44%
Separated, Divorced, or Widowed	14.63%	17.39%	11.77%	12.96%	12.73%	18.16%	11.70%	15.19%
Veteran	33.03%	25.36%	33.16%	31.48%	30.03%	26.85%	21.68%	19.76%
Less Than High School	11.28%	10.87%	12.12%	14.81%	15.98%	19.82%	21.08%	24.06%
High School	51.73%	49.28%	42.61%	49.54%	56.86%	51.66%	48.39%	50.24%
Some College	32.52%	32.61%	33.80%	28.24%	23.68%	24.42%	23.60%	20.90%
College or Higher	3.76%	5.80%	9.22%	6.48%	2.94%	3.43%	5.74%	3.93%
Experience	23.22	22.72	22.61	22.68	23.49	23.99	18.55	18.90
Experience-squared	648.36	597.80	652.69	660.38	677.23	713.25	495.39	511.06

(*continued*)

Table 2.1 (*continued*)

| | Monopoly | | | | Competitive | | | |
| | Union | | Nonunion | | Union | | Nonunion | |
	White	Black	White	Black	White	Black	White	Black
Occupation								
Technical	4.78%	2.90%	14.55%	5.09%	2.16%	1.77%	6.00%	3.32%
Administrative	6.50%	5.80%	10.78%	11.11%	4.47%	4.65%	7.23%	6.87%
Craft	41.87%	31.88%	39.07%	32.41%	31.51%	20.54%	32.67%	20.33%
Operative	36.99%	45.65%	27.48%	33.80%	42.41%	50.50%	37.04%	42.17%
Service	2.64%	5.07%	2.78%	5.56%	2.14%	3.16%	2.15%	4.23%
Transportation	3.05%	2.17%	2.38%	4.17%	8.83%	9.80%	6.76%	9.57%
Laborer	4.17%	6.52%	2.96%	7.87%	8.48%	9.58%	8.15%	13.46%
Macroeconomic Climate								
Unemployment Rate	6.45%	6.52%	6.51%	6.51%	6.40%	6.36%	6.45%	6.50%
Industry Characteristics								
Union Density	29.12%	30.56%	25.42%	25.13%	28.77%	29.78%	18.90%	18.91%
Plant Size	433.17	393.93	429.66	352.14	113.19	112.99	76.98	83.24
Capital-Labor Ratio	6.04	6.42	6.28	6.95	7.77	7.69	5.50	5.61

Separation of data by race, market structure, and union membership status allows the comparison of worker characteristics in each subcategory. Earnings of unionized blacks are roughly 90 percent of the earnings of their white counterparts—this is true for union blacks in both monopolistic and competitive industries. Nonunion blacks in monopolistic and competitive industries earn roughly 80 percent of their white counterparts. Thus, descriptive statistics of earnings of manufacturing workers in this period support the notion of standardized union wages (Freeman, 1980).

Table 2.1 also reveals that black workers, in general, are less likely than their white counterparts to be in craft occupation and are disproportionately represented in operative and laborer occupations. Consistent with past analysis, blacks are also less likely to be married or veterans.

Table 2.2 indicates the percent black in manufacturing industries in the 1991 to 1996 period at different quantiles of the wage distribution, providing insight into the labor supply of black workers at different skill levels. Overall, table 2.2 illustrates that high-skill blacks may indeed be in short supply. Blacks are prevalent in low-skill, low-paying jobs in the 1st to 25th quantile, comprising 15 percent of all manufacturing workers (column 1). Although well represented in unionized employment in noncompetitive industries (17 percent; column 2), low-skill blacks are most prevalent in nonunion employment in noncompetitive industries (20 percent; column 3), and union employment in competitive industries (18.9 percent; column 4).

As the skill level increases, black representation declines dramatically. Blacks constitute 10.7 percent of all workers in the 25th to median

Table 2.2   Percent of Black Workers in Manufacturing Industries, 1991–1996

	All	Monopolistic		Competitive	
		Union	Nonunion	Union	Nonunion
0–25th Quantile	15.4%	17.4%	20.3%	18.9%	14.8%
25th–50th Quantile	10.8%	9.6%	8.9%	10.4%	10.6%
50th–75th Quantile	8.1%	12.1%	5.9%	9.1%	7.5%
75th–100th Quantile	7.2%	10.1%	7.3%	10.2%	5.3%

quantile, 8 percent of workers from the median to the 75th quantile, and only 7.5 percent in the highest quantile (from the 75th to the 100th). Although the pattern of decreased black representation as earnings increases is not as smooth for all subcategories by market structure and union membership (columns 2–5), in all instances, black representation decreases roughly 40 to 70 percent from the lowest earnings quantile to the highest.

This pattern illustrates a reduced supply of blacks as earnings and skill level increases. The limited supply of black, high-skill workers will place upward pressure on the market wage for this group, thereby, reducing the racial wage gap created by market structure–driven discrimination. On the other hand, the abundant supply of low-skill blacks will decrease the market wage for this group, increasing the racial wage gap created by market structure–driven discrimination. Under this scenario we expect to find a weaker relationship between market structure and earnings discrimination for high-skill workers relative to their low-skill counterparts, indicating the decreased effectiveness of market structure–driven discrimination as the skill level increases.

Unionization may play a role in altering discrimination's effect on racial earnings inequality. Prior work suggests that the standardized work rules and wages in unionized employment gives employers less latitude to engage in earnings discrimination (Freeman, 1980). Further, recent work finds that there is negative selectivity to union employment for high-skill workers (Card, 1996). Taken together, these findings indicate that while unions discourage earnings discrimination among its members, many of the highly trained are not protected by collective bargaining agreements. Given that blacks are underrepresented among high-skill labor, then it is plausible that black, nonunion, high-skill workers are rare. Again, this group's high skill and limited supply increases its market wage (assuming a separate demand for black workers) and reduces wage gaps created by discriminatory employers in noncompetitive industries.

Methodology and Results

To estimate the relationship between market structure and racial wages we utilize ordinary least squares to estimate the following wage equation for manufacturing workers for the period 1991 to 1996. Specifically:

$$ln(wage_{i,un}) = a + bX + cY + dZ + f(black) + g(monopoly) \qquad (2.1)$$
$$+ h(monopoly*black) + u_i$$

$$ln(wage_{i,nu}) = a + bX + cY + dZ + f(black) + g(monopoly) \qquad (2.2)$$
$$+ h(monopoly*black) + u_i$$

where X is a matrix of worker characteristics, Y is a matrix of industry characteristics, and Z is a matrix of time controls. The worker characteristics include dummies for marital status (married and separated and divorced or widowed, with single omitted), region (Northeast, South, and West, with Midwest omitted), education (less than high school, some college, and college degree or higher, with high school diploma omitted), veteran, and union status. Dummy variables are also included for occupation (technical, administrative, craft, operative, transport, and laborer, with service omitted). In addition, experience (measured as age-education-6) and its square are included. Industry-level variables include plant size and the capital-labor ratio as well as union density. The controls for time include annual dummy variables. The omitted year is 1991. The monthly unemployment rate is also included to control for macroeconomic conditions.

The variables of particular interest are the dummy variables for black racial status (*black*), monopolistic market structure (*monopoly*), and the interaction between the two. The coefficient on black, *f*, captures the black–white wage differential in competitive industries. If discrimination persists in competitive industries then we would expect this coefficient to be negative. The coefficient on monopoly, *g*, captures the change in earnings as a result of employment in monopolistic industries. If workers share the rents of monopolistic market structure, then we would expect this coefficient to be positive.

The interaction between monopolistic market structure and black captures the differential impact of market structure on the racial wage differential. We would expect the coefficient to be negative if monopoly power allows firms to engage in more wage discrimination. Additionally, the sum of coefficients *f* and *g* provides the measurement of the black–white wage differential in monopolistic industries.

Table 2.3 (see p. 26) presents OLS estimates of racial earnings separate for union and nonunion workers. The coefficient on *black* is negative and significant across union status. Black union workers in competitive industries earn 10.0 percent less than their white counterparts. Nonunion blacks in competitive industries earn 11.7 percent less than nonunion whites. The slightly smaller racial wage gap in union employment relative to nonunion again provides some support for the notion that by standardizing wages unions reduce earnings disparity (Freeman, 1980).

Adding the coefficient on the interaction term, *monopoly*black*, to the *black* coefficient yields the black–white wage gap for workers in noncompetitive industries. The interaction term is significant for nonunion workers, but not significant for union workers.[3] Nonunion blacks in monopolistic industries earn 16.6 percent less than their white counterparts. This is larger than the racial wage gap for nonunion workers in competitive industries of 11.6 percent, providing support for Becker's hypothesis. The racial wage gap for union workers in monopolistic industries is slightly smaller than that for competitive industries and, again, is not significantly different.

The coefficient on *monopoly* measures the wage premium from noncompetitive industries that accrues to white workers. This is positive and significant for both union and nonunion workers (12.1 percent and 11.3 percent, respectively), indicating the presence of substantial rents for workers in monopolistic industries. Unionized blacks in monopolistic industries receive similar rents from monopolistic structure as whites.[4] In contrast, the sum of the *monopoly* and interaction coefficients for nonunion workers indicates that the returns to employment in a monopolistic industry is 6.4 percent for black nonunion workers, which is substantially less than the returns for whites.

These results support Becker's hypothesis for nonunion workers. Additionally, white nonunion workers are the primary beneficiaries of labor rent sharing in noncompetitive industries. In contrast, the black–white wage gap for union workers is slightly smaller in monopolistic industries, providing further evidence of the ability of unions' standardized wages to protect minorities from wage discrimination.

A shortcoming of using OLS is that it estimates the mean effects of correlates on the dependent variable. In our model, OLS reveals how market structure affects the black–white wage gap of the average union and nonunion worker, providing no information regarding market structure's impact on the wage gap elsewhere in the distribution of earnings. We have hypothesized that shifts in labor demand from employer discrimination may have different effects on earnings and employment depending on the relative racial labor supply of low-skill and high-skill workers. Quantile regression provides a less restrictive estimation procedure that allows the measurement of marginal effects of the covariates on earnings at different points along the distribution. We can use these results to test whether market structure's impact on the earnings gap differs for workers at various skill levels.

The quantile regression procedure estimates the θth quantile of the log of hourly earnings (y) conditional on covariates (Koenker and Bassett, 1978; Koenker and Hallock, 2001). The model denotes the θth conditional quantile of y given x as q_θ. Because y is linear in x, we can denote the conditional quantile, $q_\theta = x\beta(\theta)$ where the coeffiicent vector $\beta(\theta)$ is estimated as the solution to:

$$\min_{\beta(\theta)}\left\{ \sum_{i:y_i \geq x\beta(\theta)} \theta| y_i - x_i\beta(\theta)|+\sum(1-\theta)|y_i - x_i\beta(\theta)| \right\} \qquad (2.3)$$

where x is all of the independent variables utilized in equation (1) and y_i is the dependent variable above, the log of hourly earnings. This procedure was run separately for union and nonunion workers and standard errors that are robust against arbitrary forms of heteroskedasticity of the error distribution are obtained by bootstrapping (Buchinsky, 1994).

Table 2.3   Ordinary Least Squares Estimates of Earnings of Workers in Manufacturing Industries, 1991–1996

	Union	Nonunion
Married	0.0602***	0.1048***
	(7.29)	(21.17)
Separated, Divorced, or Widowed	0.0513***	0.0496***
	(4.94)	(7.18)
Veteran	0.0051	−0.0257***
	(0.84)	(−5.37)
Less Than High School Diploma	−0.1518***	−0.2183***
	(−19.57)	(−43.22)
Some College	0.0670***	0.0794***
	(10.59)	(17.47)
College Degree	0.1118***	0.2456***
	(7.44)	(30.96)
Experience	0.0239***	0.0247***
	(24.45)	(41.89)
Experience-squared	−0.0004***	−0.0004***
	(−18.27)	(−28.20)
Technical	0.2611***	0.4421***
	(10.90)	(30.74)
Administrative	0.0970***	0.2222***
	(4.72)	(15.87)
Craft	0.2059***	0.2994***
	(11.80)	(23.51)
Operative	0.0919***	0.1201***
	(5.32)	(9.47)
Transportation	0.0757***	0.1033***
	(4.00)	(7.32)

(*continued*)

Table 2.3　(*continued*)

	Union	Nonunion
Laborer	−0.0182	0.0270*
	(−0.96)	(1.94)
Unemployment Rate	2.1286***	1.4802***
	(6.43)	(6.38)
Union Density	0.3361***	0.0848***
	(15.96)	(4.96)
Plant Size	0.00002	0.0001***
	(0.59)	(6.03)
Capital-Labor Ratio	0.0028***	0.0035***
	(10.42)	(14.10)
Black	−0.1054***	−0.1243***
	(−12.92)	(−19.77)
Monopoly	0.1144***	0.1075***
	(8.33)	(8.82)
Monopoly*Black	0.0161	−0.0507*
	(0.53)	(−1.73)
Constant	1.8409***	1.6950***
	(60.69)	(82.50)
Number of Observations	15,979	39,332
F(21, 15957)	229.74	966.47
Adjusted R-squared	0.2311	0.3402

Note: t-statistics in parentheses. *significant at 10 percent level ***significant at 1 percent level.

We first present the regression results for the 25th, 50th, 75th, and 90th earnings quantiles for union workers (see table 2.4). The coefficient on black is negative and significant for union workers at each skill level; however, the magnitude of the coefficient declines dramatically as skill level increases. The black/white wage gap for union workers in competitive industries is 12.3, 10.1, 5.9, and 4.0 percentage points at the 25th, 50th, 75th, and 90th quantiles, respectively. These findings provide a more nuanced view than previous research on racial wage gaps for union members. The smaller average racial wage gaps for union workers in competitive industries in previous work (Peoples, 1994) are primarily the result of smaller gaps for high-skill union workers.

Table 2.4 Quantile Regressions Estimates of Earnings of Union Workers in Manufacturing Industries, 1991–1996

	Quantile			
Variable	25th	50th	75th	90th
Married	0.0926 ***	0.0554 ***	0.0542 ***	0.2586 ***
	(9.43)	(5.64)	(4.57)	(2.50)
Separated, Divorced, or Widowed	0.0768 ***	0.0409 ***	0.0444 ***	0.0124
	(6.13)	(3.23)	(3.16)	(0.96)
Veteran	0.0068	0.0015	−0.0111	−0.0197 ***
	(0.83)	(0.21)	(−1.62)	(−3.39)
Less Than High School Diploma	−0.1750 ***	−0.1546 ***	−0.1303 ***	−0.0886 ***
	(−15.37)	(−15.09)	(−12.40)	(−8.93)
Some College	0.0737 ***	0.0843 ***	0.0699 ***	0.0588 ***
	(9.34)	(12.05)	(9.62)	(8.80)
College	0.0685 ***	0.1284 ***	0.1320 ***	0.1310 ***
	(2.69)	(6.80)	(6.96)	(5.40)
Experience	0.0249 ***	0.0255 ***	0.0257 ***	0.0206 ***
	(18.99)	(20.61)	(21.57)	(13.81)
Experience-squared	−0.0004 ***	−0.0004 ***	−0.0004 ***	−0.0003 ***
	(−13.97)	(−15.47)	(−15.68)	(−10.78)
Technical	0.2963 ***	0.2351 ***	0.1862 ***	0.1840 ***
	(8.50)	(7.70)	(6.13)	(6.56)
Administrative	0.1157 ***	0.0953 ***	0.0522 ***	0.0410 ***
	(3.87)	(3.34)	(1.74)	(2.01)
Craft	0.2222 ***	0.1983 ***	0.1586 ***	0.1483 ***
	(7.93)	(7.29)	(6.22)	(8.09)

(*continued*)

Table 2.4 (*continued*)

		Quantile		
Variable	25th	50th	75th	90th
Operative	0.1196 ***	0.0908 ***	0.0589 ***	0.0501 ***
	(4.32)	(3.33)	(2.33)	(2.94)
Transportation	0.0970 ***	0.0660 ***	0.0304	0.0203
	(3.32)	(2.28)	(1.14)	(1.05)
Laborer	0.0074	−0.0195	−0.0705 ***	−0.0505 **
	(0.24)	(−0.67)	(−2.49)	(−2.48)
Plant Size	0.0001 ***	0.0001	−0.00003	−0.00002
	(2.78)	(0.63)	(−1.23)	(−0.82)
Capital-Labor Ratio	0.0032 ***	0.0032 ***	0.0027 ***	0.0020 ***
	(10.32)	(12.70)	(9.58)	(7.12)
Union Density	0.3265 ***	0.3955 ***	0.3775 ***	0.1717 ***
	(11.76)	(16.30)	(14.31)	(6.93)
Unemployment Rate	−1.755	0.6367	0.0543	−0.0373
	(−1.16)	(0.47)	(0.04)	(−0.03)
Black	−0.1315 ***	−0.1061***	−0.0612 ***	−0.0405 ***
	(−11.14)	(−9.05)	(−6.15)	(−3.97)
Monopoly	0.1173 ***	0.1422 ***	0.1256 ***	0.1031 ***
	(6.37)	(10.73)	(8.52)	(6.94)
Monopoly*Black	−0.0076	0.0609	0.0075	−0.0002
	(−0.13)	(1.42)	(0.24)	(−0.001)
Constant	1.877 ***	1.935 ***	2.215 ***	2.526 ***
	(17.27)	(20.19)	(20.64)	(30.30)

Note: t-statistics in parentheses. **significant at 5 percent level ***significant at 1 percent level.

The interaction term *monopoly*black* is not significant for union workers at any skill level; however, the magnitude of the interaction coefficient for workers at the 50th quantile is much larger than at other levels.[5] Although the individual coefficients on the interaction term are insignificant for the other quantiles, an F-test finds joint significance of the *black* and *monopoly*black* coefficients for each quantile. The coefficients on the interaction term are very small, however, suggesting there is no substantial difference in the racial wage gaps for union workers in competitive and noncompetitive industries.

The results of the quantile regressions also allow us to measure the earnings premium for employment in monopolistic industries by race, union membership, and skill level. The coefficients on *monopoly* indicate the monopoly premium for white unionized workers is 12.5, 15.3, 13.4, and 10.9 percentage points for workers at the 25th, 50th, 75th, and 90th quantiles, respectively. These findings suggest that monopoly rents are nearly evenly distributed to white union workers across skill levels

The black premium for employment in monopolistic industries for union members is indicated by the sum of the coefficients on the interactive term and *monopoly*. As before, F-tests find joint significance of *monopoly* and *monopoly*black*. The interaction term is only large at the 50th quantile. At this point in the distribution, the earnings of unionized blacks in monopolistic industries are 21.5 percent larger than those of unionized blacks in competitive industries. For all other quantiles there is little difference between the monopoly premium for unionized blacks and whites.

Quantile regression results of the earnings of nonunion workers in manufacturing industries are presented in table 2.5 (see p. 32). The black–white wage gap for nonunion workers in competitive industries remains fairly constant across skill levels, ranging from 10 to 12 percent across the earnings distribution. This is indicated by the consistently negative and significant coefficient on *black*. These findings are in contrast to the dramatic decline in the magnitude of this coefficient as the skill level increases in the regressions for union workers.

The sum of the coefficients on *black* and the interaction term *monopoly*black* indicates the black–white wage gap for nonunion workers in monopolistic industries. The racial wage gap is 21.6 percentage points for workers in the 25th quantile, 22.2 percentage points in the 50th quantile, and decreases to 12.0 percentage points in the 75th quantile. In contrast, at the 90th quantile nonunion blacks earn 1.5 percentage points more than their white counterparts.[6] These findings suggest that the effect of market structure–driven discrimination is high for low- and medium-skill workers and then diminishes as skill level increases. Note that the interaction with race is significant only for the first two quantiles.

Thus, the support for the Becker hypothesis from the median OLS regressions hides the fact that such support is limited to those with medium and low skills. Though this appears to contradict the original skills-based hypothesis (Heywood and Peoples, 1994), we again suggest that the limited supply of high-skill black workers decreases the racial earnings gap for high-skill workers. Recall that blacks are underrepresented in high-wage, high-skill employment (see table 2.2). Although market structure–driven discrimination produces larger racial earnings disparity for high-skill workers, the limited supply of high-skill blacks diminishes the resulting racial earnings gap.

We next examine the premium for employment in monopolistic industries for nonunion workers by market structure, race, and skill level. Again, the coefficient on *monopoly* indicates the white premium for employment in monopolistic industries for nonunion workers at each skill level. The white premium is 11.2, 14.3, 11.7, and 11.8 percentage points for workers at the 25th, 50th, 75th, and 90th quantiles, respectively. These findings are similar to those for union whites, indicating that monopoly rents are evenly distributed to white workers across skill levels.

The monopoly premium for black union workers is the sum of the coefficients on the interaction term and *monopoly*. The coefficient on the interactive term is negative, large, and significant for low-skill workers in the 25th and median quantiles (-9.75 and -9.49 percentage points, respectively).[7] The coefficient on the interactive term for workers at the 75th quantile is small and not significant. The coefficient on the interactive term is positive, large, and weakly significant for the highest skill workers at the 90th quantile (11.9 percentage points). These findings suggest that among noncompetitive workers, high-skill blacks are disproportionately the beneficiaries of blacks' share of the rents of monopolistic market structure (as low as 1 percentage point for low-skill blacks and 23 percentage points for the highest skilled).

Conclusion

This study uses quantile regressions to extend prior research on the relationship between market structure and discrimination. An advantage of quantile regressions is that they allow the measurement of the effect of market structure on the black–white wage gap for workers at different earnings and skill levels. The skills-based hypothesis anticipates that the racial wage gap would be larger for high-skill workers; however, we hypothesize that this gap will be diminished due to the relatively small number of blacks in high-skill jobs.

Table 2.5 Quantile Regressions Estimates of Earnings of Nonunion Workers in Manufacturing Industries, 1991–1996

	Quantile			
Variable	25th	50th	75th	90th
Married	.1157 ***	.1116 ***	.0931 ***	.0652 ***
	(21.30)	(20.11)	(16.10)	(8.52)
Separated, Divorced, or Widowed	0.0595	0.0557 ***	0.0407 ***	0.0176
	(6.90)	(6.09)	(4.67)	(1.38)
Veteran	−.0255 ***	−.0316 ***	−.0339 ***	−.0253 ***
	(−4.44)	(−5.81)	(−5.32)	(−3.46)
Less Than High School	−.2184 ***	−.2266 ***	−.2263 ***	−.2141 ***
	(34.38)	(-35.61)	(−30.39)	(−25.04)
Some College	.0799 ***	.0853 ***	.0916 ***	.0996 ***
	(13.67)	(16.45)	(16.80)	(13.80)
College	.1830 ***	.2626 ***	.3390 ***	.3915 ***
	(14.21)	(18.90)	(26.25)	(27.00)
Experience	.0211 ***	.0262 ***	.0304 ***	.0337 ***
	(28.02)	(36.70)	(38.92)	(35.96)
Experience-squared	−.0003 ***	−.0004 ***	−.0004 ***	−.0005 ***
	(−17.42)	(−25.10)	(−25.42)	(−23.92)
Technical	.4683 ***	.4502 ***	.4088 ***	.3967 ***
	(20.50)	(27.30)	(18.72)	(14.43)
Administrative	.2237 ***	.2161 ***	.1960 ***	.2289 ***
	(10.35)	(12.90)	(9.25)	(8.51)
Craft	.3115 ***	.3079 ***	.2800 ***	.2819 ***
	(15.56)	(21.33)	(14.49)	(10.93)

(continued)

Table 2.5 (*continued*)

	Quantile			
Variable	25th	50th	75th	90th
Operative	.1379 ***	.1289 ***	.1046 ***	.1113 ***
	(6.72)	(8.76)	(5.52)	(4.24)
Transportation	.1300 ***	.1081 ***	.0722 ***	.0656 **
	(5.53)	(6.60)	(3.61)	(2.29)
Laborer	.0624 ***	.0301	−.0019	.0078 ***
	(2.91)	(1.79)	(−0.09)	(0.28)
Plant Size	.0002 ***	.0001 ***	.0001 ***	.0001 **
	(3.92)	(3.94)	(4.19)	(2.81)
Capital-Labor Ratio	.0030 ***	.0040 ***	.0040 ***	.0041 ***
	(7.94)	(13.25)	(12.26)	(10.23)
Union Density	0.1005 ***	0.0943 ***	0.0955 ***	0.0448
	(4.36)	(4.42)	(4.15)	(1.70)
Unemployment Rate	−2.6331 ***	−1.1127	−0.5042	0.4601
	(−2.63)	(−1.25)	(−0.48)	(0.32)
Black	−.1263 ***	−.1359 ***	−.1184 ***	−.1099 ***
	(−17.84)	(−20.04)	(−15.76)	(−9.70)
Monopoly	.1054 ***	.1340 ***	.1106 ***	.1116 ***
	(6.28)	(7.93)	(7.59)	(6.32)
Monopoly*Black	−.1026 **	−.0997 **	.0080	.1126
	(−2.36)	(−2.06)	(0.18)	(1.78)
Constant	1.792 **	1.872 ***	2.039 ***	2.178 ***
	(25.77)	(30.12)	(26.72)	(21.16)

Note: t-statistics in parentheses. **significant at 5 percent level   ***significant at 1 percent level.

We find that unionization shields both high- and low-skill blacks from market structure–driven earnings discrimination. Further, the limited supply of nonunion, high-skill blacks neutralizes the wage gap created by employer discrimination of this group, while market structure–driven discrimination causes a black–white wage gap of more than 20 percentage points for both medium- and low-skill workers. These results suggest that past findings from multiple-industry studies that support the Becker hypothesis for nonunion workers are largely driven by the effect of market structure on the earnings outcomes of medium- and low-skill workers (Peoples, 1994).

The results of this analysis, taken in conjunction with previous work (Agesa and Monaco, 2004), have policy implications regarding racial discrimination of workers at each skill level. First, union membership in the United States has declined dramatically over the last three decades (Farber, 1990; Farber and Western, 2000) and we find that unionization protects black workers from discrimination in noncompetitive markets, suggesting that medium- and low-skill blacks are quickly losing a refuge from market structure–driven discrimination. Second, as long as low- and medium-skill blacks are abundant in the labor market, then nonunion blacks with these skill levels will disproportionately bear the brunt of the burden of market structure–driven discrimination. This is illustrated in both their employment and earnings outcomes. And last, if the lack of discrimination faced by high-skill blacks is largely the result of the dearth of highly trained blacks in the labor market, then policies that increase black representation in high-skill occupations may have the unintended consequence of increased earnings discrimination for this group.

A word of caution is warranted in the interpretation of our results. Our findings do not indicate that nonunion low- and medium-skill blacks are the only blacks who experience earnings discrimination. Indeed, we find evidence of racial earnings disparity for almost all groups of blacks (by skill level and union status). However, our findings provide original evidence that medium- and low-skill, nonunion blacks are the victims of racial wage disparity that can be directly attributed to employers' increased latitude to discriminate in noncompetitive markets.

Notes

We are grateful to John Heywood and James Peoples for thoughtful discussions and unending moral support.

1. See Holzer and Neumark (1999) for a review of the literature on affirmative action.

2. We recognize that while the use of such concentration ratios are common in this literature they may not accurately identify the exact extent of the market, properly account for imports, or be equally representative of all firms in the industry (see Belfield and Heywood, chapter 3 of this volume).

3. F-tests for joint significance of *black* and *monopoly*black* are significant (p < 0.001) for both union and nonunion estimations.

4. F-tests for joint significance of *monopoly* and *monopoly*black* are significant (p < 0.001) for both union and nonunion estimations.

5. F-tests for joint significance of *black* and *monopoly*black* are significant for each quantile (p < 0.001).

6. It is quite plausible that the black earnings premium for workers in the 90th quantile is the result of a compensating wage differential for unmeasured attributes. Indeed, underrepresented groups typically must outperform the norm when lucrative job opportunities are initially opened to a small set of underrepresented workers. In a discussion about female underrepresentation in the economics profession, Milton Friedman (1998, 199) articulates this view: "I have no doubt that there has been discrimination against women. I have no doubt that one of its results has been that those women who do manage to make their mark are much abler than their male colleagues."

7. F- tests of joint significance of *monopoly* and *monopoly*black* are significant (p < 0.001) for each quantile.

References

Agesa, Jacqueline, Richard U. Agesa, and Gary Hoover. "Market Structure and Racial Earnings: Evidence from Job Changers." *American Economic Review* 91 (2001): 169–73.

Agesa, Jacqueline, and Anita Brown. "Regulation, Unionization and Racial Wage Discrimination: An Analysis of the Trucking Industry." *American Journal of Economics and Sociology* 57 (1998): 285–305.

Agesa, Jacqueline, and Darrick Hamilton. "Competition and Earnings Discrimination: The Effects of Inter-industry Concentration and Import Penetration." *Social Science Quarterly* 85 (2004): 121–37.

Agesa, Jacqueline, and Kristen Monaco. "Industry Racial Employment by Skill Level: The Effects of Market Structure and Racial Wage Gaps." *Journal of Labor Research* 25 (2004): 315–28.

Becker, Gary S. *The Economics of Discrimination.* Chicago: University of Chicago Press, 1957.

Buchinsky, Moshe. "Changes in the U.S. Wage Structure 1963–1987: Application of Quantile Regressions." *Econometrica* 62 (1994): 405–58.

Card, David. "The Effect of Unions on the Structure of Wages: A Longitudinal Analysis." *Econometrica* 64 (1996): 957–79.

Edwards, Franklin. "Managerial Objectives in Regulated Industries: Expense Preference Behavior in Banking." *Journal of Political Economy* 85 (1977): 147–61.

Farber, Henry S. "The Decline of Unionization in the United States: What Can Be Learned from Recent Experience." *Journal of Labor Economics* 8 (1990): S75–S105.

Farber, Henry S., and Bruce Western. "Round Up the Usual Suspects: The Decline of Unions in the Private Sector, 1973–1998." Princeton University, Industrial Relations Section Working Paper 437, 2000.

Freeman, Richard. "Unionism and the Dispersion of Wages." *Industrial and Labor Relations Review* 34 (1980): 3–23.

Friedman, Milton. "A Comment on CSWEP." *Journal of Economic Perspectives* 12 (1998): 197–99.

Fuji, Edwin, and John J. Trapani. "On Estimating the Relationship between Discrimination and Market Structure." *Southern Economic Journal* 26 (1978): 556–71.

Hannan, Timothy. "Expense Preference Behavior in Banking: A Reexamination." *Journal of Political Economy* 87 (1979): 891–1009.

Hannan, Timothy, and Ferdinand Mavinga. "Expense Preference and Managerial Control: The Case of the Banking Firm." *Bell Journal of Economics* 87 (1979): 891–1009.

Heywood, John S. "Wage Discrimination and Market Structure." *Journal of Post-Keynesian Economics* 9 (1987): 617–27.

———. "Regulated Industries and Measures of Earnings Discrimination." In *Regulatory Reform and Labor Markets*, ed. James Peoples, 287–324. Boston: Kluwer Academic Publishers, 1998.

Heywood, John S., and James H. Peoples. "Deregulation and the Prevalence of Black Truck Drivers." *Journal of Law and Economics* 37 (1994): 133–55.

Holzer, Harry, and David Neumark. "Assessing Affirmative Action." National Bureau of Economic Research Working Paper 7323, 1999.

Husbands, Kaye. "Commentary on Regulated Industries and Measures of Earnings Discrimination." In *Regulatory Reform and Labor Markets*, ed. James Peoples, 325–62. Boston: Kluwer Academic Publishers, 1998.

Johnson, William. "Racial Wage Discrimination and Industry Structure." *Bell Journal of Economics* 9 (1978): 70–81.

Koenker, Roger, and Gilbert Bassett. "Regression Quantiles." *Econometrica* 46 (1978): 33–50.

Koenker, Roger, and Kevin Hallock. "Quantile Regression." *Journal of Economic Perspectives* 15 (2001): 143–56.

Peoples, James. "Monopolistic Market Structure, Unionization, and Racial Wage Differentials." *Review of Economics and Statistics* 76 (1994): 207–11.

———. "Deregulation and the Labor Market." *Journal of Economic Perspectives* 12 (1998): 111–30.

Peoples, James, and Rhoda Robinson. "Market Structure and Racial and Gender Discrimination: Evidence from the Telecommunications Industry." *American Journal of Economics and Sociology* 55 (1996): 309–26.

Peoples, James, and Lisa Saunders. "Trucking Deregulation and the Black/White Wage Gap." *Industrial and Labor Relations Review* 47 (1993): 23–35.

Peoples, James, and Wayne K. Talley. "Black–White Earnings Differentials: Privatization versus Deregulation." *American Economic Review* 91 (2001): 164–68.

Rose, Nancy L. "Labor Rent Sharing and Regulation: Evidence from the Trucking Industry." *Journal of Political Economy* 95 (1987): 1146–78.

Williamson, Oliver. "Managerial Discretion and Business Behavior." *American Economic Review* 53 (1963): 1032–57.

Chapter 3

Product Market Structure and Gender Discrimination in the United Kingdom

Clive Belfield and John S. Heywood

Introduction

In his classic study of nearly a half century ago, Gary Becker (1957) identified that nonwhite males held a lower proportion of manufacturing jobs in the southern United States in those sectors that were monopolistic than in those that were more nearly competitive. His study began a long line of empirical studies focusing on the association between monopolistic product market structure and racial and gender differences in the labor market. Despite the passing decades, this literature has been largely a North American literature and has not included contributions from other industrial democracies even though Becker's basic theory applies to any country. The purpose of this chapter is to examine the role of product market structure in the determination of gender wage differentials in the United Kingdom.

The rationale for such a study is particularly strong. First, there is continuing evidence of a persistent gender earnings differential in the United Kingdom, along with increases in wage dispersion and increases in female participation rates (Machin, 1996; Prasad, 2002). Second, there is substantial variation in product market structure across industries in the United Kingdom. Finally, and perhaps most importantly, the publicly available data in the United Kingdom are in many ways superior to that in the United States. The use of linked employee–employer data allows the wages of individual workers to be tied to the product market structure associated with their specific employer. Thus, unlike typical U.S. studies that simply match a worker to his or her broad three-digit industry and its market structure, the errors-in-variables problem can be minimized through a more direct link between worker treatment and market structure.

To limit our attention we focus in this chapter on estimating the influence of product market structure on gender discrimination as the variety of racial minorities in the United Kingdom is great and specific racial minorities comprise only a small share of the total labor force. In the next section we review the basic theory, predicting a role for product market structure in determining discrimination, and review studies that have estimated the link between structure and earnings discrimination. In the third section we introduce our data source and method. The initial results are in the fourth section and they confirm the role of market structure in determining the gender wage gap as measured by individual worker wages. In the fifth section we present two additional inquiries at the aggregated establishment level. First, we explore the share of women workers as a determinant of earnings and whether market structure influences the strength of this determinant. Second, we follow recent work in the United States to test whether gender employment patterns influence firm performance in the way predicted by Becker's theory of discrimination. The sixth section concludes.

The Link between Discrimination and Structure

Following Becker (1957), economists have long identified personal prejudice as the source of labor market discrimination. This prejudice might be held by the customers (Borjas and Bronars, 1989) or by the coworker (Buffum and Whaples, 1995) or by the employer. While each of these possibilities may result in equally productive workers receiving different labor market treatment because of their demographic group, it is prejudice by the employer that has received the greatest attention. Becker argues that discrimination is costly to the employer who faces a trade-off between satisfying prejudices and earnings profits. The extent of observed discrimination reflects the intensity of prejudice on the one hand and the cost of discrimination on the other hand. Firms operating in more competitive product markets have smaller rents and are less able to afford discrimination. Put somewhat differently, the cost of discrimination is higher in the competitive product market as reductions in profits threaten the viability of the firm. Thus, this popular view of discrimination differs from the view that discrimination is an information problem, that is, statistical discrimination, and from the view that discrimination is a profitable tool in which firms engage as a matter of explicit strategy as suggested by some renderings of the dual labor market hypothesis.

As Heywood (1998) argues, it is only the possibility of employer prejudice that generates strong predictions about the role of product market structure. If the prejudice rests with customers or coworkers, the firm has a cost-based rationale for discrimination that does not easily change with product market structure. For instance, if workers prefer to work with other workers of their own gender, it remains cheaper for the firm to hire a single gender workforce independent of market structure. Thus, confirmation of the association between measured discrimination and product market structure supports the contention that employers have prejudice while clearly not ruling out prejudice from other sources.

The link between earnings discrimination and market structure has been tested by a number of studies with varying success. Fuji and Trapani (1978) and Johnson (1978) investigated whether a less competitive market structure is associated with larger measures of earnings discrimination. The study by Johnson is particularly relevant as it foreshadows the extensive examination of regulated industries. Johnson concludes there are no differences in the extent of earnings discrimination across three broad sets of industries: competitive, oligopolistic, and regulated. Yet, Johnson's use of the 1972 Panel Study of Income Dynamics (PSID) forces him to assign workers to one of the three broad sectors based on two-digit industry classifications. In doing so, many of the relevant differences in market structure are lost and some workers are clearly incorrectly assigned (see Heywood, 1987b). Similarly, Fuji and Trapani are forced to divide manufacturing into only sixteen industries creating an error-in-variables problem and limiting the variance in the market structure variable, making it difficult to uncover an influence even if it exists.

Heywood (1987b) returned to the PSID once three-digit industry details became available. He assigned each manufacturing industry the relevant concentration ratio and identified a critical level through a switching regression technique. The extent of racial wage discrimination in the less competitive industries was substantially and significantly larger than that in the more competitive industries. Peoples (1994) used the larger samples of the Current Population Survey (CPS) to undertake a similar study that focused on the role of unionization. Despite a large overall sample size, some individual cells emerged with a low number of observations resulting in mixed patterns of statistical significance. Nonetheless, the overall pattern is generally supportive. Across many specifications and estimation variations, the extent of racial earnings discrimination for nonunion members is larger in the highly concentrated (ratios above 65 percent) industries. No differences in discrimination by market structure were found among unionized workers.

Rather than examine broad cross-sections of workers as these four studies did, more recent studies have tended to follow individual industries as their market structures changed. The change in market structure in these studies has been the deregulation of U.S. industries in communications and transportation. The idea that regulated industries might engage in greater discrimination is at least as old as Alchian and Kessel (1962). The presumption is that regulated industries are less competitive and that deregulation forces them to become more competitive (see Peoples, 1998). Thus, the researchers examine whether the extent of earnings discrimination decreased following deregulation as this presumption, together with Becker's basic insight, would predict.

Rose (1987) used the CPS and a single equation model that pooled union and nonunion workers to find that the white–nonwhite earnings gap in the trucking industry fell as a result of the deregulation of that industry. Peoples and Saunders (1993) estimated separate union and nonunion equations for those in the private carrier market and the for-hire carrier market. Deregulation was associated with declines in real earnings but these declines were largely among white workers. The conclusion according to Peoples and Saunders was that deregulation had "the apparently unintended consequence of ending black/white wage differences" (34). Agesa and Brown (1998) echo this conclusion, confirming that deregulation in trucking reduced racial earnings differences. Peoples and Robinson (1996) examined the consequences of the divestiture of AT&T, breaking out earnings patterns for a wide variety of race, gender, and occupational groupings. Earnings differentials did decline for nonblack minority men, black men, and white women in the telecommunications industry following divestiture. Yet, in fairness a similar pattern was evident for white women in the broader economy over the period they investigated. Heywood (1998) investigates the earnings differentials for blacks among samples of males in four deregulated industries: trucking, telecommunications, railroads, and airlines. Using CPS data from 1973 to 1991, in three of the four industries, deregulation was associated with a significant decline in the size of the black earnings differential. Only in airlines was no evidence of decline found. This is perhaps not surprising as the airline industry was engaged in competition before deregulation but it was a wasteful service competition. Thus, while deregulation changed the nature of competition in the airline industry, it did not make profound changes in underlying structure or behavior. Agesa (2001) makes just this point in explaining why deregulation did not change the racial composition of airlines as it did for other deregulated industries such as trucking.

Thus, while the evidence is not monolithic, there exists a variety of evidence linking more competitive product market structure with smaller racial and gender earnings differentials. As this short review makes clear, the empirical testing of this link has been largely focused on the United

States. Yet, as Hamermesh (2002) suggests, focusing on other countries provides the opportunity for testing theories with alternative data and institutional frameworks. We now turn to our examination of evidence from the United Kingdom and we will emphasize the advantages of doing so.

Data and Method

The data are drawn from the 1998 Workplace Employment Relations Survey (WERS), a nationwide survey of 2,191 workplaces across the United Kingdom. Information is collected from managers, from union representatives, and from a random sample of up to twenty-five workers per plant. Questions were asked on matters such as management of personnel, representation at work, collective disputes and procedures, and pay systems and pay determination (per Cully et al., 1999). We limit the sample to only those workplaces in the trading sector as market structure is often not meaningful in much of the public and nonprofit sector. This reduces the sample to 1,607 workplaces.

The managerial respondents for each workplace identify a number of crucial dimensions about the product market structure in which they operate. The three most relevant dimensions are detailed in table 3.1. Perhaps the most comprehensive question asks the manager to identify their primary product or service and then assess the degree of competition in that market. As shown, there is a distribution across the five possible responses but over 45 percent identify the extent of product market competition as "very high." Similarly, 55 percent of firms identify that they have "many" competitors in their primary market. Importantly, the degree of competition may be only poorly related to the number of competitors. Thus, a dominant firm may have many small competitors but the overall market may not be as competitive as if all firms were roughly the same size. A third measure identifies the market share for the firm's primary product across broad bands. Essentially half of the firms identify their market share as 10 percent or less.

The availability of workplace-specific measures of market structure in the WERS is crucial for at least three reasons. First, the relevant measure of product market structure may well be at the firm level. Shepherd (1972) contends that market power is a firm rather than industry concept.[1] Indeed, in their examination of market structure and employment discrimination, Shepherd and Levine (1973) argue for using firm-specific measures of market share. Second, the self-assessed firm measure avoids the inevitable problem of assigning firms to specific industries based on aggregated industrial codes. These codes often combine many

Table 3.1   Description of Market: Manager Responses

Description of Market	Percent
[A] How would you assess the degree of competition in this market?	
Very High	45.4
High	30.6
Neither High nor Low	10.2
Low	6.2
Very Low	7.7
N	*1,607*
[B] How many competitors do you have for your main product or service?	
None	11.2
Some	33.7
Many	55.1
N	*1,601*
[C] What is your company's UK market share for its main product or service?	
<5%	39.4
5–10%	11.3
11–25%	16.8
26–50%	14.4
>50%	18.1
N	*1,366*

Note: Data are unweighted. Only establishments in the trading sector.

detailed industries with very different market structures. As an illustration, in the United States the broad industrial code for food manufacturing" includes four-digit industries that range from soft drinks with a 15 percent four-firm concentration ratio to breakfast cereals with a 90 percent concentration ratio (Heywood, 1987b). Most current U.S. micro data include only three-digit industrial codes but the relevant market structure is surely determined at a far less aggregate level. The firm assessed measures avoid this problem. Third, the firm measures of the WERS can be combined with the individual workers of the firms. This allows tying the market structure of specific firms to the earnings of the workers in that firm. Despite this obvious advantage, linked employer–employee data has not been used to isolate the influence of market structure on earnings discrimination.

The market structure data are transformed into dichotomous variables to ease interpretation and estimation. The results are not particularly sensitive to modest variations in the cut-points. The transformed variables are shown in table 3.2 and reflect the sampling weights given in WERS. The three measures are positively correlated with each other but not so closely that they could be combined or a single measure used. Thus, we will proceed using each separately.

The individual workers within the workplaces form the ultimate units of observation and generate a sample size of 15,172. The individual hourly wages of each worker form the dependent variable to be explained by a large list of earnings determinates. These controls include the worker's union status, years of tenure and its square, marital status, ethnicity, education level (3), and occupation (8). Workplace-level control variables are whether the workplace is unionized, the age of the establishment, whether the firm has representative participation, a suggestion scheme, downward communication, and upward problem-solving. Also included are whether the firm uses profit-related pay, has share-ownership, is UK owned, is a single establishment, the share of manual (blue-collar) workers, the share of freelance workers, the share of shift work, and the percent of costs from labor. Finally, we include employer size and broad industrial sector dummies (12). This unusually long list of controls should allow us to accurately isolate the influence of market structure on earnings. Descriptive statistics for the key variables are presented in table 3.3.

Table 3.2   Measures of Competition: Manager Responses

Measures of Competition	Percent
[A] Very High Competition	0.47
[B] Number of Competitors	0.56
[C] Company's UK Market Share under 25%	0.64
Correlations:	
[A] and [B]	0.39***
[A] and [C]	0.05*
[B] and [C]	0.21***

Note: Weighted analysis. Only establishments in the trading sector.
    *p < 0.1 level   *** p < 0.01 level.

Table 3.3 Critical Variables: Workplace Level and Worker Level

	Mean	SD
Worker Level		
Log Hourly Wage	1.86	0.19
N	*15,172*	
Workplace Level		
Percent Female Workers	0.48	0.29
Log Median Wage at Workplace	9.55	0.32
Financial Performance Above Industry Average	0.60	0.49
Labor Productivity Above Industry Average	0.51	0.50
N	*1,361*	

Note: Weighted frequencies. Only full-time workers. Only workplaces in the trading sector.

The basic methodology is to estimate two log-linear wage equations: one for the more competitive sector and one for the less competitive sector as indicated by each of the dichotomous variables in table 3.2. In each case the extent of the gender differential will be estimated and comparisons across sectors will be made.

Initial Results

The basic results are captured in table 3.4. The long list of explanatory controls results in very high R-squared for cross-sectional wage equations indicating a good fit.[2] The overall estimate of the gender differential combines both sectors and is .155 log wages. For each of the three market structure variables, the gender differential is smaller in the more competitive sector. The most comprehensive measure, the assessed extent of competition, shows the largest change. The gender differential in the less competitive sector emerges as .175 while that in the more competitive sector is only .122. This difference of .053 is statistically significant and indicates that the differential in the competitive sector is roughly two-thirds of that in the less competitive sector. The differences generated by the other two measures of market structure are smaller but go in the same direction, suggesting the importance of market structure in the labor market treatment of women.

Table 3.4 Effect on Log Hourly Pay for Female Workers

Dependent Variable:

Log Hourly Pay	Female Worker		LR	R^2	N
	Coeff.	(S.E.)			
Full Sample	−0.1547	(0.0100)***	259.99	0.4934	15,172
High Competition Sector	−0.1216	(0.0133)***	140.54	0.5739	6,522
Low Competition Sector	−0.1751	(0.0102)***	166.62	0.5440	8,245
Some Competitors for Main Product	−0.1448	(0.0120)***	157.49	0.5605	7,599
No Competitors for Main Product	−0.1521	(0.0110)***	144.44	0.5576	7,074
Low Market Share Workplaces	−0.1518	(0.0116)***	163.90	0.5541	8,411
High Market Share Workplaces	−0.1592	(0.0136)***	106.56	0.5673	4,368

Note: Weighted estimation. OLS. Robust Huber-White standard errors. Worker-level controls are union worker, tenure, tenure-squared, marital status, ethnicity, education level (3), occupation (8). Workplace-level control variables are union site, age of establishment, representative participation, suggestion scheme, downward communication, upward problem-solving, profit-related pay, share-ownership, UK owned, single firm, ratio manual workers, freelance workers, shiftwork, percent labor costs (3), employment size, sector (12). ***p < 0.01 level.

Table 3.5 reproduces the earlier estimates but further separates the samples by union status. In U.S. studies this separation has proved important. Typically, unionized sectors in the United States have reduced race and gender differentials and the influence of market structure is substantially smaller or nonexistent (Peoples 1994; on wage dispersion effects for the United Kingdom, see Gosling and Machin, 1995). As the combined estimate shows, the extent of the gender differential among the union and nonunion subsamples is virtually identical and, if anything, slightly larger in the union sector.

The evidence presented by the first measure of market structure largely confirms what has been presented with both the union and nonunion sectors showing significantly lower gender differentials in the competitive sector than in the less competitive sector. Yet, the magnitude of this difference is not shared. The differential in the nonunion less competitive sector is a very large .195 log wage points while that in the nonunion competitive sector is only .084 log wage points. Thus, the difference associated with market structure is .111 log wage points. Put differently, the gender differential in the competitive sector is only about two-fifths of that in the less competitive sector. The evidence from the unionized sector is less dramatic but goes in the same direction. The gender differential in the less competitive sector is .163 while that in the unionized more competitive sector is .137.

The other two measures of market structure present a somewhat mixed picture. The number of competitors again shows that the more competitive sector has smaller gender earnings differentials in both the union and nonunion sectors. Moreover, as before, the difference between the sectors is larger in the nonunion sector. As with the combined union and nonunion estimations, the influence of market structure appears smaller using this second measure. Nonetheless, both of the first two measures support the importance of market structure in determining gender differentials and largely mimic the U.S. evidence that it is more important in the nonunion sector. The final measure presents a contrasting pattern with virtually no difference by market structure in the union sector and an anomalous reversal in the nonunion sector.

The initial results presented in this section largely confirm the prediction that more competitive market structures are associated with lower gender earnings differentials. This effect seems to be stronger among nonunion workers. In general, the evidence fits the notion that employer prejudice gets translated into discriminatory treatment in the labor market and that more competitive market structure limits this translation.

Table 3.5 Gender Earnings Difference for Female Workers

Dependent Variable: Log Hourly Pay	Female Worker Nonunion Sector		Female Worker Union Sector	
	Coeff.	(S.E.)	Coeff.	(S.E.)
Full sample	−0.1449	(0.0136)***	−0.1489	(0.0103)***
High Competition Sector	−0.0841	(0.0187)***	−0.1373	(0.0173)***
Low Competition Sector	−0.1951	(0.0193)***	−0.1627	(0.0118)***
Some Competitors for Main Product	−0.1308	(0.0169)***	−0.1423	(0.0158)***
No Competitors for Main Product	−0.1444	(0.0220)***	−0.1469	(0.0126)***
Low Market Share Workplaces	−0.1601	(0.0243)***	−0.1589	(0.0156)***
High Market Share Workplaces	−0.1306	(0.0181)***	−0.1586	(0.0148)***

Note: Weighted estimation. OLS. Robust Huber-White standard errors. Worker-level controls are union worker, tenure, tenure-squared, marital status, ethnicity, education level (3), occupation (8). Workplace-level control variables are union site, age of establishment, representative participation, suggestion scheme, downward communication, upward problem-solving, profit-related pay, share-ownership, UK owned, single firm, ratio manual workers, freelance workers, shiftwork, percent labor costs (3), employment size, sector (12). ***$p < 0.01$ level.

Further Estimations

This section follows up on two related ideas. First, we move to the establishment level to examine the influence of establishment gender composition on the median wages of the workplace. Second, we examine the links between firm performance and gender composition.

Gender composition of the workplace can be associated with lower wages for at least two related reasons. First, the greater the share of women, the more the median wage will reflect the consequences of individual earnings discrimination against women. Second, the greater the share of women, the more likely women in that workplace may be subject to crowding, which is thought to lower the wage. Thus, if women are pushed into a narrow set of workplaces, labor supply will be increased and the equilibrium wage will be lower (Bergmann, 1974; Blau, Ferber, and Winkler, 2002). Again, our methodology will be to divide the establishments according to the measures of market structure and estimate the determinants of the median wage.[3] The results of two sets of estimations are shown in table 3.6. In each case the share of women is associated with a lower median wage. Using both the self-assessed measure of competition and the measure of market share, the results are consistent. The influence of the share of women is smaller in the more competitive market structures. This serves to further confirm the results already presented and fits with the notion that women suffer more disparate earnings treatment in more monopolistic industries.

Our second investigation follows recent research by Hellerstein, Neumark, and Troske (2002) who investigate the consequences of discrimination for plant and firm profitability. Following Becker, they argue that employers give up current profits to indulge their tastes for discrimination. As a result, the marginal revenue product of male labor is below its input price, because male labor increases the employer's utility while the marginal revenue product of female labor is above its input price, reflecting the nonpecuniary cost of female labor to the employer. In essence, female labor is "on sale" for nondiscriminatory employers and their employment should increase the short-run profitability of the nondiscriminatory employers. Assuming the presence of such employers, the wage of women will, in the long run, be bid up and discrimination eliminated. Indeed, this is the argument frequently used by those who see earnings residuals between men and women as a reflection of unmeasured productivity differences (O'Neill, 1994). Hellerstein, Neumark, and Troske directly examine the link between the employment of women and profitability, testing whether there is money to be made by employing women.

Table 3.6   Workplace-Level Effects of Percent Female on Log Median Wage at Workplace

Dependent Variable: Log Median Wage

	High Competition		Low Competition	
Percent Female Workers	−0.4158	(0.057)***	−0.4966	(0.053)***
LR Chi(29)	38.21		35.01	
Pseudo R-squared	0.5195		0.5320	
N	666		785	

	Low Market Share		High Market Share	
Percent Female Workers	−0.4775	(0.0491)***	−0.5292	(0.063)***
LR Chi(29)	30.76		21.66	
Pseudo R-squared	0.5176		0.5206	
N	840		406	

Note: Weighted analysis. Only establishments in the trading sector. Workplace-level control variables are union, age of establishment, representative participation, suggestion scheme, downward communication, upward problem-solving, profit-related pay, share-ownership, UK owned, single firm, ratio manual workers, freelance workers, shiftwork, percent labor costs (3), employment size, sector (12). ***$p < 0.01$ level.

Linking household responses to the 1990 Census long form with the Standard Statistical Establishment List, they create a sample of manufacturing workers in the United States and their employers that is further linked to the Census and Annual Survey of Manufactures. The worker data is used to construct the share of women workers in each establishment along with other aggregated human capital and demographic variables. The employer data provides details on plant age, four-digit industry, market share, and price-cost margins. Initial regressions show that profitability is positively associated with the share of women workers. Those firms in an industry employing more women, all else equal, earn higher profits. Using the market structure variables, they find that this relationship is unique to the less competitive product markets. The share of female workers brings additional profits only among the set of establishments with market power. It is irrelevant among those firms in competitive market structures. Among the establishments with market power, an increase in the share of women workers of 10 percentage points (and a corresponding decrease in the share of men workers) generates an increase of 1.6 percentage points in profitability.

As profitability is a direct performance measure, Hellerstein, Neumark, and Troske argue that this evidence is more persuasive than typical earnings-based regressions of wage gaps. These estimated gaps are always subject to interpretation as they may reflect discrimination or they may reflect unmeasured ability. The fact that employing women increases profitability among firms with market power confirms that female labor is "on sale," a direct implication of Becker's theory. Moreover, the fact that this finding is confined to the less competitive sector confirms that competition brings each gender's earnings in line with productivity, ending the sale and discrimination.

In what follows, we use the available data in the WERS to replicate the essence of the Hellerstein, Neumark, and Troske U.S. study. The WERS establishment-level data provides us with two measures of performance taken from the managerial survey. Specifically, we know whether managers see their establishment's financial performance above their industry's average and whether they see their establishment's labor productivity above their industry's average (see table 3.3). These subjective measures have been used in previous studies, they correlate reasonably well with objective measures of firm performance (such as employment change and plant closings), and they are influenced by a similar set of determinants, such as union status (see Addison and Belfield, 2001; Machin and Stewart, 1996; McNabb and Whitfield, 1998). This past work shows that although it is possible to identify the direction of any influence on firm performance, it is hard to explain a large proportion of the variation in subjective performance measures.

Table 3.7 presents the baseline estimates using the two measures of market power and the share of women workers. In all cases the dichotomous performance indicators are used as dependent variables in profit estimations including the full list of establishment-level controls from previous specifications.[4] The evidence is consistent across both measures as well as across both performance indicators. Performance is weaker in competitive market structures (as suggested by the structure-conduct-performance hypothesis) and establishments employing greater shares of women do better all else equal. Thus, the UK data mirrors that for the United States by showing that female labor is "on sale" and as reflected by financial performance and, for the first time, labor productivity.

Table 3.7   Workplace-Level Effects of Percent Female Workforce on Financial Performance and Labor Productivity

	(1)		(2)	
Financial Peformance				
Percent Female Workers	0.3243	(0.1782)*	0.3771	(0.1901)**
High Competition [A]	−0.1407	(0.0757)*		
Low Market Share [C]			−0.3692	(0.0843)***
LR Chi(30)	70.23		75.94	
Pseudo R-squared	0.0374		0.0464	
N	1,390		1,205	
Labor Productivity				
Percent Female Workers	0.4478	(0.1772)**	0.3534	(0.1882)*
High Competition [A]	−0.0162	(0.0765)		
Low Market Share [C]			−0.2545	(0.0839)***
LR Chi(30)	91.49		83.93	
Pseudo R-squared	0.0496		0.0518	
N	1,332		1,169	

Note: Probit estimation. Weighted analysis. Only establishments in the trading sector. Workplace-level control variables are union, age of establishment, representative participation, suggestion scheme, downward communication, upward problem-solving, profit-related pay, share-ownership, UK owned, single firm, ratio manual workers, freelance workers, shiftwork, percent labor costs (3), employment size, sector (12). *$p < 0.1$ level   **$p < 0.05$ level   ***$p < 0.01$ level.

Table 3.8 divides the results by market structure, presenting a mixed picture. The evidence for labor productivity shows the expected pattern with the coefficient on the share of women workers positive in all cases and larger when both market structure measures indicate less competitive markets. Yet, the only significant coefficient for the share of women workers is among the less competitive markets when using the self-assessed measure. The evidence for financial performance is reversed. The share of women workers retains a positive coefficient in all cases but it now appears larger in the more competitive market structures. The only significant coefficient is for the less competitive structure as measured by low market share.

Table 3.8 Workplace-Level Effects of Percent Female on Financial Performance and Labor Productivity by Market Competitiveness

Dependent Variable: Financial Performance

	High Competition		Low Competition	
Percent Female Workers	0.4187	(0.2624)	0.2646	(0.2557)
LR Chi(29)	58.99		35.78	
Pseudo R-squared	0.0665		0.0362	
N	653		736	

	Low Market Share		High Market Share	
Percent Female Workers	0.3926	(0.2289)*	0.2613	(0.3691)
LR Chi(29)	57.43		27.96	
Pseudo R-squared	0.0506		0.0582	
N	822		383	

Dependent Variable: Labor Productivity

	High Competition		Low Competition	
Percent Female Workers	0.2471	(0.2667)	0.6032	(0.2525)**
LR Chi(29)	72.64		61.32	
Pseudo R-squared	0.0836		0.0628	
N	627		705	

	Low Market Share		High Market Share	
Percent Female Workers	0.2989	(0.2290)*	0.3685	(0.3593)
LR Chi(29)	82.07		33.15	
Pseudo R-squared	0.0748		0.0645	
N	794		375	

Note: Probit estimation. Weighted analysis. Only establishments in the trading sector. Workplace-level control variables are union, age of establishment, representative participation, suggestion scheme, downward communication, upward problem-solving, profit-related pay, share-ownership, UK owned, single firm, ratio manual workers, freelance workers, shiftwork, percent labor costs (3), employment size, sector (12). *$p < 0.1$ level   **$p < 0.05$ level.

The smaller sample size in each cell may explain some of the lack of significance but in general the mixed pattern must be taken as such. Yet, it is worth noting that the only statistically significant difference across market structures is that larger shares of women are associated with greater profitability in the less competitive sector when compared with the more competitive sector. This result fits that from the U.S. study, arguing the importance of competition in reducing discrimination.

Conclusions

The evidence from this chapter supports the presence of gender discrimination among UK workplaces. It also, on balance, supports the notion that product market competition reduces the extent of that discrimination. The earnings of individual workers were tied to the product market characteristics of their employers. Typical log linear earnings equations revealed a significant gender differential. Moreover, the size of this gender differential varied by the nature of the product market structure. The differential was significantly smaller among establishments in the more competitive sector. The role of unionization retains ambiguity but, in general, the role of product market structure appears greater in the nonunion sector, confirming U.S. evidence.

Moving to the establishment level, the median level of earnings responded as anticipated with a greater share of women workers associated with a smaller median wage, all else equal. Moreover, the establishment results mimic those from the individual workers with the strength of this association being much greater in the less competitive sector. Finally, we followed recent U.S. work, examining the influence of gender composition on the performance of establishments. As in the United States, a larger share of women workers is associated with stronger performance. While the evidence on market structure is mixed, the strongest result is that labor productivity is more strongly associated with women workers in the less competitive sector. Thus, in aggregate, the establishment-level results chime in with those from the individual level, reinforcing the importance of product market structure.

While the apparent lesson is that increased product market competition reduces gender discrimination, some argue that such competition need not be required as other market forces will be at work. More profitable nondiscriminatory establishments will grow more rapidly among those with market power. Similarly, those seeking profit will buy out discriminatory firms with market power, or profit-maximizing shareholders will replace discriminatory managers. The dynamics of the market structure–discrimination relationship are poorly under-stood but it is clear that these predictions of reduced discrimination depend on a series of assumptions about the market for corporate con-trol (Heywood, 1998). If agency problems are such that discriminatory managers are not replaced by profit-maximizing stockholders, dis-crimination may persist among firms with market power. Indeed, Hellerstein, Neumark, and Troske (2002) found that U.S. firms with market power employing small shares of women were not punished over time with either lower growth or takeover. This conclusion only serves to heighten the importance of product market competition as a curb on discrimination.

Notes

1. The proper measure of market structure is a highly contested theoreti-cal and empirical issue. See Heywood (1987a) and Salinger (1990) for reviews and additional evidence on this point.

2. The full estimations are available from the authors.

3. Descriptive statistics for the share female and median wage are pre-sented in table 3.3.

4. The unionization of the establishment is critical among these controls. Hellerstein, Neumark, and Troske have no controls for unionization in their sample of manufacturing establishments despite its likely association with prof-itability, the gender composition of the workforce, and the market structure.

References

Addison, John T., and Clive R. Belfield. "Updating the Determinants of Firm Per-formance: Estimation Using the 1998 U.K. Workplace Employee Relations Survey." *British Journal of Industrial Relations* 39 (2001): 341–66.

Agesa, Jacqueline. "Deregulation and the Racial Composition of Airlines." *Jour-nal of Policy Analysis and Management* 20 (2001): 223–37.

Agesa, Jacqueline, and Anita Brown. "Deregulation, Unionization and Racial Dis-crimination: An Analysis of the Trucking Industry." *American Journal of Economics and Sociology* (1998) 57: 285–305.

Alchian, Armen, and Rubin Kessel. "Competition, Monopoly and the Pursuit of Pecuniary Gain." In *Aspects of Labor Economics*, Universities-National Bu-reau Committee for Economic Research, 156–83. Princeton, NJ: Prince-ton University Press, 1962.

Becker, Gary S. *The Economics of Discrimination.* Chicago: University of Chicago Press, 1957.

Bergmann, Barbara. "Occupational Segregation, Wages and Profits When Employers Discriminate." *Eastern Economic Journal* 1 (1974): 103–10.

Blau, Francine, Marianne Ferber, and Anne Winkler. *The Economics of Women, Men and Work.* Upper Saddle River, NJ: Prentice-Hall, 2002.

Borjas, George, and Stephen Bronars. "Consumer Discrimination and Self-Employment." *Journal of Political Economy* 97 (1989): 581–605.

Buffum, David, and Robert Whaples. "Fear and Lathing in the Michigan Furniture Industry: Employee-Based Discrimination." *Economic Inquiry* 33 (1995): 234–52.

Cully, Mark, Stephen Woodland, Andrew O'Reilly, and Gill Dix. *Britain at Work.* London: Routledge, 1999.

Fuji, Edwin, and John Trapani. "On Estimating the Relationship between Discrimination and Market Structure." *Southern Economic Journal* 26 (1978): 556–71.

Gosling, Alison, and Stephen Machin. "Trade Unions and the Dispersion of Earnings in British Establishments." *Oxford Bulletin of Economics and Statistics* 57 (1995): 167–84.

Hamermesh, Daniel. "International Labor Economics." *Journal of Labor Economics* 20 (2002): 709–32.

Hellerstein, Judith, David Neumark, and Kenneth Troske. "Market Forces and Sex Discrimination." *Journal of Human Resources* 37 (2002): 351–80.

Heywood, John. "Market Share and Efficiency—A Reprise." *Economics Letters* 24 (1987a): 171–75.

———. "Wage Discrimination and Market Structure." *Journal of Post Keynesian Economics* 9 (1987b): 617–28.

———. "Regulated Industries and Measures of Earnings Discrimination." In *Regulatory Reform and Labor Markets* ed, James Peoples, 287–323. Boston: Kluwer Academic Publishers, 1998.

Johnson, William. "Racial Wage Discrimination and Industrial Structure." *Bell Journal of Economics* 9 (1978): 71–81.

Machin, Stephen. "Wage Inequality in the United Kingdom." *Oxford Review of Economic Policy* 2 (1996): 47–64.

Machin, Stephen, and Mark B. Stewart. "Trade Unions and Financial Performance." *Oxford Economic Papers* 48 (1996): 213–41.

McNabb, Robert, and Keith Whitfield. "The Impact of Financial Participation and Employee Involvement on Financial Performance." *Scottish Journal of Political Economy* 45 (1998): 171–87.

O'Neill, June. "Discrimination and Income Differences." In *Race and Gender in the American Economy*, ed. Susan F. Feiner, 13–37. Englewood Cliffs, NJ: Prentice-Hall, 1994.

Peoples, James. "Monopolistic Market Structure, Unionization, and Racial Wage Differentials." *Review of Economics and Statistics* 76 (1994): 207–11.

———. "Deregulation and the Labor Market." *Journal of Economic Perspectives* 12 (1998): 111–30.

Peoples, James, and Rhoda Robinson. "Market Structure and Racial and Gender Discrimination: Evidence from the Telecommunications Industry." *American Journal of Economics and Sociology* 55 (1996): 309–26.

Peoples, James, and Lisa Saunders. "Trucking Deregulation and the Black/White Wage Gap." *Industrial and Labor Relations Review* 47 (1993): 23–35.

Prasad, Edward S. "Wage Inequality in the United Kingdom, 1975–1999. IZA Working Paper 510, 2002.

Rose, Nancy. "Labor Rent Sharing and Regulation: Evidence from the Trucking Industry." *Journal of Political Economy* 95 (1987): 1146–78.

Salinger, Michael. "The Concentration-Margins Relationship Reconsidered." *Brookings Papers on Economic Activity: Microeconomics Special Issue* (1990): 287–335.

Shepherd, William G. "Elements of Market Structure." *Review of Economics and Statistics* 54 (1972): 25–38.

Shepherd, William G., and Sharon Levine. "Managerial Discrimination in Large Firms." *Review of Economics and Statistics* 55 (1973): 412–19.

Chapter 4

Gender and Wages in Germany
The Impact of Product Market Competition and Collective Bargaining

Uwe Jirjahn and Gesine Stephan

Introduction

A substantial literature confirms the existence of a significant gender wage differential, even controlling for productive worker characteristics. Yet, the size of the gender wage differential varies substantially across countries.[1] These remarkable differences raise an interesting question, Do differences in institutions and markets influence the extent of discrimination? We address the question by studying blue-collar workers in West German establishments facing different market forces and institutional influences. Specifically, we investigate the impact of product market competition and collective bargaining agreements on the gender wage differential.

In the theoretical part of this chapter, we argue that it is important to consider the agents of discrimination and the channels through which discrimination occurs. In the presence of equal employment opportunity and equal pay laws, actors cannot avowedly discriminate against women. To continue in the practice they need to hide discriminatory practices. Hiding discrimination requires discretion in hiring, job evaluation, or performance appraisal. Market forces and institutions influence the degree of discretion and, thus, the degree of discrimination. These forces and institutions may influence the use of payment schemes within establishments that reduce the degree of discretion. Thus, product market competition may force management to reduce slack and improve efficiency by adopting payment schemes. Collective bargaining agreements reduce the degree of discretion in performance appraisal if they contain detailed regulations concerning the design of payment schemes. Moreover, collective bargaining may influence the creation of a trustful employer–employee relationship within establishments, which is crucial for the adoption of particular payment schemes.

The empirical analysis uses matched employer–employee data from manufacturing establishments in the German federal state of Lower Saxony. The analysis proceeds in three steps. First, we investigate the determinants of piece rates. The focus on piece rates is motivated by the idea that piece rates provide less discretion for performance appraisals since the quantity of produced output can be easily verified (see Heywood and O'Halloran in chapter 9 of this volume). In the second step, we estimate wage regressions with fixed establishment effects on wages to analyze the impact of performance pay on wages of male and female employees at the individual level. However, performance pay is only one element of the firm wage policy and further unobserved elements may influence the gender wage gap too. The impact of the unobserved firm wage policies on the gender wage gap is reflected by differences in fixed firm effects on the wages for male and female workers. Thus, in a third step we analyze determinants of the gender-specific differences in establishment effects on wages. In particular we investigate the role of collective bargaining and product market competition.

Theoretical Background and Hypotheses

There are two controversial interpretations of the unexplained gender wage gap. While some researchers view this gap as a result of unobserved productivity differences between men and women, others view it as evidence of gender discrimination. A theory of gender discrimination has to answer three crucial questions, Who discriminates? What are the channels through which discrimination occurs? How do market forces and the structure of collective bargaining influence the channels of discrimination? We organize our theoretical discussion around these three questions.

THE AGENTS OF DISCRIMINATION

Becker (1957) distinguishes between discrimination by employers, employees, and customers. Prejudice is the source of labor market discrimination in each of the three cases. If members of the majority group are prejudiced against the minority group, they prefer not to interact with members of the minority group. Employers with distaste for female employees will hire fewer women than profit maximization would imply.

If male employees are prejudiced against female colleagues, they will not work with women without a compensating payment. If consumers dislike women, they receive less utility, and will pay less, when they purchase from women.

In considering the role of the employer in more detail, it is important to emphasize that since Berle and Means (1932) the separation of ownership and control has received attention by economists. If the owners of the firm can monitor the executive managers' actions only imperfectly, managers have scope to pursue their own goals. Ashenfelter and Hannan (1986) argue that managers can use this scope to discriminate against workers beyond the level preferred by the owners. Even if owners are solely interested in profits, discrimination may persist if managers have prejudice. This argument can be generalized. In most organizations, the agency problem is multilayered. Superiors at the various levels of hierarchy have some scope and discretion. Thus, discrimination may occur even in owner-led firms where owners, and the senior management, are not prejudiced against women.

The incorporation of agency relationships yields implications that differ from those of Becker. A decrease in discrimination is always profitable in Becker's analysis. However, in the presence of agency problems, a reduction of discrimination entails not only benefits but also costs for firm owners. Reducing discrimination requires additional expenditures to monitor managers and supervisors to reduce their discretion. In a later subsection, we will discuss the market factors that influence the optimal level of monitoring undertaken by the owners.

In addition, a more differentiated discussion of employee discrimination is required. Becker's analysis of employee discrimination refers to collaboration on the job. Individual members of the majority group dislike working with members of the minority group. Unions may also have an impact on discrimination, but it is not clear whether unions exert a positive or a negative influence on the gender wage gap. Sap (1993) presents a theoretical model of intraunion bargaining in which wage increases negotiated with an employer are divided between male and female unionists. The gender wage gap results in this model from differences in the bargaining strength of men and women.[2] Alternatively, one can apply a median voter approach. Union leaders who are interested in reelection care more about the tastes and the income situation of the majority group—men—than about the interests of the minority group—women.

These models contradict the declared goal of unions in Germany: equal pay for work of equal value. Discrimination undermines cohesion within the workforce, weakening the unions' bargaining position against the employers.[3] This is particularly important for industrial unions that represent heterogeneous workers in broad industrial sectors. Indeed, an international comparison by Rowthorne (1992) confirms that the centralization of collective bargaining (across larger and diverse groups of workers) is associated with smaller gender wage gaps. This finding suggests that the influence of unions on the gender wage gap depends on the structure of collective bargaining. In another subsection we discuss the structure of the industrial relations in Germany.

CHANNELS OF DISCRIMINATION

Having identified possible agents of discrimination, we now examine the channels through which discrimination occurs. We emphasize that agents will be more successful in discrimination when they can hide their actions. First, equal employment opportunity and equal pay laws make it difficult for agents to directly reveal their distaste and prejudices. Second, supervisors who will be sanctioned by owners cannot avowedly discriminate beyond the level preferred by the owners. We now turn to an evaluation of discretion in hiring, job evaluation, or performance appraisal and the opportunities such discretion plays to practice covert discrimination.

In Becker's analysis of employer discrimination, prejudiced employers hire fewer women than profit maximization would imply. Obviously, this presumes some degree of discretion in hiring standards.[4] Discretion in hiring standards allows systematically favoring male job applicants over equally skilled female job applicants. This discrimination in hiring worsens the labor market opportunities of female workers compared to those of men resulting in a wage gap between equally skilled men and women. According to Becker, unprejudiced employers can gain a cost advantage by hiring women and paying them less than men. Yet, in the presence of an equal pay law, unprejudiced employers need discretion to treat equally skilled men and women differently. If the law is successful in eliminating the ability to pay men and women differently, an additional avenue is to hire male and female workers for different jobs, which allows for gender-specific payments. This requires discretion in job evaluation.

Jobs differ in their contribution to the output of a firm. Therefore, a worker's wage depends on the job he or she holds. The goal of job evaluation is to determine the importance of the various jobs for the firm's production. Lazear (1995, chapter 8) identifies two sources of arbitrariness associated with job evaluation. First, there is the problem of how to scale indexes for the various job characteristics. A job can be characterized by several items such as required education, tenure, job experience, and responsibility. The worker's wage depends on the weights given to each of the items. Discretion in job evaluation exists because the choice of the weighting scheme is often not clear-cut. Second, the evaluators' subjective opinions may influence the ranking of jobs. If subjective opinions play a role in determining the indexes of the various job characteristics, evaluators with prejudice may influence job rankings.

Job evaluation can be a channel of discrimination. One possibility is that female-dominated and male-dominated jobs requiring the same skill and responsibility are not ranked identically by evaluators. Lazear (1995, 102) reports evidence of gender bias in the ranking of jobs. Women tend to rank female-dominated jobs more highly, whereas men tend to rank male-dominated jobs more highly. To the extent that men are disproportionately represented on evaluations committees, job rankings will disadvantage women.

Another possibility is that female-dominated and male-dominated jobs systematically differ in some requirements and that a weighting scheme favors characteristics typical of male-dominated jobs beyond their contribution to production. Women are more likely to have lower labor force attachment than men due to their disproportionate responsibility for household production. If job experience or tenure with the firm is overly weighted, male-dominated jobs will be favored.

Considering discretion in job evaluation as a potential source of discrimination has several implications. In Becker's model of employer discrimination, women are sorted into unprejudiced firms since prejudiced employers are less willing to hire female employees. Female-dominated jobs coupled with discretion in job evaluation may explain how unprejudiced employers can still take advantage of women's unfavorable labor market opportunities to pay them less than equally skilled men despite equal pay laws.

Moreover, discretion in job evaluation sheds light on discrimination within firms where prejudice against female workers is prevalent. Even prejudiced employers may hire women to a certain degree. First, male and female labor may not be perfect substitutes. Second, equal employment opportunity laws may require a share of female employees higher than preferred by a prejudiced employer. Third, prejudiced managers of the firm may not always be able to avoid hiring female workers when the owners are unprejudiced. In these situations, the agents of discrimination can use their discretion in job evaluation to disadvantage female workers. Analogous implications result from discretion in performance appraisal.

Providing incentives for workers requires performance evaluation. Incentive systems such as promotions, merit pay, and piece rates are based on different performance measures. Performance measures can be divided into objective and subjective measures (Baker, Jensen, and Murphy, 1988). Objective performance measures such as sales or the quantity of output can be verified. However, complex tasks are associated with dimensions of performance that cannot be easily verified or quantified. Examples include building long-term relationships with customers, helping on the job, and asset maintenance. To reward performance along these dimensions, individual incentives are typically based on subjective evaluations by superiors.

Obviously, subjective performance measures imply discretion in performance appraisal. This discretion may result in performance appraisals based on the superiors' subjective opinions. Arbitrary performance appraisals lead to an efficiency loss. If workers feel that the superiors' discretion results in favoritism, they will withhold effort and cooperation or they will refuse to work in jobs where incentives are based on subjective performance measures. However, in most organisations, agency relationships are multilayered. Since superiors share only a small part of the efficiency loss resulting from their arbitrary performance evaluations, they have an incentive to allocate rewards in favor of their personally preferred subordinates. Thus, subjective performance evaluation provides a channel of discrimination. This notion is supported by Elvira and Town (2001) who find a race bias in performance evaluations. White supervisors rate black subordinates lower, while black superiors rate white employees lower. If supervisory jobs are dominated by whites, this leads to an average disadvantage of blacks. A similar argument may hold for male and female workers.

Piece rates reward the quantity of produced output. Since units of output can easily be verified, piece rates are associated with less discretion in performance appraisal. Thus, piece rates present less scope for wage discrimination. This hypothesis has received support by a handful of studies. Belman and Heywood (1988) and Heywood and O'Halloran (chapter 9 in this volume) show for the United States that racial earning differentials are smaller when workers are paid piece rates. Jirjahn and Stephan (2004) find for blue-collar workers in Germany that the unexplained gender wage gap is substantially smaller among those paid piece rates than those paid straight time rates.

Of course, piece rates also may suffer from employer opportunism. A well-known example is the ratchet effect in which workers withhold effort fearing that the employer will reduce the piece rate in light of the workers' past performance. However, this kind of opportunism affects all workers remunerated by piece rates and not just women. Moreover, works councils in Germany may prevent employers from altering the terms of the piece rate scheme (Heywood, Hübler, and Jirjahn, 1998; Heywood and Jirjahn, 2002). Preventing the ratchet effect may be easier for works councils than preventing superiors from showing favoritism, because the terms of a piece rate scheme are more observable and verifiable in contrast to idiosyncratic performance appraisals by superiors.

Thus, while we admit that there may be other ways for employers to discriminate even when paying piece rates, we emphasize that the performance standards of piece rates are more observable and verifiable than subjective performance evaluations. The expected consequence is reduced gender discrimination among employers paying piece rates. Yet, not all employers can use piece rates. Individual-based piece rates require that a worker's individual output can be identified. Thus, piece rates are more suitable for production technologies characterized by the absence of team production (Heywood and Wei, 1997). Moreover, piece rates may distort the allocation of effort if workers have to perform multidimensional tasks and the quality of produced output is important (Holmström and Milgrom, 1991). Therefore, piece rates are more likely to be found for simple tasks (MacLeod and Parent, 1999). However, the use of piece rates is determined by factors other than technology. Owners' incentives to improve efficiency within firms, due to competitive market structure, and the extent of trust in employer–employee relations are also likely to play a role.

PRODUCT MARKET COMPETITION

Product market competition is often thought to provide incentives to increase efficiency within firms. This includes a reduction in discriminatory practices. In Becker's analysis, prejudiced employers forgo profit maximization and should be competed out of the market by the entry of unprejudiced firms. Similarly, prejudiced owners may be bought out by unprejudiced owners (Hellerstein, Neumark, and Troske, 2002). Yet, such conclusions may depend on the functioning of the labor market. Altonji and Blank (1999, 3172) argue that discrimination is unlikely to be eliminated by unprejudiced firms when there are labor market imperfections. Search costs or mobility costs may hinder the move of discriminated workers to unprejudiced employers.[5]

Further, principal–agent problems within firms may influence the link between product market competition and discrimination. Even if the owners of the firm are unprejudiced, managers or superiors may have their own prejudices and preferences toward employees. Owners who want to reduce discrimination have to invest in measures that reduce managers' or superiors' discretion. Put differently, measures to reduce discrimination within firms can be viewed as a special case of investments in improving the internal efficiency of organizations. Theoretical analyses show that competition may increase or decrease the incentives to improve efficiency. On the one hand, an increased number of competitors provides additional information the owners can use for a relative performance evaluation of their managers (Bertoletti and Poletti, 1997). Also, competition may imply a threat of liquidation, which induces efficiency-enhancing investments in order to reduce the probability of bankruptcy (Schmidt, 1997). On the other hand, product market competition reduces incentives to control production costs when a shrinkage effect dominates (Martin, 1993). While a greater number of competitors increases industry output, the output of each individual firm may decrease. Similarly, Boone (2000) shows that product market competition may involve a discouragement effect when a firm faces superior competitors.

While the theoretical link between competition and firm performance is not clear-cut, empirical studies usually find that firms facing high product market competition have greater productivity and technical efficiency (see Nickell, 1999, for a survey). Correspondingly, recent studies for the United States show that the gender wage gap is smaller due to deregulation (Black and Strahan, 2001) and to import competition (Black and Brainerd, 2002). Empirical studies on the link between competition and discrimination in Europe are extremely rare. One exception is Winter-Ebmer (1995) who finds that increased industrial concentration in Austria is associated with higher wages for women but not for men. This result contrasts sharply with the evidence from the United States.

An alternative research strategy is to investigate the concrete measures that we anticipate will reduce discrimination. The findings by Belman and Heywood (1988), Heywood and O'Halloran (2005), and Jirjahn and Stephan (2004) suggest that piece rates are associated with less discretion in performance appraisal. International evidence from Australia (Drago and Heywood, 1995), the United Kingdom (Burgess and Metcalfe, 2000), and Germany (Heywood, Hübler, and Jirjahn, 1998; Heywood and Jirjahn, 2002; Jirjahn, 2002) shows establishments in sectors with low industrial concentration are more likely to use piece rates. Based on the sum of past evidence and theory, we anticipate that competition may reduce discrimination by forcing firms to introduce piece rates and that product market competition might more generally increase investments in reducing discretion in job evaluation.

THE GERMAN SYSTEM OF INDUSTRIAL RELATIONS

Industrial relations in Germany are characterized by a dual structure of employee representation through both unions and works councils (Hübler and Jirjahn, 2003). Works councils provide a highly developed mechanism for establishment-level participation that is formally independent of the process of collective bargaining. Councils have full codetermination rights on a broad set of issues, which include the introduction of new payment methods, the fixing of job and bonus rates, and the introduction and use of technical devices designed to monitor employee performance. They have consultation rights in matters such as changes in equipment and working methods that affect job requirements. Their participation rights include the provision of financial and economic information.

Collective bargaining agreements regulate wage rates and general aspects of the employment contract such as working hours. Typically, they are negotiated between unions and employers' associations on a broad industrial level. Members of employers' associations are covered by these industry-wide bargaining agreements. However, a smaller proportion of firms is covered by firm level contracts that are directly negotiated between the firm and a union. In this case, firms that are not members of an employers' association are also covered. Employers covered by industry-level or firm-level agreements have an incentive to pay the negotiated wage rate not only to union members but also to employees who are not union members. This incentive results because otherwise nonmembers would join the union (Fitzenberger and Franz, 1999). In West Germany less than one-third of employees are union members, but 77 percent of workers are covered by either industry-wide collective agreements or firm-level contracts (Pfeiffer, 2003, for the year 2000). Note that collective agreements define minimum standards. Of course, covered firms are free to pay wages or to improve working conditions above the level specified by the agreements.

The role industrial relations plays in the gender wage gap is controversial. One view is that unions increase discrimination (e.g., Sap, 1993). Yet, a contrasting view is that the role of unions depends on the structure of collective bargaining (Rubery and Fagan, 1995). We hypothesize that the characteristics of the industrial relations system in Germany implies reduced wage discrimination in firms covered by collective bargaining agreements. Unions in Germany are large industrial unions that cut across firms and industries. In contrast to craft unions or narrow industrial unions, they represent a highly heterogeneous workforce. Creating worker cohesion across different occupations and firms is crucial for strengthening the bargaining position of each of the industrial unions. Increased discrimination is likely to dilute cohesion and, thus, to weaken a union's bargaining power. Accordingly, one central objective of German unions is "equal pay for work of equal value." There are several ways unions can contribute to a reduction of the gender wage gap.

Collective bargaining agreements contain wage groups. Each wage group specifies a certain wage level and is associated with different levels of required skills and responsibility. Bargaining agreements assign typical jobs to each wage group. Therefore, they set the general conditions for job evaluation within covered establishments. If unions are interested in reducing discrimination, coverage by a collective bargaining implies less discretion in job evaluation.

Collective bargaining also exerts an impact on the use of pay-for-performance schemes, including piece rates. First, bargaining agreements often contain more or less detailed regulations concerning the design of these payment schemes.[6] Second, collective bargaining has an indirect effect by reducing distributional conflicts between employers and works councils (Freeman and Lazear, 1995; Hübler and Jirjahn, 2003). Works councils in covered establishments are less engaged in rent-seeking. They are more likely to be engaged in building trust and cooperation, which is important for positive incentive effects of pay-for-performance schemes. This prediction is supported by Heywood, Hübler, and Jirjahn (1998) and Heywood and Jirjahn (2002). They find that the presence of a works council exerts a positive impact on the use of pay-for-performance schemes within the industrial relations regime covered by collective bargaining agreements but not within the uncovered industrial relations regime. Thus, covered establishments with works councils have in place a mechanism to build trust and share information, making the adoption of performance pay more likely. This includes piece rates, which are associated with less discretion in performance appraisal. If piece rates contribute to a reduced discrimination and to improved efficiency within establishments, a works council in covered establishments can help to establish this form of performance payment.

In sum, we expect a smaller gender wage gap in covered establishment due to reduced discrimination. Blau and Kahn (2003) also argue that collective bargaining implies a lower gender pay gap. However, they contend that this results from a gender-unspecific influence that is not related to discrimination. Since women have, on average, less labor market experience, they are at the bottom of the wage distribution. If collective bargaining produces a compressed wage structure, it automatically reduces the gender wage gap. Yet, the international study by Blau and Kahn supports this view only partially. While it confirms that countries with a more compressed male wage structure have a smaller gender wage gap, collective bargaining coverage remains a strong negative determinant of the gap even when controlling for the wage structure and other influences. We interpret this as an indication for a gender-specific role of collective bargaining that may be related to a reduction in discrimination.

Data, Variables, and Methods

To investigate the impacts of product market competition and collective bargaining on the gender wage gap in Germany, we use linked employer–employee data from the Lower Saxony Salary and Wage Structure Survey for the year 1995 (see Stephan, 2001, 2002, for a detailed description of the data). Lower Saxony is one of the larger federal states of Germany, with an industry composition that is typical for West Germany and it includes around 11 percent of all West German workers. The data are drawn as a two-stage random sample from all establishments in the entire manufacturing sector and parts of the service sector. The percentage of employees included per establishment depends on firm size (from 100 percent for small establishments to 6.25 percent for very large establishments).

The wage structure survey includes a number of questions on wages, working time, and worker characteristics. Information on the establishment includes firm size, sector, region, and the presence of an industry-level or a firm-level collective bargaining agreement. Two variables serve as indicators for national and international product market competition: official statistics on industrial concentration CR6 (sales of the six largest companies in each industrial sector as a share of total sales in the sector) and on international competition (the extent of the German output sold internationally at the four-digit industry level) are matched to each establishment. Further, regional labor market conditions are captured by the local unemployment rate (three-digit regional level "Kreisebene").

The study restricts itself to blue-collar workers in the production sector with a contractual working time of at least twenty-five weekly hours and employed in establishments with at least ten employees, for whom at least two observations for male or two observations for female workers were available. The hours restriction is taken as a lower bound for full-time work (some Lower Saxony plants introduced a full-time week of twenty-eight weekly hours in 1995). The resulting data set consists of approximately 24,000 blue-collar workers employed in 400 different establishments. Descriptive statistics of the variables are shown in table 4.1. A gross gender wage gap of around 30 percent exists. Performance pay is found more often among female blue-collar workers. Men are more often employed in establishments applying collective wage contracts and men have, on average, more tenure than women.

Table 4.1 Descriptive Statistics of Performance Pay

	Men		Women	
Variable	Mean	Standard Deviation	Mean	Standard Deviation
Log Hourly Wage	3.2372	(0.2246)	2.9684	(0.2270)
Piece Rate	0.2043	(0.4032)	0.2449	(0.4301)
Premium Pay	0.0930	(0.2904)	0.0974	(0.2965)
Remuneration Occasionally Based on Performance Pay	0.0424	(0.2016)	0.0913	(0.2880)
Industry-Level Bargaining Agreement	0.6093	(0.4879)	0.5862	(0.4925)
Firm-Level Bargaining Agreement	0.2399	(0.4270)	0.1532	(0.3602)
Log CR6	1.3211	(1.1707)	1.1243	(1.0807)
Export Share	30.511	(16.952)	25.837	(14.556)
Log Firm Size	6.3507	(1.9126)	5.8650	(1.5202)
Regional Unemployment Rate	11.626	(2.6380)	11.019	(2.3346)
Years of Schooling	11.455	(1.1057)	10.617	(1.2844)
Years of Potential Experience	21.521	(1.0294)	22.500	(1.1051)
Years of Tenure	12.466	(0.9141)	9.861	(0.7983)
Number of Workers	19,772		4,249	

As the first step, we analyze the determinants of working under piece rates by estimating probit equations. The dependent variable indicates if a worker is paid a piece rate or not. The control group includes those workers who receive time rates or any other form of performance payment. The focus on piece rates is motivated by previous empirical studies that show a smaller gender wage gap for employees working under piece rates. The purpose of the probit estimates is to examine the impact of product market competition and industrial relations on a form of performance pay that is associated with less scope for discrimination.

In the second step, we run pooled and gender-specific wage regressions with fixed firm effects on wages:

$$w_{ij} = \beta'x_{ij} + \phi_j + v_{ij} \tag{4.1}$$

where w_{ij} is the log hourly wage of worker i at employer j, β is the vector of coefficients, x_{ij} is the vector of independent variables, ϕ_j is a "global" establishment wage effect, and v_{ij} is an i.i.d. error term. The vector of independent variables includes variables for the workers' human capital and for the method of pay. If we find an influence of competition or collective bargaining on the likelihood of receiving piece rate in the first step and higher returns to working under piece rates for female workers in the second step, it can be argued that competition or collective bargaining have an effect on the gender wage gap by influencing the use of piece rates.

However, other elements of the firm wage policy such as job evaluation are not observed and are captured by the fixed wage effect ϕ_j. The establishment wage effect ϕ_j in equation (4.1) can be interpreted as the approximate percentage deviation of mean wages within a firm from expected wages and thus as a measure for firm-specific compensation politics, conditional on observed employee characteristics. This brings us to the third step of our study. From gender-specific regressions of equation (4.1) we obtain gender-specific estimates, $\hat{\phi}_j^M$ and $\hat{\phi}_j^F$, for the fixed establishment effects on wages. The difference in the gender-specific fixed establishment effects, $(\hat{\phi}_j^M - \hat{\phi}_j^F)$ reflects elements of the firm wage policy. This difference is used as the dependent variable in firm-level regressions:

$$(\hat{\phi}_j^M - \hat{\phi}_j^F) = \gamma'z_j + \varepsilon_j \tag{4.2}$$

where γ is the vector of coefficients, z_j is the vector of independent variables, and ε_j is an i.i.d. error term. To take into account the unbalanced nature of the hierarchical data, equation (4.2) is estimated by Weighted Least Squares. Equation (4.2) enables us to investigate the impact of product market competition and collective bargaining on unobserved firm wage policies that influence the gender wage gap.

Empirical Results

Table 4.2 investigates the determinants of receiving piece rates for the pooled sample and separately by gender. Confirming international evidence, female workers are more likely to be remunerated by piece rates. Further, we control for the presence of children, schooling, experience, and tenure, but will concentrate the following discussion on the impact of industrial relations and product market competition. The first important result is that workers are more likely to receive piece rates when the establishment applies a collective bargaining agreement. The gender-specific estimates show that collective contracts at the industrial level increase the probability for men and for women to receive piece rates, while firm-level wage contracts do this only for male workers. The second important result is that the likelihood of receiving piece rates is higher for workers employed in industries with greater international competition. Thus, both collective bargaining and the competitive pressure of international markets are positively linked with a method of pay that is based on a more objective performance measure.

Table 4.3 shows the results of pooled and gender-specific wage regressions with fixed establishment effects on wages. Wage effects that are constant across all employees of a firm such as product market competition and the application of a collective bargaining agreement are captured in the fixed establishment effects. As well as the usual human capital variables and occupational dummies,[7] we consider three variables for performance pay: regular piece rates, regular premium pay, and occasional performance pay. Premium pay rewards the quantity of output or the speed of completion but it is more often linked to the quality of workmanship or the sparing use of raw materials. Occasional performance pay means that a worker receives performance payments such premium pay or piece rates only an irregular basis.

The pooled estimates in column (1) obtain an unexplained gender wage gap of 11 percent when controlling for human capital, method of pay, and fixed firm effects.[8] However, separate wage regressions for male and female blue-collar workers show that the gender wage gap is influenced by the method of pay. Piece rates increase wages more strongly for women (5 percent) than for men (1 percent). This result implies that the gender wage gap is smaller for those employees who regularly receive piece rates. It is consistent with the notion that piece rates reduce discretion from performance appraisals. Together with the estimates of table 4.2, the results of table 4.3 confirm the notion that collective bargaining and international product market competition reduce the gender wage gap by increasing the use of piece rates.

Table 4.2 Determinants of Receiving Piece Rates (Method: Probit-ML Estimates)

Variable	All $\hat{\beta}$	|t|	Men $\hat{\beta}$	|t|	Women $\hat{\beta}$	|t|
Constant	−3.1778***	(23.20)	−2.9728***	(19.05)	−3.6991***	(12.99)
Man with Children	−0.0171	(0.70)	−0.1651	(0.66)		
Woman with Children	0.0167	(0.31)			0.0629	(1.11)
Woman	0.4152***	(12.85)				
Schooling	−0.0655***	(7.03)	−0.0789***	(7.38)	−0.0102	(0.54)
Experience/10	0.0111	(0.22)	0.0249	(0.41)	0.0413	(0.39)
(Experience/10)^2	−0.0094	(0.87)	−0.0060	(0.48)	−0.0301	(1.39)
Tenure/10	0.1625***	(3.81)	0.0620	(1.29)	0.3470***	(3.56)
(Tenure/10)^2	−0.0611***	(4.99)	−0.0496***	(3.64)	−0.0424	(1.38)
Industry-Level Bargaining Agreement	0.4962***	(12.57)	0.5776***	(10.88)	0.3936***	(6.28)
Firm-Level Bargaining Agreement	0.5038***	(10.15)	0.6684***	(10.63)	0.0110	(0.11)
Log CR6	0.0068	(0.63)	0.0155	(1.26)	−0.0340	(1.42)
Export Share	0.0053***	(6.53)	0.0051***	(5.66)	0.0065***	(3.39)
Log Firm Size	0.2589***	(28.84)	0.2547***	(25.25)	0.2836***	(13.61)
Regional Unemployment Rate	0.0558***	(11.06)	0.0492***	(8.67)	0.0719***	(6.33)
McFadden R^2	0.2161		0.2328		0.1647	
Number of Workers	24,021		19,772		4,249	

***p < .01.

Table 4.3 Determinants of the Log Hourly Wage at the Individual Level (Method: Fixed Effects Estimates with Fixed Establishment Effects)

Variable	All		Men		Women	
	$\hat{\beta}$	|t|	$\hat{\beta}$	|t|	$\hat{\beta}$	|t|
Piece Rate	0.0178***	(6.30)	0.0088***	(2.81)	0.0454**	(7.06)
Premium Pay	0.0169***	(3.90)	0.0189***	(3.91)	0.0199**	(1.98)
Remuneration Occasionally Based on Performance Pay	0.0270***	(4.51)	0.0307***	(4.46)	0.0105	(0.88)
Woman	−0.1208***	(52.38)				
Schooling	0.0200***	(35.30)	0.0215***	(27.25)	0.0103***	(7.06)
Experience/10	0.0425***	(13.21)	0.0486***	(13.54)	0.0119*	(1.80)
(Experience/10)^2	−0.0094***	(14.17)	−0.0105***	(14.14)	−0.0034**	(2.49)
Tenure/10	0.0724***	(24.77)	0.0752***	(23.48)	0.0663***	(9.55)
(Tenure/10)^2	−0.00945***	(11.65)	−0.0098***	(11.19)	−0.0132***	(6.05)
Control for 2-digit occupations	Yes		Yes		Yes	
R^2	0.3249		0.1717		0.1253	
Number of workers	24,021		19,772		4,249	

Note: R^2 refers only to variables at the individual level. *p < .1   **p < .05   ***p < .01.

In contrast to piece rates, regular premium payment has similar effects on the wages of men and women (2 percent). One interpretation of this result is that the performance measures associated with premium pay are not standardized in the same degree as the performance measures for piece rates. Occasional performance pay has no significant impact on female workers' wages, but increases male workers' wages (3 percent). An interpretation for this result is that irregular performance pay provides discretion in the decision when to base a worker's remuneration on his or her performance. In sum, the results indicate that both a standardization of performance measures and regular performance payment are required to reduce the gender wage gap.

Table 4.4 presents the estimation of the determinants of the firm-dimension of the gender wage gap, $(\hat{\phi}_j^M - \hat{\phi}_j^F)$. We present two specifications: Model (1) restricts itself on the impact of collective bargaining and product market competition. Model (2) adds controls for the use of pay for performance schemes, the share of female workers, firm size, and the unemployment rate.

In both specifications international competition but not the concentration ratio is significantly and negatively correlated with the gender difference in firm effects on wages. The gender wage gap decreases if the international presence and, thus, pressure from international product market competition increases. Second, the application of a collective contract at the industrial and at the firm level is associated with a significantly smaller wage gap (6 percent in the second specification) and thus advantageous for women. The findings are consistent with the hypothesis that competition and collective bargaining result in a firm wage policy based on a more standardized job evaluation.

The augmented specification (2) shows that the use of piece rates or premium pay is not correlated with other unobserved firm wage policies influencing the gender wage gap. However, the use of occasional performance payment is associated with unobserved firm wage policies reducing the gender wage gap. This result indicates that firms initiate other actions to reduce discrimination if occasional performance payments are required.

Further, an interesting result is that an increasing share of female employees within the firms increases the establishment part of the gender wage gap. Thus, female-dominated establishments do not pursue firm wage policies that aim to reduce the gender wage gap. Firm size and the regional unemployment rate do not have a significant impact on the difference in gender-specific establishment effects on wages. Finally, controlling for firm size, regional unemployment, the share of female workers, and the use of performance payment does not strongly influence the significance of the product market variables and the wage-setting regime.

Table 4.4 Determinants of Gender Differences in Establishment Effects on Wages (Method: Weighted Least Squares Estimates)

Variable	(1) $\hat{\beta}$	(1) $|t|$	(2) $\hat{\beta}$	(2) $|t|$
Constant	−0.0215*	(1.94)	−0.0449*	(1.74)
Industry-Level Bargaining Agreement	−0.0743***	(6.81)	−0.0608***	(5.38)
Firm-Level Bargaining Agreement	−0.0888***	(6.52)	−0.0636***	(4.04)
Log CR6	0.0024	(0.66)	0.0039	(1.07)
Export Share	−0.0007***	(2.65)	−0.0006**	(2.24)
Firm Uses Piece Rates			−0.0016	(0.11)
Firm Uses Premium Pay			−0.0184	(1.16)
Firm Bases Workers' Remuneration Occasionally on Performance Pay			−0.0484**	(2.47)
Share of Female Workers			0.0752***	(3.88)
Log Firm Size			−0.0013	(0.44)
Regional Unemployment Rate			0.00009	(0.05)
R^2	0.1770		0.2213	
Number of Firms	406		406	

*p < .1   **p < .05   ***p < .01.

Conclusions

Recent studies show that an unexplained gender wage gap continues to exist and remains of substantial size. This chapter has explored the extent to which institutions and markets influence the gender wage gap. The theoretical part of the chapter starts by identifying potential agents of gender-specific wage discrimination and the channels through which discrimination can occur. Discrimination requires discretion in hiring, job evaluation, or performance appraisal, which is in turn influenced by market forces and institutions. Increased product market competition induces efficient production and may thus foster the use of performance schemes that reduce slack and restrict possibilities for discrimination. Collective bargaining agreements standardize wage-setting procedures, which reduce the degree of discretion in performance appraisal, and furthermore help create trusting employer–employee relationships, which are often a prerequisite for the use of performance pay.

Based on linked employer–employee data for blue-collar workers from Germany, we first show that there is in fact a positive link between the coverage by collective bargaining agreements and the likelihood of working under piece rates. Moreover, workers in industries with extensive international competition are more likely to receive piece rates. In a second step we estimate wage regressions with fixed establishment effects on wages. The results confirm findings from earlier work (Jirjahn and Stephan, 2004): piece rates for women are associated with a larger wage increase than piece rates for men. Together with the results from the first step, this suggests that both international competition and the collective bargaining reduce discrimination indirectly by fostering the use of piece rates. In a last step we investigate gender-specific differences in establishment effects on wages. The findings indicate that the competitive pressure of international markets and collective bargaining reduce the gender wage gap at the firm level beyond the implementation of performance pay. We suspect that an important aspect may be that they spur additional efforts to reduce discretion in job evaluation.

Notes

The authors are grateful to Bernd Höptner, Uwe Rode, and Dietrich Schwinger (Niedersächsisches Landesamt für Statistik) for their help in working with the Lower Saxonian Wage Structure Survey.

1. See the studies by Black, Trainor, and Spencer (1999); Brookes, Hinks, and Watson (2001); and Blau and Kahn (2003). For instance, Black, Trainor, and Spencer obtain an unexplained gender wage gap of 0.32 for West Germany compared to 0.47 for Great Britain.

2. A study for the United States by Budd and Na (2000) provides some supporting evidence. The union membership wage premium is larger for men than for women.

3. The link between wage dispersion and cohesion is discussed by Levine (1991).

4. Darity and Mason (1998) provide evidence for visible discrimination in hiring from help wanted advertisements in the United States before the Civil Rights Act of 1964. Court cases and audit studies indicate that discrimination in hiring continued in more covert and subtle forms since then.

5. For formal models on the role of search costs, see Black (1995) and Bowlus and Eckstein (2002).

6. For a description of these regulations, see Bispinck (2000).

7. To save space, the ninety-nine dummy variables for the occupations (two-digit classification) are not reported.

8. Calculated as $e^\beta - 1$.

References

Altonji, Joseph G., and Rebecca M. Blank. "Race and Gender in the Labor Market." In *Handbook of Labor Economics*, vol. 3, ed. Orley Ashenfelter and David Card, 3143–259. Amsterdam: Elsevier Science, 1999.

Ashenfelter, Orley, and Timothy Hannan. "Sex Discrimination and Product Market Competition: The Case of the Banking Industry." *Quarterly Journal of Economics* 101 (1986): 149–73.

Baker, George, Michael C. Jensen, and Kevin J. Murphy. "Compensation and Incentives: Practice vs. Theory." *Journal of Finance* 18 (1988): 593–616.

Becker, Gary S. *The Economics of Discrimination*. Chicago: University of Chicago Press, 1957.

Belman, Dale, and John S. Heywood. "Incentive Schemes and Racial Wage Discrimination." *Review of Black Political Economy* 17 (1988): 47–56.

Berle, Adolf, and Gardiner Means. *The Modern Corporation and Private Property*. Chicago: Commerce Clearing House, 1932.

Bertoletti, Paolo, and Clara Poletti. "X-Inefficiency, Competition and Market Information." *Journal of Industrial Economics* 45 (1997): 359–75.

Bispinck, Reinhard. "Tarifentgelt nach Leistung und Erfolg: Regelungen in ausgewählten Tarifbereichen." WSI Informationen zur Tarifpolitik 43, 2000.

Black, Dan A. "Discrimination in an Equilibrium Search Model." *Journal of Labor Economics* 13 (1995): 309–34.

Black, Sandra E., and Elizabeth Brainerd. "Importing Equality? The Impact of Globalization on Gender Discrimination." Institute for the Study of Labor (IZA), Discussion Paper 556, Bonn, 2002.

Black, Sandra E., and Philip E. Strahan. "The Division of Spoils: Rent-Sharing and Discrimination in a Regulated Industry." *American Economic Review* 91 (2001): 814–31.

Black, B., Mary Trainor, and J. E. Spencer. "Wage Protection Systems, Segregation and Gender Pay Inequalities: West Germany, the Netherlands and Great Britain." *Cambridge Journal of Economics* 23 (1999): 449–64.

Blau, Francine D., and Lawrence M. Kahn. "Understanding International Differences in the Gender Pay Gap." *Journal of Labor Economics* 21 (2003): 106–44.

Boone, Jan. "Competitive Pressure: The Effects on Investments in Product and Process Innovation." *RAND Journal of Economics* 31 (2000): 549–69.

Bowlus, Audra J., and Zvi Eckstein. "Discrimination and Skill Differences in an Equilibrium Search Model." *International Economic Review* 43 (2002): 1–37.

Brookes, Mick, Timothy Hinks, and Duncan Watson. "Comparisons in Gender Wage Differentials and Discrimination between Germany and the United Kingdom." *Labour* 15 (2001): 393–414.

Budd, John, W., and In.-Gang Na. "The Union Membership Wage Premium for Employees Covered by Collective Bargaining Agreements." *Journal of Labor Economics* 18 (2000): 783–807.

Burgess, Simon, and Paul Metcalfe. "Incentive Pay and Product Market Competition." CMPO Working Paper 00/28, Bristol, 2000.

Darity, William A., and Patrick L. Mason. "Evidence on Discrimination in Employment: Codes of Color, Codes of Gender." *Journal of Economic Perspectives* 12 (1998): 63–90.

Drago, Robert, and John S. Heywood. "The Choice of Payment Schemes: Australian Establishment Data." *Industrial Relations* 34 (1995): 507–32.

Elvira, Maria, and Robert Town. "The Effects of Race and Worker Productivity on Performance Evaluations." *Industrial Relations* 40 (2001): 571–90.

Fitzenberger, Bernd, and Wolfgang Franz. "Industry-Level Wage Bargaining: A Partial Rehabilitation—The German Experience." *Scottish Journal of Political Economy* 46 (1999): 437–57.

Freeman, Richard B., and Edward P. Lazear. "An Economic Analysis of Works Councils." In *Works Councils—Consultation, Representation and Cooperation in Industrial Relations*, ed. J. Rogers and W. Streeck, 27–52. Chicago: University of Chicago Press, 1995.

Hellerstein, Judith K., David Neumark, and Kenneth R. Troske. "Market Forces and Sex Discrimination." *Journal of Human Resources* 37 (2002): 353–80.

Heywood, John S., Olaf Hübler, and Uwe Jirjahn. "Variable Payment Schemes and Industrial Relations: Evidence from Germany." *Kyklos* 51 (1998): 237–57.

Heywood, John S., and Uwe Jirjahn. "Payment Schemes and Gender in Germany." *Industrial and Labor Relations Review* 56 (2002): 44–64.

Heywood, John S., and Patrick O'Halloran. "Racial Earnings Differentials and Performance Pay." *Journal of Human Resources* 40 (2005): 435–53.

Heywood, John S., and Xiangdong Wei. "Piece Rate Payment Schemes and the Employment of Women: The Case of Hong Kong." *Journal of Comparative Economics* 25 (1997): 237–55.

Holmström, Bengt, and Paul Milgrom. "Multitask Principal–Agent Analyses, Incentive Contracts, Asset Ownership, and Job Design." *Journal of Law, Economics, and Organization* 7 (1991): 24–52.

Hübler, Olaf, and Uwe Jirjahn "Works Councils and Collective Bargaining in Germany: The Impact on Productivity and Wages." *Scottish Journal of Political Economy* 50 (2003): 1–21.

Jirjahn, Uwe. "The German Experience with Performance Pay." In *Paying for Performance: An International Comparison,* ed. Michelle Brown and John S. Heywood, 148–78. New York: M. E. Sharpe, 2002.

Jirjahn, Uwe, and Gesine Stephan. "Gender, Piece Rates and Wages: Evidence from Matched Employer–Employee Data." *Cambridge Journal of Economics* 28 (2004): 683–704.

Lazear, Edward, P. *Personnel Economics.* Cambridge, MA: MIT Press, 1995.

Levine, David I. "Cohesiveness, Productivity, and Wage Dispersion." *Journal of Economic Behavior and Organization* 15 (1991): 237–55.

MacLeod, W. Bently, and Daniel Parent. "Job Characteristics and the Form of Compensation." In *Research in Labor Economics*, vol. 18, ed. S. W. Polachek, 172–242. Greenwich, CT: JAI Press, 1999.

Martin, Stephen. "Endogenous Firm Efficiency in a Cournot Principal–Agent Model." *Journal of Economic Theory* 59 (1993): 445–50.

Nickell, Stephen. "Product Markets and Labour Markets." *Labour Economics* 6 (1999): 1–20.

Pfeiffer, Friedhelm. *Lohnrigiditäten in Gemischten Lohnbildungssystemen.* Mannheim: Nomos, 2003.

Rowthorne, R. E. "Centralisation, Employment and Wage Dispersion." *Economic Journal* 102 (1992): 506–23.

Rubery, Jill, and Collete Fagan. "Comparative Industrial Relations Research: Towards Reversing the Gender Bias." *British Journal of Industrial Relations* 33 (1995): 209–36.

Sap, Jolande. "Bargaining Power and Wages: A Game-Theoretic Model of Gender Differences in Union Wage Bargaining." *Labour Economics* 1 (1993): 25–48.

Schmidt, Klaus M. "Managerial Incentives and Product Market Competition." *Review of Economic Studies* 64 (1997): 191–213.

Stephan, Gesine. "Employer Wage Differentials in Germany: A Comparative Note." *Labour* 16 (2002): 491–512.

———. "The Lower Saxonian Salary and Wage Structure Survey—Linked Employer–Employee Data from Official Statistics." *Schmollers Jahrbuch: Journal of Applied Social Science Studies* 121 (2001): 267–73.

Winter-Ebmer, Rudolf. "Sex Discrimination and Competition in Product and Labour Markets." *Applied Economics* 27 (1995): 849–57.

Chapter 5

Gender Composition and Market Structure in Hong Kong

John S. Heywood and Xiangdong Wei

Introduction

This chapter uses original data to examine the connection between the gender composition of firms' employees and the market structure in which those firms operate. We were involved in the collection of the data and it has not been previously used for this purpose. We argue that Hong Kong just prior to the establishment of the Special Administrative Region provides an interesting test case and that the results reflect a highly flexible and deregulated labor market. As such, the findings from Hong Kong are not just one more data point but rather evidence from an environment more closely fitting the ideal of the neoclassical economist.

The argument that market structure influences discrimination has a long history. Originally modeled by Becker (1957), discriminating firms incur higher costs and, if markets are competitive and entry is free, find it difficult to compete with lower cost nondiscriminating firms. Milton Friedman (1962, 109) elegantly presents this view: "[T]he preserves of discrimination in any society are the areas that are most monopolistic in character, whereas discrimination against groups of particular color or religion is least in those areas where there is the greatest freedom of competition." Thus, at its most extreme, discrimination persists because of market imperfections.

From these early beginnings a substantial empirical literature has attempted to estimate the influence of product market structure on the extent of measured discrimination. This literature often examines racial discrimination, which we will not consider (see Heywood and O'Halloran in chaper 9 of this volume) and often examines earnings discrimination, which we will not consider (see Belfield and Heywood in chapter 3 of this volume). Our focus will be the influence of market structure on the gender composition of firms (used as a proxy to measure the extent of employment discrimination by gender). Despite this narrow focus, there exists a substantial empirical literature that we review in the next section. In that section we also present the importance of the Hong Kong case study. The third section reviews our data, the critical dependent and independent variables, and outlines our methodology. The fourth section isolates the anticipated role for our control variables and presents the heart of the empirical estimations, and the fifth section concludes.

Past Studies and the Case of Hong Kong

Studies from the United States suggest, on balance, that the employment opportunities of women are enhanced by increased product market competition. We first review these studies and then indicate the importance of our studying this relationship in Hong Kong.

PREVIOUS EMPIRICAL RESEARCH

A series of studies during the 1970s examined the relationship between market structure and the relative employment of women by examining the variation across industries and firms. Lyle and Ross (1973) examine female employment in 246 firms, showing that larger firms that dominate their market tended to concentrate their employment of women in lower-level positions when compared to other firms. Levin and Levin (1976) examine gender discrimination in white-collar employment, finding that the extent of employment discrimination increases as the extent of "discretionary profit" increases. They identify one of the sources for such profit as monopolistic market structure. Luksetich (1979) examines female white-collar employment across forty-four industries and nine Standard Metropolitan Statistical Areas (urban areas) in the United States. He shows that the concentration ratio has a robust and negative partial correlation as a determinant of the share of female white-collar workers. Oster (1975) presents somewhat mixed findings. She examines the variation in the female worker to male worker ratio across industries within eight professional occupations. She includes as a determinant of this ratio the four-firm concentration ratio for each industry. The sign of the coefficient on concentration emerges as negative for seven of the eight professions but is statistically significant for only two professions: those in personnel and those doing drafting. While limited to professional occupations and to those industries for which concentration ratios are readily available, we take this as at least weak confirmation for the role of product market structure.

These results are largely mirrored by those found from examining minority employment in the same time period. Shepherd (1969), Comanor (1973), and Haessel and Palmer (1978) each find that more monopolistic market structure is associated with reduced relative employment of racial minorities.

Yet, all of the studies from this period, those on both race and gender, suffer from seeking the variation in market structure from cross-industry differences. Ashenfelter and Hannan (1986) use the variation in structure across separate geographical markets in the same industry—banking. Their finding that more concentrated banking markets hire a smaller proportion of women as managers despite an extensive list of relevant controls is important for at least three reasons. First, the measure of market structure is more likely to have a similar meaning across markets in the same industry than it does across different industries. The elasticity of demand, the nature of the product, the extent of scale economies, and many other variables that influence the ability to exert market power are more likely to be held constant within a single industry. Second, and related, the omitted industry variables are much less likely to be driving the resulting correlation. Differences across industries such as skill requirements and working differences are among the potential excluded industry variables that might influence the racial composition and may also be correlated with market structure. Third, the findings are of particular interest as they arise from a regulated industry. Regulation may provide particular protections, barriers to entry for example, that insulate discriminatory firms that fail to profit maximize (Heywood, 1998). This raises the possibility of identifying the influence of market structure by examining the influence of deregulation.

In the United States, trucking deregulation dramatically changed the structure of the industry, creating a far more competitive market for trucking services. Heywood and Peoples (1994) and Agesa (1998) confirm that minority employment increased markedly following this change in market structure.[1] While less work has been done on the influence of deregulation on gender composition, Peoples and Robinson (1996) show that the relative employment of women in the telecommunications industry after the U.S. deregulation remained largely unchanged. They emphasize the role played by a series of successful discrimination lawsuits, resulting in pred-eregulation AT&T implementing strong affirmative action policies. They conclude, in part, that increased competition associated with deregulated industry without the affirmative action policies performed essentially as well as the regulated industry with those policies.

In summary, the evidence is not monolithic but the emerging consensus suggests that the relative employment opportunities of women are enhanced by increased product market competition. Importantly, these findings come only from the examination of the U.S. labor market despite the fact that gender discrimination remains an issue in most developed nations (Blau and Kahn, 2003). We next argue for the pertinence of such a study for Hong Kong.

THE CASE OF HONG KONG

Hong Kong provides an important test case as one of the world's most competitive labor markets. As measured by the number of International Labor Organization conventions it observes, Hong Kong has the world's least regulated and most flexible labor markets. As of the early 1990s, Hong Kong observed zero of the organization's conventions, often taken as a measure of government intervention in the labor market (see Edwards and Lustig, 1997), while the United States observed 11, Singapore 21, Argentina 67, Germany 74, and France 114. In more recent years more of the conventions have been recognized but the fundamental flexibility remains. In 2000 the International Monetary Fund continued to identify Hong Kong's labor market as substantially more flexible than the nations of the Organization for Economic Cooperation and Development (OECD) (Aziz et al., 2000).[2]

In general this former colony is identified as the "epitome of capitalism" and provides an example of a highly successful economy operating with less government regulation than is common in most developed countries including the United States (Enright, Scott, and Dowell, 1997). A good share of this success has been attributed to a highly flexible and competitive labor market, one in which "real wages adjust as quickly if not quicker than anywhere else in the World" (Enright, Scott, and Dowell, 1997, 110). Trade unions are largely absent and, when present, are largely ineffective (Snape and Chan, 1997). Moreover, government regulation of employer's hiring and wage policies is very limited by international standards (see Heywood, Ho, and Wei, 1999). While the "one country, two systems" policy was designed to retain Hong Kong's economic dynamism after absorption by China in 1997, our data provide a snapshot of the labor market in the year just prior to this absorption.[3]

Specifically, the regulation of hiring is based on the principle of equality between men and women as articulated in the Sex Discrimination Ordinance (SDO). The SDO renders hiring discrimination unlawful

on the grounds of gender, marital status, or pregnancy and further identifies sexual harassment as illegal. The responsibility for enforcing the
SDO falls to an independent statutory body, the Equal Opportunities
Commission. In understanding the issue of gender in the workplace, it is
critical to understand that the SDO was the first legislation against discrimination in Hong Kong. Yet, the commission was not established and
in operation until September 1996 and the SDO, including the employ-
ment-related provisions, did not take full effect until December 1996.
Thus, our snapshot of the labor market taken very early in 1996 occurred
during a period in which there was no prohibition on gender discrimination but in which legislation was in the process of creating such a prohibition. To the extent that the pattern we identify predates the legal
prohibition on gender discrimination, it shows a picture that many of the
U.S. studies do not. It identifies the influence that product market competition may play in reducing discrimination in an environment in which
the government is not actively supporting that reduction.[4] The Hong
Kong labor market prior to December 1996 has been examined by researchers who are interested by a large influx of women workers in the absence of governmental prohibitions on gender discrimination. Sung
(2001) notes that in the fifteen years prior to the SDO an increasing share
of women participated in the Hong Kong labor force and that the relative
education of women also increased dramatically. This was combined with
an industrial shift toward the traditionally less male-dominated service sector. With this as institutional background, he examines the female–male
earnings ratio, showing that it increased from 0.710 in 1981 to 0.839 in
1996. The author emphasizes that the overall magnitude of the ratio and
its growth are larger than that for similar ratios in the United States,
Canada, and the United Kingdom despite the absence of antidiscrimination legislation in Hong Kong. Sung does emphasize that the majority of
the remaining gender wage gap in Hong Kong is "unexplained" by typical
human capital or demographic controls. Yet, in related work Suen and
Chan (1997, 51) chronicle the relative improvement of women workers
prior to the SDO, expressing the view that while the SDO may help decrease the disadvantage of women, "continued progress will ultimately depend on their increasing commitment and attachment to the workforce."

More generally, the Hong Kong economy is highly diversified, with
every sector well represented except agriculture and mining. It shares
with other developed economies the fact that service industries have
replaced manufacturing as the sector with the largest employment. The
growth in financial services has been particularly large.[5] The per capital,
gross domestic product in 1996 stood at US$25,000, placing it ahead of

many other industrial countries, including Canada, the United Kingdom, and Australia.

Data and Methodology

In February 1996 our survey was mailed to a random sample of establishments in Hong Kong. The initial list of establishment names and addresses came from the master list maintained by the Census and Statistics Department and was made available to us. The surveys were addressed to the ranking human resource manager, recognizing that in smaller firms this person may have broader duties. We were fortunate to have a cover letter from the Manpower and Education Branch of the Hong Kong government that encouraged all establishments to respond and to have the help of a professional survey firm, Survey Research Hong Kong. By the end of March a total of 770 responses had been returned, for a gross response rate of about 31 percent. Officials from the Census and Statistics Department suggested to us that the characteristics of the sample aligned well with those in the full population. More detail on the questionnaire and the survey methodology are available from the Centre for Public Policy Studies (1996).

The original purpose of the survey was to examine the age distribution of new hires and of existing workers among Hong Kong establishments. Evidence from the survey suggested that there exists a set of establishments that employ older workers but fail to hire older workers. In addition to whatever role discrimination might play, it was clear that this pattern was motivated by both concerns over specific human capital and internal labor markets (see Heywood, Ho, and Wei, 1999). Included in the questionnaire, but largely not used in the above examination, was a question asking the gender composition of the workplace, as measured by the percent of female employees. This variable has proven important in other contexts in Hong Kong as Heywood and Wei (1997) show that establishments with a greater share of female employees are more likely to provide more immediate rewards through payment schemes like piece rates but are less likely to delay rewards through deferred compensation. Yet, despite previous work on age discrimination and previous concern over the gender composition of the workplace, these unique survey data have not been used to examine the determinants of that composition.

We limit our attention to those establishments that report the full set of information needed for our inquiry. This results in a sample size of 641 establishments. As shown in table 5.1, the critical dependent variable indicates that, on average, an establishment's workforce is approximately 44 percent female workers.

The critical independent variable is an establishment-specific measure of market structure, taking a value of one if managers respond that either their product dominates the market or that they have few competitors. The availability of the establishment-specific measure distinguishes this research from much of the related work in the United States, which is only able to match an industry or market-wide measure of industrial concentration to individual data. It might be argued that a manager's perception is subjective but it should be emphasized that it is the manager's perception of market latitude that influences the extent of discrimination in a Becker-type model of discrimination. Put differently, those managers who feel insulated from the competitive market may well be those who are more likely to discriminate. In any event, table 5.1 shows that approximately one-quarter of the establishments report dominating their market or having few competitors.

Table 5.2 presents a simple cross tabulation of these two critical variables. It shows that establishments that have market power are more likely to have shares of women 40 percent or less than establishments without market power. At the same time, establishments with market power are less likely to have shares of women above 40 percent than establishments without market power. A difference of means test reveals the average share of women workers among the firms with market power to be about 4 percentage points lower but that the difference is statistically significant at only the 10 percent level.

The methodology in what follows presents two series of regression estimates. The first series will be simple ordinary least squares with the share of women, α, as the dependent variable explained by controls and the critical market structure variable. The second series recognizes that the share of women is constrained to be between one and zero and assumes a logistic formulation. The resulting log-odds estimation transforms the dependent variable:

$$A = \ln \alpha \ / \ \ln(1 - \alpha) \tag{5.1}$$

The transformed variable A becomes the dependent variable in a linear specification:

$$A_i = X_i'\beta + \varepsilon_i \tag{5.2}$$

Table 5.1 Variable Description and Descriptive Statistics for Hong Kong

Variables	Mean	Std. Dev.	Description
% FEMALE	44.1%	0.237	% female employees in the firm
MPOWER	0.252	0.434	Dummy=1 for firms that dominate or have few competitors in the market
LSIZE	3.622	1.653	Log firm size1 for firms that dominate or have few competitors in the market
LSIZE	3.622	1.653	Log firm size
AGE	17.060	17.770	Firm age
SALES	0.175	0.380	Dummy=1 for firms with majority employees in sales occupations
PROF	0.145	0.352	Dummy=1 for firms with majority employees in professional and managerial occupations
SKILL	0.416	0.493	Dummy=1 for firms with majority employees in skilled workers occupations
UNSKILL tions	0.249	0.433	Dummy=1 for firms with majority employees in unskilled workers occupa-
UNION	0.033	0.180	Dummy=1 for firms recognizing a union for collective bargaining
MEET	0.320	0.470	Dummy=1 for firms holding regular meetings with employee representatives
PTEN5	38.3%	42.785	% of employees with 5 and over years tenure
PERPAY	0.323	0.468	Dummy=1 for firms having a performance-related pay scheme for any group of employees
PENSION	0.480	0.500	Dummy=1 for firms having a pension scheme for employees
APPRAI	0.556	0.497	Dummy=1 for firms carrying out regular job appraisals
TURNCOST	2.123	1.319	1 (low) −5 (high) categorical measure of firms' turnover cost

(*continued*)

Table 5.1 (*continued*)

Variables	Mean	Std. Dev.	Description
OWNCH	0.092	0.290	Dummy=1 for firms with ownership change during the last 3 years
TECHCH	0.310	0.460	Dummy=1 for firms with technology change during the last 3 years
MANCH	0.316	0.465	Dummy=1 for firms with change of management styles during the past 3 years
% OLD	16.9%	26.844	% of employees over 44 years old

Industry dummies (omitted industry: manufacturing):

IND2	0.068	0.250	Dummy=1 for construction
IND3	0.210	0.400	Dummy=1 for wholesale and import/export trade
IND4	0.076	0.270	Dummy=1 for retail
IND5	0.100	0.300	Dummy=1 for hotel and restaurants
IND6	0.085	0.280	Dummy=1 for transportation, storage, and communication
IND7	0.170	0.370	Dummy=1 finance, insurance, real estate, and business service
IND8	0.046	0.210	Dummy=1 for community, social, and personal services

Sample size: 641

Table 5.2 Cross Tabulation of Gender Share and Market Structure

	MPOWER = 0	MPOWER = 1	Observations
0–20% Female	18.5	19.3	120
21–40% Female	26.9	32.7	181
41–60% Female	31.0	28.0	194
61–80% Female	15.9	14.7	100
81–100% Female	7.7	5.3	46
Total	100.0	100.0	641

Note: The entry in each cell is the share of all observations within that market structure.

Here the marginal effect of a particular independent variable X^j on the underlying proportion α is as follows:

$$\partial\alpha/\partial X^j = \hat{\beta}^j\bar{\alpha}(1 - \bar{\alpha}) \tag{5.3}$$

where $\hat{\beta}^j$ is the estimated coefficient on the jth independent variable from equation (5.2) and where $\bar{\alpha}$ is the mean level from the sample of the dependent variable, the share of women. As some of the establishments have shares of women equal to one or zero, we adopt arbitrarily small epsilon values above zero and below one so these observations can be included.

For each series we will begin with a parsimonious specification, then present an augmented specification, an even further extended specification, and then a final refinement in which we drop the observations that have shares of women equal to one or zero. The full set of explanatory variables and their descriptive statistics are presented in table 5.1.

Regression Results

Our parsimonious specification includes as controls the size of the establishment, the age of the establishment, dummy variables to control for the four broad occupational groups available to us in the survey, a set of one-digit industrial controls, and an indicator of whether a union is recognized for collective bargaining. To the extent that women are concentrated in particular broad occupations or industries, these controls will allow us to more narrowly identify the role of market structure. The results are presented in table 5.3.

The industrial controls play an important role, with women less likely in manufacturing and construction but more likely across the service industries. The age and size of the establishment play no role in the regressions but the presence of a recognized union plays a large role. There are very few unions in Hong Kong but those that exist are concentrated in traditionally male occupations. Thus, it is not surprising that establishments with unions report a lower share of women workers, all else equal. The broad occupational controls show only a very modest role with establishment, with mostly professional workers reporting a higher share of women workers in the log-odds estimation.

Table 5.3   Regressions with the Parsimonious Model

Dependent Variable

Independent Variables	% FEMALE		Log-Odds of % FEMALE	
	Coefficients	t-statistics	Coefficients	t-statistics
Constant	0.493	15.651**	0.082	0.460
MPOWER	−0.046	−2.146**	−0.348	−4.933**
LSIZE	0.001	0.231	0.007	0.267
AGE	0.001	0.926	0.002	1.560
SALES	−0.005	−0.182	0.220	1.668*
PROF	0.032	1.078	0.292	2.362**
SKILL	−0.018	−0.756	0.069	0.746
UNION	−0.138	−2.454**	−1.232	−7.421**
IND2	−0.300	−7.788**	−1.593	−7.196**
IND3	−0.025	−0.917	−0.438	−2.743**
IND4	−0.035	−0.863	0.220	1.335
IND5	−0.103	−3.093**	−0.687	−5.869**
IND6	−0.105	−2.926**	−0.565	−4.386**
IND7	−0.062	−2.168**	−0.336	−3.537**
IND8	0.188	3.855**	0.500	3.073**
Adjusted R^2	0.131		0.285	
Sample Size	641		641	

*significant at 10 percent level   **significant at 5 percent level.

The market structure variable is large and highly significant in both estimations. In the linear estimation the presence of market power is associated with a 4.6 percentage points lower share of women in the establishment holding all else equal. In the log-odds formulation the influence of market power is a reduction in the share of women workers of 8.6 percentage points.[6] For comparison this is not as large as the influence of an establishment recognizing a union but larger than the influence of having professionals as the largest occupational group. The explained variation is reasonable for cross-sectional data but it is interesting to note that the log-odds specification does have a higher R-squared.

Our extended specification includes all of the variables already discussed but adds the share of workers with long tenure; whether the firm holds regular meetings, uses performance-related pay, offers a pension, and carries out regular appraisals of employees; and the manager's evaluation of the extent of turnover costs. We anticipate that longer tenure is more likely in jobs and firms with greater specific human capital requirements and that those firms will be less likely to hire women because of their lower expected tenure (Heywood, Ho, and Wei, 1999). Performance pay may be positively associated with the share of women as it is a more immediate form of reward compared to deferred compensation that women more greatly discount (Goldin, 1986). Similarly, as a type of deferred compensation, pensions may be associated with lower shares of women workers. Appraisals may be evidence of an internal labor market that plays the same role as deferred compensation and, again, may be associated with lower shares of women workers. High turnover cost may make women less valuable because of their shorter tenure and so may be associated with lower shares of women workers.

The results of the augmented specification are presented in table 5.4. Of the new variables in the linear specification, only the tenure variable emerges with a statistically significant coefficient. It indicates that establishments with a large share of high tenure workers have significantly lower shares of women workers. As in the earlier log-odds estimation, the current linear estimation shows that establishments with professional workers as their largest occupational category have significant greater shares of women workers. The R-squared of the linear estimate is only modestly higher than in the parsimonious specification. Importantly, the influence of market structure remains statistically significant. Firms that dominate their market or have few competitors have 5.3 percentage points lower shares of women workers, all else constant.

In the log-odds formulation the share of high tenure workers again emerges as a strong negative partial correlate. The role of the professional

Table 5.4 Regressions with the Augmented Model

| | Dependent Variable | | | |
| | % FEMALE | | Log-Odds of % FEMALE | |
Independent Variables	Coefficients	t-statistics	Coefficients	t-statistics
Constant	0.481	12.383**	0.193	0.989
MPOWER	−0.053	−2.374**	−0.480	−6.589**
LSIZE	0.006	0.757	0.033	1.055
AGE	0.001	1.129	0.006	3.845**
SALES	0.002	0.068	0.274	1.937*
PROF	0.066	1.972*	0.329	2.578**
SKILL	0.001	0.029	0.091	1.002
MEET	0.008	0.369	−0.042	−0.649
PTEN5	−0.0004	−2.238**	−0.003	−2.442**
PERPAY	−0.005	−0.265	0.075	0.974
UNION	−0.202	−3.271**	−2.029	−11.049**
PENSION	0.030	1.339	−0.100	−0.937
APPRAI	−0.019	−0.779	−0.028	−0.213
TURNCOST	−0.012	−1.657*	0.001	0.034
IND2	−0.279	-6.923**	−1.527	−6.695**
IND3	−0.012	−0.397	−0.625	−3.901**
IND4	−0.032	−0.754	−0.009	−0.056
IND5	−0.069	−1.782*	−0.806	−6.673**
IND6	−0.107	−2.686**	−0.583	−4.546**
IND7	−0.046	−1.477	−0.496	−4.824**
IND8	0.156	2.728**	0.247	1.269
Adjusted R^2	0.136		0.431	
Sample Size	508		508	

Note: Three change variables and the percent of older workers were included but were not statistically significant. *significant at 10 percent level   ***significant at 5 percent level.

occupational group remains as do the roles for union recognition and the industrial dummies. The extended specification shows the older firms have significantly larger shares of women workers. This may reflect the fact that some of the older firms include textile, sewing, and other female-dominated jobs. The R-squared increased substantially as a result of the added variables.

In any event, the market structure coefficient emerges with one of the largest t-statistics and indicates that firms with market power have almost 12 percentage points lower shares of women workers holding all else constant. To emphasize this point we estimate the share of female workers in establishments with average characteristics but with and without market power. The share with market power is 35 percent and that in competitive firms is 47 percent. This is roughly the difference between an establishment that is one-third women and an establishment that is one-half women.

In addition to these variables we have measures of the extent of older workers as older workers have lower rates of female participation in the Hong Kong labor market. We also add three measures of change at the establishment level. These measures indicate whether there has been ownership change, technological change, or management change in the last three years. Adding these additional variables to the specification gives the full extended specification in table 5.5.

In the linear specification, the extent of older workers seems to be positively associated with the extent of women workers as the participation pattern would suggest. None of the change variables emerge as statistically significant. Despite the continued modest loss of sample size as additional variables are added, the pattern of other results remains roughly as before. The coefficient on the market power variables increases further, indicating that firms with market power have 5.7 percentage points lower share of women workers.

The log-odds specification gives a slightly different portrait of the new variables. Change of any sort—ownership, technology, or management—is associated with a larger share of women workers. We suspect that these change variables are negatively associated with firm age and that younger firms have greater shares of women as they have done most of their hiring more recently when the female labor force participation rate is higher. Interestingly, the share of old workers does not emerge as significant in this specification. The general pattern of results remains as before and the very strong role of market structure is repeated. The even larger coefficient translates into a reduction of more than 13 percentage points in the share of women workers for those establishments with market power.

Table 5.5 Regressions with the Extended Model

| | Dependent Variable | | | |
| | % FEMALE | | Log-Odds of % FEMALE | |
Independent Variables	Coefficients	t-statistics	Coefficients	t-statistics
Constant	0.394	8.011**	0.076	0.348
MPOWER	−0.057	−2.509**	−0.530	−7.156**
LSIZE	0.002	2.317**	0.040	1.151
AGE	0.001	0.936	0.005	3.104**
SALES	0.005	0.147	0.218	1.540
PROF	0.073	2.134*	0.384	3.054**
SKILL	0.003	0.122	0.022	0.237
MEET	0.004	0.176	−0.018	−0.277
PTEN5	−0.0004	−2.282**	−0.003	−1.979**
PERPAY	−0.0005	−0.023	0.035	0.426
UNION	−0.237	−3.531**	−2.382	−11.33**
PENSION	0.029	1.263	−0.143	−1.343
APPRAI	−0.015	−0.631	−0.073	−0.558
TURNCOST	−0.013	−1.737*	0.022	0.809
OWN CHG	0.032	0.966	0.400	3.179**
TECH CHG	−0.002	0.087	0.173	2.331**
MANG CHG	0.012	0.566	0.159	2.215**
% OLD	0.002	2.686*	0.004	0.530
IND2	−0.279	−6.834**	−1.407	−6.249**
IND3	−0.017	−0.609	−0.365	−2.173**
IND4	−0.035	−0.802	0.187	1.077
IND5	−0.076	−1.915*	−0.631	−4.783**
IND6	−0.110	−2.719**	−0.427	−3.252**
IND7	−0.053	−1.678*	−0.311	−2.875**
IND8	0.131	2.224**	0.281	1.471
Adjusted R^2	0.149		0.466	
Sample Size	497		497	

*significant at 10 percent level   **significant at 5 percent level.

Finally, we recognize that some of the establishments, mostly smaller ones, have shares of women that are either zero or one. These may be critical observations that bias the results. In other words the basic decision to have a gender-integrated workplace may have different determinants than the decision once integrated to have a larger or smaller share of women workers. To test this we again estimate the extended specification but eliminate all values of the dependent variable that are either zero or one.

This refinement gives us greater confidence in our results as the new specification changes none of the patterns already identified. The same controls retain their importance and market structure remains statistically significant. Here the establishments that dominate their market have 5.6 percentage points lower shares of women workers as indicated by the linear estimate and, again, more than 13 percentage points lower shares of women by the log-odds estimate.

Conclusions

We have argued that our snapshot of the Hong Kong labor market provides a valuable laboratory. It is a laboratory characterized by a highly flexible and unregulated labor market in a highly competitive and entrepreneurial society. In reviewing our findings it is interesting to recall that others examining Hong Kong have found that despite the absence of antidiscrimination laws, women seemed to fare about as well as in countries with such laws. Yet, our inquiry was not an examination across countries but an examination across market structures within Hong Kong.

Using original data we have details on market structure and gender composition for a sample of Hong Kong establishments. The descriptive statistics suggested that establishments that dominate their market appeared to hire fewer women. As we went through progressively more refined estimation, this result endured. Indeed, the magnitude of the relationship actually grew as we added variables and refined our sample.

Assuming this relationship accurately reflects the labor market in Hong Kong, several implications emerge. First, in the absence of antidiscrimination laws, there is substantial variation in the share of female workers across firms. Second, this variation has consistent patterns by industry and occupational group. Third, and most critical, the tenants of the neoclassical theory of discrimination are supported by the evidence from a labor market most closely resembling the neoclassical ideal. The share of women workers is larger in establishments operating in more competitive product markets. While it might be easy to simply call for competitive product markets in all cases, this may not be easily achieved if there exist substantial scale economies, patents, or other government intervention. More constructively, it might be suggested that the Equal Opportunities Commission dedicated to enforcing the SDO might best concentrate its resources on firms operating in less competitive product markets as it is there that the extent of discrimination appears to be greatest.

Notes

1. It is important to stress that the change flows from the increased competition not from deregulation per se. Agesa (2001) shows that deregulation in the U.S. airline industry did not dramatically change the extent of competition and, consequently, had little influence on the relative hiring of minorities.

2. The International Monetary Fund report contends that even though Hong Kong product markets have moved away from being highly competitive relative to OECD countries, the flexibility of the labor market remains unrivaled.

3. Lee and Warner (2002) present the view that since absorption there is an emerging, but still small, degree of convergence between the labor market in Hong Kong and those in other large Chinese cities.

4. For details on the SDO, see the government-provided information at its Web site: http://www.info.gov.hk/info/women.htm.

5. For more detail on these sectoral shifts and their employment consequences, see Suen (1995).

6. We recognize these are based on coefficients on a dummy variable and represent approximations.

References

Agesa, Jacqueline. "Deregulation and the Racial Composition of Airlines." *Journal of Policy Analysis and Management* 20 (2001): 223–37
———. "The Impact of Deregulation on Employment Discrimination in the Trucking Industry." *Atlantic Economic Journal* 26 (1998): 288–303.
Ashenfelter, Orley, and Timothy Hannan. "Sex Discrimination and Product Market Structure: The Case of Banking." *Quarterly Journal of Economics* 101 (1986): 149–74.
Aziz, Jahangir, Peter Breuer, Yukatka Nishigaki, and Peter Strum. "People's Republic of China–Hong Kong SAR: Selected Issues and Statistical Appendix," IMF Staff Country Report 00/30, 2000.
Becker, Gary. *The Economics of Discrimination.* Chicago: University of Chicago Press, 1957.
Blau, Francine, and Lawrence Kahn. "Understanding International Differences in the Gender Pay Gap." *Journal of Labor Economics* 21 (2003): 106–45.

Centre for Public Policy Studies, Lingnan University. "Age Discrimination in Employment." A Fact-Finding Study Commissioned by the Education and Manpower Branch, 1996.

Comanor, William. "Racial Discrimination in American Industry." *Economica* 40 (1973): 363–80.

Edwards, Sebastian, and Nora Lustig. Introduction. In *Labor Markets in Latin American: Combining Social Protection with Market Flexibility*, ed. Sebastian Edwards and Nora Lustig, 1–26. Washington, DC: Brookings Institutions Press, 1997.

Enright, Michael, Edith Scott, and David Dowell. *The Hong Kong Advantage.* Oxford, UK: Oxford University Press, 1997.

Friedman, Milton. *Capitalism and Freedom.* Chicago: University of Chicago Press, 1962.

Goldin, Claudia. "Monitoring Costs and Segregation by Sex: A Historical Analysis." *Journal of Labor Economics* 4 (1986): 1–27.

Haessel, Walter, and John Palmer. "Market Power and Employment Discrimination." *Journal of Human Resources* 13 (1978): 545–59.

Heywood, John S. 1998. "Regulated Industries and Measures of Earnings Discrimination." In *Regulatory Reform and Labor Markets*, ed. James Peoples, 287-324. Boston: Kluwer Academic Publishers, 1988.

Heywood, John S., Lok Sang Ho, and Xiangdong Wei. "Determinants of Hiring Older Workers: Evidence from Hong Kong." *Industrial and Labor Relations Review* 52 (1999): 444–59.

Heywood, John S., and James Peoples. "Deregulation and the Prevalence of Black Truck Drivers." *Journal of Law and Economics* 37 (1994): 133–55.

Heywood, John S., and Xiangdong Wei. "Piece Rate Payment Schemes and the Employment of Women." *Journal of Comparative Economics* 25 (1997): 237–55.

Lee, Grace, and Malcolm Warner. "Labour-Market Policies in Shanghai and Hong Kong: A Study of 'One Country, Two Systems.'" *International Journal of Manpower* 23 (2002): 505–26.

Levin, Sharon, and Stanford Levin. "Profit Maximization and Discrimination." *Industrial Organization Review* 2 (1976): 108–16.

Luksetich, William. "Market Power and Sex Discrimination in White-Collar Employment." *Review of Social Economy* 37 (1979): 211–24.

Lyle, Jerolyn, and Jane Ross. *Women in Industry.* Lexington, MA: Lexington Books, 1973.

Oster, Sharon. "Industry Differences in the Level of Discrimination against Women." *Quarterly Journal of Economics* 89 (1975): 215–29.

Peoples, James, and Rhonda Robinson. "Market Structure and Racial and Gender Discrimination: Evidence from the Telecommunications Industry." *American Journal of Economics and Sociology* 55 (1996): 209–26.

Shepherd, William. "Market Power and Racial Discrimination in White Collar Employment." *Antitrust Bulletin* 14 (1969): 141–61.

Snape, Ed, and Andy Chan. "Whither Hong Kong's Unions: Autonomous Trade Unionism or Classic Dualism?" *British Journal of Industrial Relations* 37 (1997): 39–64.

Suen, Wing. "Sector Shifts: Impact on Hong Kong Workers." *Journal of International Trade and Economic Development* 4 (1995): 135–52.

Suen, Wing, and William Chan. *The Labour Market in a Dynamic Economy.* Hong Kong: City University of Hong Kong Press, 1997.

Sung, Yun-Wing. "Gender Wage Differentials and Occupational Segregation in Hong Kong." *Pacific Economic Review* 6 (2001): 345–59.

Chapter 6

Privatization and Racial Earnings Differentials

James H. Peoples and Wayne K. Talley

Introduction

A lack of competition can lead to positive racial wage differentials in local public sector labor markets. Such wage differentials may occur despite municipal employers' strict adherence to equal employment opportunity laws that prohibit earnings and employment discrimination. Racial earnings differentials may arise because black and white municipal employees work (and live) in different metropolitan locations. Thus, municipal workers of one race may work disproportionately in municipalities that rent-share by passing high labor costs on to tax payers. Recent privatization can radically alter the labor market environment for local government employees by introducing competition. If racial wage differentials reflect rent-sharing, competitive pressure may reduce the wages of the race benefiting from working in rent-sharing communities.

Past research has reported a significant link between racial wage differentials and privatization. Peoples and Talley (2002) show that public transit drivers receive a premium associated with residency in a city. This city wage advantage contributes to a substantial wage premium for black drivers over their white counterparts. Privatization creates greater incentives to employ drivers from outside the city and had the unintended effect of eliminating the apparent earnings advantage of black drivers. Given the racially segmented residency patterns that persist in many metropolitan areas, past findings on racial earnings differentials and privatization may not be unique to public transit. The pre-privatization black wage advantage in public transit, though, is highly unlikely in other segments of the public service sector. The importance of examining the influence of privatization on racial earnings is highlighted by the fact that the public sector has historically been a major source of high wage jobs for minorities.

This study contributes to the understanding of public sector wage determination by examining the association between privatization and racial wage differentials in five public service sectors. The next section describes the different methods local governments use to privatize services, revealing how privatization exerts downward pressure on the cost of providing public services. The third section uses Sam Peltzman's (1976) model of government policy to identify the determinants of privatization. Special emphasis is given to residential location as a potential determinant of the pattern of racial wage differentials among municipal employees. The fourth section presents the data and empirical approach used to test the hypotheses derived from using Peltzman's model. Labor earnings equations are estimated in the fifth section, and concluding remarks are presented in the sixth section.

Privatization and Labor Cost Savings

Methods for reducing the costs, and in particular the labor costs, of the public provision of services include (1) labor incentive programs for eliciting greater productivity (e.g., rewarding superior performance) from existing government employees; (2) asset privatization, the transfer of government assets of a publicly provided service to the private sector for its provision; and (3) service privatization, the transfer of a publicly provided service (but not public sector assets) to the private sector for its provision. The motivation for privatization is the assumption that the private sector will be more efficient at providing the service than the public sector. "Private sector managers are subject to incentives and disciplines different from, and more demanding than, those which apply to their public sector counterparts" (Kay and Thompson, 1986, 18). Savas (1998) found that the primary sources of cost savings achieved from privatizing public services are private owners providing private employees less paid time off, less vacation time, and fewer paid absences compared to public employees. Compared to public owners, private contractors were also more likely to employ younger workers as well as part-time and lower-skilled workers. Privatization also may be a means by which government can reduce the rent-seeking power of public sector labor unions.

Examples of service privatization include contracting-out, competitive (or franchising) tendering, and privatization competition. Contracting-out occurs when a public authority (e.g., a municipality, state government, or a public firm) transfers one or more of its services to a private provider(s).

Competitive tendering occurs when a franchise authority (distinct from the public authority) auctions the transfer of a public authority's service to the private sector. If the public authority can participate in the tendering of its service, the tendering is privatization competition. If an outside contractor is the lowest bidder, the service is privatized. If the public authority is the lowest bidder, the service is not privatized, but cost savings will still occur if the authority's cost bid is lower than its current cost of provision.

Contracting-out privatization can be viewed as a principal–agent issue. The principal is the public authority, the agent is the private service provider, and the contract is the mechanism by which the principal induces the agent to act in its interests. Contracting-out has both direct and indirect effects on the labor costs of publicly provided services. The direct effect is the labor cost-saving effect from substituting lower-cost labor of privately provided services for the higher-cost labor of publicly provided services. In a U.S. survey of contracted-out public transit services, Teal (1988) found cost savings in the range of 9 to 23 percent from substituting private for public transit services. "The private companies achieve lower labor costs mainly because they use non-union labor, pay lower wages, and offer fewer benefits" (Black, 1991, 73).[1]

The indirect (or threat) effect is the labor cost-saving effect attributed to cost discipline: the private provider sets a visible standard on what services should cost. Public workers providing similar services to those of private providers are expected to moderate their demands from fear they might be replaced—not only because they face actual competition for their jobs (from further contracting-out) but also because they face potential competition, that is, they are employed at a public authority where services are not currently, but have the potential to be, privatized. For the U.S. public transit industry, there is little evidence of an indirect effect from contracting-out. Talley (1998) found that public transit union premiums did not change markedly following the introduction of contracting-out. His finding is attributed to public transit firms having to make union wage concessions for the right to privatize services.

As for contracting-out, competitive tendering has also resulted in direct labor cost savings for privatized public services. Competitive tendering, however, is more likely to exhibit an indirect labor cost-saving effect than contracting-out. Specifically, since a franchise authority, rather than the public authority, determines the transference of a public authority's service to the private sector, public unions are less likely to obtain wage concessions for service privatization. In the United Kingdom the Transport Act of 1985 deregulated the local public bus service industry (excluding London) as well as provided for competitive tendering of subsidized services. UK bus operators are generally free to offer whatever commercial bus services they wish. An independent agency was established to decide which services are to be tendered and which private providers will provide the services. Wage reductions in the UK local bus service industry following passage of the 1985 act are attributable to (1) cost-saving work-rule concessions, (2) wage-tier concessions, and (3) the payment of minibus drivers at lower rates than big bus drivers. It appears that the "mere threat of competition from entrants . . . was sufficient to force unions to cave in on the introduction of minibus wage rates and working practices" (Heseltine and Silcock, 1990, 251).

An investigation by Snyder, Trost, and Trunkey (2001) of cost savings from privatization competition estimates that the U.S. Department of Defense saved $1.46 billion from the 3,500 privatization competitions that were conducted from 1978 to 1994. The cost savings not only arose from transferring Defense work to private contractors that were more efficient than in-house teams (savings from privatization) but also from the teams submitting bids substantially lower than current in-house costs (savings from competition). Privatization competitions are particularly useful for reducing the costs of public sector work projects for which similar projects are found in the private sector. The bidding may be less competitive for work projects that require sunk investments. Nonetheless, "privatization competitions may be more efficient than either maintaining public ownership or straight privatization" (Snyder, Trost, and Trunkey, 2001, 109).[2]

Determinants of Local Government Privatization

Despite the potential for cost savings, evidence presented in table 6.1 reveals that many municipalities continue to rely on public ownership to provide public services. The table indicates that less than one-half of public employees providing construction, recreation, or health services reside in municipalities that have privatized at least part of these service sectors. The same pattern holds for private sector workers who are employed in these same sectors. Public transit and public utilities are the only heavily privatized services of the five presented in this table.[3] Apparently, privatization has not generated the requisite political support for a wholesale shift to using private owners even though high public wages present taxpayers with the incentive to support privatization officials. The failure to generate support results in large part from resistance by the beneficiaries of public policies that encourage high wage payments to municipal workers (Chandler and Feuille, 1991). Strong resistance can arise even if the beneficiary municipal workers are not a majority of the voting public.

Table 6.1   Mean Residency Patterns

Panel 1. Mean percentage of *local government workers* residing in localities that have privatized part of the sector in which worker is employed

Sector	Privatization Concentration	Sample Population
Construction	16.67%	1,015
Public Transit	88.23	620
Energy Utilities	76.26	1,369
Recreation	28.68	1,013
Health Services	38.30	1,697

Panel 2. Mean percentage of *private sector workers* residing in localities that have privatized part of the sector in which worker is employed

Sector	Privatization Concentration	Sample Population
Construction	18.22%	23,527
Public Transit	88.12	1,687
Energy Utilities	91.45	3,626
Recreation	23.75	4,510
Health Services	42.79	26,188

Source: Bureau of Economic Analysis 1999 Census of Government and 1999–2001 Annual Current Population Survey–Outgoing Rotation Group files.

Peltzman's model on public policy determinants would assume that the chances of municipal workers defeating pro-privatization candidates depends on attaining a majority vote depicted by the following equation:

$$n \cdot \alpha(\varphi) > (N-n) \cdot \beta\,(\tau,\pi) \tag{6.1}$$

In this equation n denotes the number of voters supporting the public employment of workers providing municipal services, N is the number of potential voters, $\alpha(\varphi)$ is the probability that supporters of public employment vote for the public system, and β is the probability that supporters of privatization vote against public employment of workers. The probability of support for the public system is dependent on the "net" gain to the beneficiaries of this system as depicted by the variable φ, where

$\varphi = (T-K-C(n))/n$, K is the campaign funding provided to gain political support, and $C(n)$ is the cost of organizing supporters of the public
system. The variable T is the consumer surplus transferred to the beneficiaries of the public system. Such surplus is used to fund the earnings of
publicly employed municipal workers. It is assumed that the probability
that workers from the public system vote yes increases with increasing consumer surplus transferred to them in the form of higher earnings.

Within Peltzman's framework municipal workers depict an ideal
pressure group to successfully support its candidate. They have easy access to funds for advertising campaigns to promote antiprivatization candidates, since these workers are generally represented by municipal
unions. Municipal unions also have low per capitia campaign organization costs due to the ease of mobilizing their membership. Furthermore,
municipal unions can take advantage of representing a relatively small
interest group who benefit from sustaining a public system that supports
high public wages as long as such labor compensation results in a small
per capitia cost for taxpayers

Peltzman's model also reveals that municipal unions' advantages as
a pressure group erodes at high enough public wage rates. This wage effect is captured by including the variables τ and π as determinants of opposition resistance. The variable τ denotes the local per capita tax rate
and π denotes the cost to municipal workers to inform voters of the benefits of sustaining a public system. Negotiating high public wage rates requires funding from high tax receipts, which increases the probability of
opponents voting against the use of public employment. Such a tax burden also requires greater promotional expenditure from municipal
workers to convince taxpayers that the benefits of operating a high wage
public system outweighs contracting-out to low wage workers from the
private sector. Indeed, Kodrzycki (1994) indicates that municipalities
with higher public wages usually serve large metropolitan areas and are
more likely to contract-out.

A potential labor market effect associated with the increased likelihood of privatization in high wage and large metropolitan areas is that
privatization will alter racial earnings differentials because black municipal workers disproportionately reside in these localities. Labor market information on major U.S. metropolitan areas presented in table 6.2
confirms that black workers are disproportionately employed by municipalities in nine of the ten largest urban areas and these areas generally
pay high public wages.[4] As indicated in column (3), all of these metropolitan areas, except Dallas, pay public wages above the national average
of $373 for public municipal workers. The possibility that the concentra-
tion of black municipal workers in high wage areas helps explain racial

Table 6.2 Metropolitan Area Labor Earnings and Racial Residency Patterns of Public Municipal Employees

Ten Largest Metropolitan Areas by Rank	(1) Percentage of All Black Public Municipal Employees (1999–2001)	(2) Percentage of All White Public Municipal Employees (1999–2001)	(3) Mean Public Municipal Employees' Weekly Earnings (1999–2001; 1987 Dollars)
New York	16.53%	4.94%	$436
Los Angeles	5.29	3.93	456
Chicago	6.15	4.93	413
Philadelphia	3.15	2.03	398
San Francisco	0.43	0.39	519
Detroit	4.41	1.77	410
Boston	0.58	1.60	391
Houston	2.31	1.07	426
Washington, D.C.	9.51	1.07	405
Dallas	1.39	0.85	351
Mean Weekly Earnings of Municipal Employees for the U.S.	—	—	373

Source: 1999–2001 Annual Current Population Survey–Outgoing Rotation Group files.

earnings differentials when municipalities privatize has been explored in past research, yet such analysis was limited to public transit drivers (Peoples and Talley, 2001, 2002). Examination of racial earnings differentials in other sectors of the public system is needed for a broader analysis of privatization's influence on these differentials.

Data and Wage Estimation Procedure

Two data sources reporting municipality and individual worker information are used to examine privatization and racial earnings differentials.

Municipality information is taken from the Bureau of Economic Analysis (BEA) 1999 Census of Government. This source includes privatization information on twenty-six public services at the township level. Municipalities contracting-out to workers in the private sector are identified by assigning a value of one for the privatized service. Municipalities employing their own in-house employees are assigned a value of zero. A major shortcoming encountered when using the BEA's dichotomous measure for privatization is it precludes distinguishing municipalities by the extent to which they rely on private contractors. Thus, municipalities using both a small and a large percentage of workers from the private sector are simply identified as privatized. Nonetheless, reporting privatization information at the municipality level is an important advance for examining privatization and racial earnings differentials as information used in past research did not identify privatized municipalities but simply relied on time dummies to identify policy shifts favoring privatization.

Individual worker information is taken from 1999–2001 Current Population Survey–Outgoing Rotation Group files (CPS–ORG). Files from this data source report information on worker characteristics, weekly earnings, regional and local residency, and the individual worker's industry and occupation of employment. The population sample taken from these files are limited to individual respondents who are employed and are sixteen years of age or older. This sample is merged with the BEA file by using local residency identifiers. The CPS uses four-digit metropolitan statistical area (MSA) codes, while the BEA uses its own coding system for townships. Codes are matched using the Census Bureau's *Government Integrated Directory* to convert township BEA codes to census MSA codes. Since such matching requires aggregating township level information at the MSA level, privatization is identified as a weighted percentage of privatized townships within an MSA.[5] Merging these CPS and BEA files also limits the population sample to only include individuals who report working for thirteen of the twenty-six public services reported in the BEA. This reduction in the number of public services reported in the sample arises because CPS files only report worker information for the more limited set of public services.[6] In addition, due to small sample sizes, data of closely related service categories are combined such that of the remaining thirteen services only worker information for individuals employed in construction, public transit, power utilities, parks and recreation, and health services are included in this study.[7]

Mean weekly earnings compiled from using information from the merged files are presented in table 6.3.[8] These results suggest two key labor earnings patterns. Excluding health services, privatization is associated with smaller racial wage differentials for municipal workers. For instance, the findings in panel 1 indicate that black–white labor earnings differentials for nonprivatized versus privatized municipalities falls from

Table 6.3   Mean Weekly Earnings

	Resides in Nonprivatized Locality			Resides in Privatized Locality		
Sector	(1) White	(2) Black	(3)# Black–White Earnings Differential (Percentage)	(4) White	(5) Black	(6) Black-White Earnings Differential (Percentage)
Panel 1. Mean Weekly Earnings of Municipal Workers (1987 dollars)						
Construction	$396	$306	−29.41	$397	$356	−11.51
Public Transit	418	469	12.20	408	390	−4.61
Energy Utilities	420	317	−32.49	409	341	−19.94
Recreation	273	222	−22.97	258	239	−7.49
Health Services	375	333	−12.61	391	306	−27.77
Panel 2. Mean Weekly Earnings of Private Sector Workers (1987 Dollars)						
Construction	$381	$300	−27.00	$401	$328	−22.25
Public Transit	308	292	−5.49	295	287	−2.88
Energy Utilities	466	290	−60.68	530	415	−27.71
Recreation	250	250	0	229	219	−4.56
Health Services	338	253	−32.80	351	268	−30.97

Source: BEA 1999 Census of Government and 1999–2001 Annual CPS–ORG files.
Note: #: Black–white earnings differentials are derived by taking the difference of the mean earnings for blacks and whites and dividing by the lower of the two mean earnings.

29.41 to 11.51 percent, 32.49 to 19.94 percent, and 22.97 to 7.94 percent for public municipal workers who provide construction, energy utility, and recreation services, respectively. The racial earnings differential also declines for public transit; however, in contrast to the findings for other municipal services, this differential depicts a black earnings advantage for transit workers residing in nonprivatized localities. This black earnings advantage does not arise for transit workers who reside in privatized localities. This finding on public transit racial differentials fits with past findings, indicating the racial residency patterns contribute to higher black earnings in the absence of privatization (Peoples and Talley, 2002).

The other key finding in panel 1 is the contrasting black and white earnings pattern for public municipal workers residing in privatized localities. For instance, black public municipal workers in construction, energy utility, and recreation who reside in privatized localities receive higher earnings than blacks providing these same services who reside in nonprivatized localities. White public municipal workers who provide any of these three services and reside in privatized localities receive the same or lower earnings than white public municipal workers who provide these services and reside in nonprivatized localities. The findings reported in panel 1, though, may be part of a more general earnings pattern such that privatization is associated with lower black–white earnings differentials for private sector workers who provide these same services.

Mean labor earnings results for service providers in the private sector are presented in panel 2 of table 6.3. The private sector results suggest a much different racial earnings pattern. The findings in panel 2 reveal that excluding energy utilities racial earnings differentials do not differ appreciably for private sector workers residing in nonprivatized localities compared to workers from this sector who reside in privatized localities. In sum, findings in panels 1 and 2 of table 6.3 generally support the notion that privatization is associated with smaller racial earnings differentials for public municipal workers and that this association is unique to the public sector.

It remains possible that worker characteristics vary by privatized and nonprivatized localities. For example, the high earnings paid to white public municipal workers who reside in nonprivatized localities may reflect compensation for highly valued observable worker characteristics. The earnings results presented earlier are likely to be biased if such compensation is practiced by municipal employers.

A standard earnings equation is estimated to address potential bias that may result from worker profiles differing among public service providers who reside in privatized and nonprivatized localities. The following equation depicts the specification used in this study:

$$LN(earnings)_j = \beta_0 + \beta_1 Z_j + \beta_2 T_j + \beta_3 Black_j + \beta_4 Private_j$$
$$+ \beta_5 (Black^* Private)_j + \varepsilon_j \qquad (6.2)$$

where j indexes individual workers and the dependent variable is the log of real weekly earnings of the jth worker. The matrix Z consists of a set of worker residency and worker profile variables and a measure of weekly hours worked. These explanatory variables include residency dummies for U.S. geographic quadrant, urban residency status, and a continuous measure of metropolitan population size. The worker profile measures are dummies depicting a worker's marital, sex, full-time, occupational, union, military veteran, and educational attainment status, as well as the age and age-squared of the individual worker. The vector T consists of a set of yearly time dummies that are included to account for the possible changes in the wage determination process over time. The variable *Black* is a dummy equaling one if the individual is black, and white otherwise.[9] The variable *Private* is a continuous variable measuring the share of townships that provide privatized service for the locality where the individual resides. The final variable presented in equation (6.2) is the interaction of the *Black* and *Private* variables.[10]

The coefficients that are of special interest to this study are β_3, β_4, and $\beta_3 + \beta_5$. They are used to measure racial earnings differentials for workers residing in privatized and nonprivatized localities. The coefficient β_3 measures the black–white log earnings differential for workers residing in nonprivatized localities.[11] The coefficient β_4 measures a 1 percentage point earnings difference for white workers associated with a 1 percentage point difference in the share of privatized townships in the metropolitan locality where these workers reside. The sum of β_3 and β_5 measures the black–white percentage earnings difference associated with a 1 percentage point difference in the share of privatized townships in the metropolitan locality where these workers reside.

Labor Earning Results

Labor earnings results from estimating equation (6.2) using the sample population of public municipal workers is presented in Table 6.4. The findings of the estimated coefficients on the control variables reveal the importance of adjusting for variations in worker profiles. For instance, the results for the standard measures of human capital investment indicate statistically significantly higher earnings for public municipal workers who attain higher levels of formal education, high-skill content jobs, and experience.[12] The estimated coefficient on the

Table 6.4 Earnings Results for Public Municipal Workers (Dependent Variable: Weekly Earnings in 1987 Dollars)

Variable	Construction	Public Transit	Energy Utilities	Recreation	Health Services
Intercept	−0.305	0.287	0.231	0.420	0.040
	(−1.030)	(0.679)	(0.888)	(2.943)	(1.471)
Private	−0.036	0.052	−0.0422	−0.0373	0.0104
	(-0.849)	(0.651)	(−1.094)	(−0.837)	(0.303)
Private*	0.082	−0.090	0.129	0.115	−0.0237
Black	(0.794)	(−0.737)	(1.689)	(1.203)	(−0.452)
Black	−0.085	0.029	−0.2207	−0.213	−0.084
	(−1.983)	(0.257)	(−3.586)	(−4.047)	(−2.452)
Union Member	0.052	0.121	0.085	0.254	0.134
	(1.987)	(2.548)	(3.435)	(6.909)	(5.542)
Married	0.085	0.0308	0.0424	0.086	0.0402
	(3.205)	(0.777)	(1.882)	(2.606)	(1.850)
Veteran	0.009	−0.040	0.0266	−0.121	0.047
	(0.332)	(−0.861)	(0.995)	(−2.509)	(0.968)
Diploma	0.145	0.167	0.177	0.055	0.188
	(3.789)	(2.329)	(4.556)	(1.340)	(3.866)
BA	0.3403	0.209	0.400	0.157	0.361
	(5.941)	(2.321)	(7.824)	(5.470)	(6.569)
College	0.164	0.221	0.179	0.281	0.269
	(3.878)	(2.953)	(4.350)	(2.747)	(5.413)
Postgrad	0.347	0.402	0.570	0.2646	0.481
	(3.981)	(3.116)	(7.993)	(3.750)	(8.200)
Midwest	0.003	−0.026	0.022	0.022	−0.072
	(0.008)	(−0.477)	(0.681)	(0.510)	(−2.263)
South	−0.084	−0.084	−0.053	0.029	−0.057
	(−2.264)	(−1.367)	(−1.469)	(0.638)	(−1.668)
West	0.037	0.077	0.031	0.0575	−0.022
	(1.014)	(1.323)	(0.891)	(1.255)	(−0.658)
Male	0.127	0.176	0.0947	0.090	0.0769
	(2.628)	(3.649)	(2.921)	(2.860)	(2.752)
Manager	0.370	0.386	0.276	0.338	1.397
	(7.708)	(2.633)	(5.924)	(4.302)	(6.446)
Pro	0.383	0.549	0.3809	0.161	1.358
	(5.821)	(3.670)	(6.715)	(2.039)	(6.315)
Tech	0.194	0.149	0.268	0.321	1.148
	(2.435)	(1.028)	(4.286)	(1.428)	(5.315)
Sales	0.012	−0.277	0.222	0.026	0.844
	(0.033)	(−1.172)	(1.615)	(0.254)	(1.777)
Clerical	−0.029	0.027	0.0805	0.120	1.009
	(−0.392)	(0.197)	(1.729)	(1.386)	(4.705)

(*continued*)

Table 6.4 (*continued*)

Variable	Construction	Public Transit	Energy Utilities	Recreation	Health Services
Service	−0.122	−0.216	−0.0013	0.040	0.778
	(−1.320)	(−1.475)	(−0.019)	(0.552)	(3.633)
Farm	−0.095	—	−0.0746	−0.043	0.531
	(−0.882)	—	(−0.814)	(−0.567)	(1.429)
Craft	0.164	0.098	0.235	0.132	1.333
	(4.406)	(0.754)	(6.321)	(1.343)	(5.951)
Trans	0.0688	−0.002	0.094	0.238	0.798
	(1.780)	(−0.018)	(2.174)	(2.081)	(3.216)
Nontrans	−0.001	−0.056	0.149	0.0248	0.899
	(−0.013)	(−0.198)	(2.306)	(0.135)	(3.798)
Age	0.052	0.034	0.055	0.0289	0.017
	(7.222)	(2.847)	(8.616)	(5.348)	(3.137)
Age2 (×1000)	−0.510	−0.330	−0.576	−0.279	−0.135
	(−6.234)	(−2.523)	(−7.632)	(−4.487)	(−2.137)
Lhour	1.137	1.108	0.986	1.031	0.893
	(14.578)	(10.985)	(14.963)	(32.698)	(21.369)
Cencity	−0.012	0.0929	0.009	−0.026	0.007
	(−0.424)	(2.254)	(0.393)	(−0.880)	(0.299)
Gas	—	—	0.114	—	—
	—	—	(3.250)	—	—
Water	—	—	−0.0001	—	—
	—	—	(−0.003)	—	—
Health	—	—	—	—	−0.064
	—	—	—	—	(−1.526)
Hospital	—	—	—	—	0.0611
	—	—	—	—	(1.350)
Y01	0.074	−0.154	0.062	0.133	0.019
	(2.091)	(−2.602)	(1.958)	(3.312)	(0.626)
Y00	0.097	−0.044	0.0932	0.0815	0.005
	(2.687)	(−0.742)	(2.936)	(1.953)	(0.160)
Fulltime	−0.0307	0.021	0.002	0.0302	0.0314
	(−0.917)	(0.403)	(0.090)	(0.725)	(0.754)
Smsasize	0.0449	0.0365	0.043	0.0364	0.0196
	(6.080)	(2.297)	(6.074)	(3.972)	(2.639)
Number of Observations	1,014	619	1,368	1,012	1,696
F-Statistic	29.371	17.388	33.434	114.767	68.469
R-squared	0.5047	0.4947	0.4747	0.7996	0.5976

Note: t-statistics are presented in parentheses.

control variable depicting union status suggests statistically significantly higher earnings for public municipal workers who belong to a union. This finding supports this study's hypothesis that municipal unions are in an advantageous position to successfully negotiate high labor compensation for their members. The estimated coefficient on the control variable depicting metropolitan population size is positive and statistically significant. The findings on metropolitan size indicate the potential earnings biases for the sample population of black public municipal workers, since relative to their white counterparts they are more likely to reside in such localities.

Findings on the race variable reported in table 6.4 indicate that adjusting for differences in worker characteristics results in some important changes in the earnings patterns. Excluding public transit the estimated coefficient on the *black* dummy variable is negative and statistically significant for each service. The nontransit findings suggest that black public municipal workers who reside in nonprivatized localities receive lower earnings than white public municipal workers in nonprivatized localities. The earnings advantage for white municipal workers mirrors that reported on mean earnings in table 6.3. However, excluding recreation services, the racial earnings differentials are markedly smaller when adjusting for differences in worker profiles. Finding smaller racial earnings differentials for the sample of municipal workers residing in nonprivatized localities suggest that white worker characteristics command higher earnings, which helps explain their earnings advantage in construction, energy utility, and health services.[13] The estimated coefficient on the *black* dummy variable for public transit services is positive and is not statistically significant. Hence, white providers of this service who reside in nonprivatized localities receive earnings that closely match the earnings of black public transit workers residing in nonprivatized localities. The lack of a racial earnings differential differs from the mean earnings advantage of black public transit workers reported in table 6.3. Apparently, black public transit workers possess observable characteristics that command high mean earnings.

Correcting for worker characteristic differences does not alter the relative earnings of whites who reside in privatized and nonprivatized localities. For instance, the estimated coefficients on the *privatization* variable are small and lack statistical significance for each service. This finding is consistent with mean earnings results and suggests that privatization is not associated with earnings differentials among white public municipal workers.

Findings that use a combination of the estimated coefficients on the race, privatization, and interaction term are presented in table 6.5. Columns (1) and (2) indicate that differences in worker profiles help

Table 6.5 Black–White Racial Earnings Differentials for Local Government Employees (Derived from Estimating Equation ([6.2])

Sector	(1) $(e^{\beta_3}-1)\times 100$ Resides in Nonprivatized Locality	(2) $\{(e^{\beta_3}-1)+\beta_5 X\}\times 100$ Resides in Locality with Mean Level of Privatization #	(3) $\{(\beta_4+\beta_5)X\}\times 100$ Privatization Earnings Premium for Blacks Residing in Localities with Mean Level of Privatization	(4) $(\beta_4 X)\times 100$ Privatization Earnings Premium for Whites Residing in Localities with Mean Level of Privatization
Construction	−8.15%**	−6.8%*	0.518%	−0.36%
Public Transit	2.94	−5.0	−3.352	0.52
Energy Utility	−19.3***	−9.46*	6.619	−0.0422
Recreation	−19.2***	−15.9**	2.23	−0.0373
Health Services	−8.06*	−8.96**	0.51	0.104

*Significant at the 10 percent level   **significant at the 5 percent level   ***significant at the 1 percent level.

The variable X denotes the mean percentage of government workers residing in municipalities that have privatized part of the sector in which the worker is employed, as listed in panel 1 of table 6.1.

explain privatization's effect on racial earnings differences. Still, racial earnings differentials decline for four of the five services examined in this study. For instance, the white wage advantage for nonprivatized workers falls from 8.15 to 6.8 percent for construction services, 19.3 to 9.46 percent for energy utility services, and 19.2 to 15.9 percent for recreation services. The black earnings advantage in public transit also declines from 2.94 percent to a white advantage of 5 percent. Even in health services where the white wage advantage did not decline, the racial earnings differentials are not markedly different for workers residing in privatized or nonprivatized localities. These labor earnings findings are consistent with the notion that privatization creates a work environment that discourages unjustifiable earnings disparities.

The third column of table 6.5 uses the estimated coefficients on *private* and the *private*black* interaction term to present results on earnings differential for black municipal workers who reside in privatized or nonprivatized localities. These findings reveal an earnings pattern that mirrors the mean earnings findings. Black public municipal workers in construction, energy utility, and recreation who reside in privatized localities receive higher earnings than blacks providing these same services who reside in nonprivatized localities. In contrast, the fourth column in this table indicates that white municipal workers providing these services are paid less if they reside in privatized localities. The findings reported in columns (3) and (4) support the hypothesis that compared to whites, black public municipal workers are more likely to be residing in localities that pay high public earnings and these localities are more likely to face privatization. However, such support is tenuous given the lack of statistical significance associated with these estimated coefficients. Rather, the results for construction, energy utility, and recreation services in column (3) suggest that compared to blacks in nonprivatized localities blacks residing in privatized localities possess attributes that command high earnings. For example, the mean privatization earnings differentials for blacks are 16.1, 7.5, and 7.6 percent for construction, energy utility, and recreation services, respectively. The privatization earnings differentials for blacks are only 0.518, 6.619, and 2.23 percent when adjusting for differences in worker characteristics.

Findings in table 6.6 present racial earnings differentials for private sector workers who provide service for the same five classifications reported in table 6.5.[14] These findings indicate that the racial labor earnings pattern for private sector workers generally resembles that found for public municipal workers. The findings in column (1) of table 6.6 indicate that excluding public transit, black private sector employees reside in nonprivatized localities that pay statistically significantly lower earnings than nonprivatized localities where white private sector workers reside. While the black–white earnings differential for public transit is not significant, black private sector employees providing this public service also reside in nonprivatized localities that pay lower earnings than nonprivatized localities where white public transit workers in the private sector reside. These nonprivatization racial earnings differentials closely resemble the differentials reported in column (2) for private sector workers who reside in privatized localities. The finding on private sector workers who provide public transit service reveals a small racial earnings differential that is not statistically significant whether public transit workers reside in privatized or nonprivatized localities. In sum, the lack of an appreciable association between privatization and racial earnings differentials for the five services presented in table 6.6 nearly mirrors that reported for public municipal workers in table 6.5. However, racial earnings differentials are more often smaller for the private sector.[15]

Table 6.6   Black–White Racial Earnings Differentials for Private Sector Employees (Derived from Estimating Equation [6.2])

Sector	(1) $(e^{\beta_3}-1)\times100$ Resides in Nonprivatized Locality	(2) $\{(e^{\beta_3}-1)+\beta_5 X\}\times10$ Resides in Locality with Mean Level of Privatization[#]
Construction	−12.68%**	−9.59%*
Public Transit	−5.44	−4.95
Energy Utilities	−1.49*	−10.49*
Recreation	−6.5*	−4.7
Health Services	−5.75***	−6.44**

*Significant at the 10 percent level   ** significant at the 5 percent level ***significant at the 1 percent level.

#The variable X denotes the mean percentage of private sector workers residing in municipalities that have privatized part of the sector in which the worker is employed, as listed in panel 2 of table 6.1.

Concluding Remarks

Privatization is commonly viewed as a public policy that presents governments with the potential to generate savings for taxpayers. The policy shift toward this approach for providing public services is almost universal, as many governments moved from state-owned operations during the last twenty years. A similar change is occurring in the United States at the local municipality level. Often the source of municipal cost savings is the avoidance of high compensation paid to public sector employees. Black public municipal workers are highly likely to face wage pressures from privatization given that they disproportionately reside in localities that pay high public wages. Privatization's potential effect on black workers is also significant because the public sector is a major source of high wage jobs for blacks.

This study examines racial earnings differentials for five local public services. Governmental information on privatization and individual information on workers providing public services are used to measure earnings differentials. The means indicate that privatization is associated with smaller racial earnings differentials for construction, public transit, energy utility, and recreation. The payment of high mean public wages by the nonprivatized localities where white municipal workers reside contributes to the larger nonprivatization racial earnings differentials for services other than public transit. Black public workers residing in privatized localities that pay high public wages compared to the public wages paid by nonprivatized localities where other black municipal workers reside explains the smaller mean privatization racial earnings differential for nontransit services. High mean public earnings of nonprivatized localities to black public workers who provide transit services explains the larger nonprivatized racial earnings differential for transit. Compared to the mean results the difference between the racial earnings differential for individuals residing in privatized and nonprivatized localities are generally smaller when controlling for worker characteristics.

This study's findings also indicate that racial earnings differentials in privatized localities persist even when controlling for differing worker profiles. These differentials, though, closely resemble the levels reported in the private sector. Hence, it seems that privatization has performed as well as the market allows for reducing earnings disparities.

Table 6.7 Description of Explanatory Variables and Their Descriptive Statistics for Public Municipal Workers Who Provide Construction, Public Transit, Energy Utility, Recreation, or Health Services

Explanatory Variable	Mean	Standard Deviation	Description
Private	0.47	0.44	A continuous variable measuring the share of townships that provide privatized service for the locality where the individual resides
Black	0.22	0.41	A dummy equaling one if the individual is black and white otherwise
Union Member	0.38	0.48	A dummy equaling one if the individual belongs to a union
Married	0.60	0.49	A dummy equaling one if the individual is married
Veteran	0.15	0.35	A dummy equaling one if the individual is an armed service veteran
Diploma	0.36	0.48	A dummy equaling one if the individual attained at most a high school diploma
College	0.31	0.46	A dummy equaling one if the individual attended college and did not attain a bachelor's degree
BA	0.15	0.36	A dummy equaling one if the individual attained a bachelor's degree
Postgrad	0.068	0.25	A dummy equaling one if the individual attained a postgraduate degree (individuals not attaining a high school diploma are the education baseline comparison group)
Midwest	0.23	0.42	A dummy equaling one if the individual resides in the midwestern United States
South	0.28	0.45	A dummy equaling one if the individual resides in the southern United States
West	0.23	0.42	A dummy equaling one if the individual resides in the western United States (individuals residing in the northeastern part of the United States are the regional baseline comparison group)

(*continued*)

Table 6.7 (*continued*)

Explanatory Variable	Mean	Standard Deviation	Description
Male	0.62	0.48	A dummy equaling one if the individual is a male
Manager	0.12	0.33	A dummy equaling one if the individual's occupation is classified as managerial
Pro	0.16	0.37	A dummy equaling one if the individual's occupation is classified as professional
Tech	0.05	0.21	A dummy equaling one if the individual's occupation is classified as technician
Sales	0.008	0.087	A dummy equaling one if the individual's occupation is classified as sales
Clerical	0.11	0.32	A dummy equaling one if the individual's occupation is classified as clerical
Service	0.13	0.33	A dummy equaling one if the individual's occupation is classified as service
Farm	0.04	0.19	A dummy equaling one if the individual's occupation is classified as farmer
Trans	0.12	0.32	A dummy equaling one if the individual's occupation is classified as transportation operative
Nontrans	0.014	0.12	A dummy equaling one if the individual's occupation is classified as nontransportation operative
Craft	0.17	0.37	A dummy equaling one if the individual's occupation is classified as craft (individuals employed as laborers are the occupation baseline comparison group)

(*continued*)

Table 6.7 (*continued*)

Explanatory Variable	Mean	Standard Deviation	Description
Age	41.82	12.03	A continuous variable measuring the individual's age
Lhour	3.60	0.33	A continuous variable measuring the natural log of the usual hours the individual works per week.
Gas	0.043	0.20	A dummy equaling one if the individual is employed in the gas or the electric utility service sector
Water	0.10	0.30	A dummy equaling one if the individual is employed in the water supply service sector (Gas and Water dummies are only used with the energy utility sample; individuals employed in sanitary services are the baseline comparison group)
Health	0.13	0.34	A dummy equaling one if the individual is employed in the nonhospital health services sector
Hospital	0.14	0.35	A dummy equaling one if the individual is employed in hospital care services (Health and Hospital dummies are only used with the health services sample; individuals employed in nursing care services are the baseline comparison group)
Y00	0.34	0.45	A dummy equaling one if the observation year is 2000
Y01	0.32	0.40	A dummy equaling one if the observation year is 2001 (1999 is the baseline observation year)
Smsasize	5.33	1.65	A continuous variable that ranks the metropolitan areas by population size; the ranking ranges from a low of one to a high of seven
Fulltime	0.76	0.42	A dummy equaling one if the individual is employed full time
Cencity	0.22	0.41	A dummy equaling one if the individual resides in the central city

Notes

The authors thank Bin Wang for his valuable research assistance.

1. There is hardly consensus on the potential privatization cost savings derived from enhanced competition. For example, Scaler (2000) argues that the public contract market is actually noncompetitive and is usually oligopolistic if not monopolistic. Hart, Shleifer, and Vishney (1997) observe that cost savings from privatization can still arise from a noncompetitive contract market since the private contractor has residual control over the service and does not need government approval for cost reduction. The profit-maximizing contractor has strong incentive to lower costs, which may not arise for government employees since he or she only receives a fraction of the returns to cost reduction.

2. For further discussion of the impacts of privatization, see Poole and Fixler (1987), Gomez-Ibanez, Meyer, and Luberoff (1991), Button and Weyman-Jones (1994), Bhaskar and Khan (1995), and La Porta and Lopez-De-Silanes (1999).

3. Strong federal incentives promoting privatization have successfully led to the use of private owners in public transit. The dominance of privately operated utilities allows for competitive contracting in this service sector.

4. Even though compared to whites a larger share of black public municipal workers are employed in the San Francisco metropolitan area, the difference between these shares is minor.

5. Township population sizes are used as weights when computing this measure of privatization.

6. The thirteen services identified by the CPS are construction, public transit, gas utility, electric utility, water supply, sewage removal, nonhospital health services, hospital care, nursing home care, library services, fire protection, corrections, and police protection.

7. Individual information on workers employed in the gas utility, electric utility, water supply, and sewage removal services is combined to form the power utility category. Information on nonhospital health services, hospital care, and nursing home care are combined to form the health services category. The sample of workers reporting library services, fire protection, corrections, and police protection are excluded from this study because of the lack of private sector observations needed to allow for intersector analysis.

8. The earnings results presented in table 6.3 do not distinguish between the earnings of union and nonunion workers.

9. CPS files report Hispanics as white or black. Information on other non-black minorities is excluded from the analysis due to extremely small sample sizes.

10. The description of all the explanatory variables is presented in table 6.7.

11. The estimated coefficient β_3 is converted to percentage earnings differentials by using the formula $(e^\beta - 1) \times 100$.

12. The estimated coefficients on the three higher educational attainment dummies listed as College, BA, and Postgrad are positive and statistically significant. The estimated coefficient on the high-skill content dummies listed as Manager, Professional Technician, and Craft are also positive and statistically

significant. Last, the estimated coefficients on the experience variable listed as Age is positive and statistically significant.

13. Only differences in worker characteristics explain the differences from mean earnings differentials because the returns to worker characteristics are held constant when estimating the earnings equation.

14. The complete estimation results using the private sector sample population are available from the authors upon request.

15. Privatization is associated with lower racial earnings differentials for public municipal workers who provide energy utility service. This finding differs from the lack of a privatization association for private sector workers who provide that service.

References

Bhaskar, V., and Mushtao Khan. "Privatization and Employment: A Study of the Jute Industry in Bangladesh." *American Economic Review* 85 (1995): 267–73.

Black, Alan. "Privatization of Urban Transit: A Different Perspective." *Transportation Research Record* 1297 (1991): 69–75.

Button, Kenneth, and Thomas Weyman-Jones. "Impacts of Privatisation Policy in Europe." *Contemporary Economic Policy* 12 (1994): 23–33.

Chandler, Timothy, and Peter Feuille. "Municipal Unions and Privatization." *Public Administration Review* 51 (1991): 15–22.

Gomez-Ibanez, Jose A., John R. Meyer, and David E. Luberoff. "Prospects for Privatising Infrastructure: Lessons form US Roads and Solid Waste." *Journal of Transport Economics and Policy* 25 (1991): 259–78.

Hart, Oliver, Andrei Shleifer, and Robert Vishney. "The Proper Scope of Government: Theory and an Application to Prisons." *Quarterly Journal of Economics* 112 (1997): 1127–61.

Heseltine, P. M., and D. T. Silcock. "The Effects of Bus Deregulation on Costs." *Journal of Transport Economics and Policy* 24 (1990): 239–54.

Kay, John A., and David J. Thompson. "Privatisation: A Policy in Search of a Rationale." *Economic Journal* 96 (1986): 18–32.

Kodrzycki, Yolanda K. "Privatization of Local Public Services: Lessons for New England." *New England Economic Review* (1994): 31–46.

La Porta, Rafael, and Florencio Lopez-De-Silanes. "The Benefits of Privatization: Evidence from Mexico." *Quarterly Journal of Economics* 114 (1999): 1193–241.

Peltzman, Sam. "Toward a More General Theory of Regulation." *Journal of Law and Economics* 19 (1976): 211–40.

Peoples, James, and Wayne K. Talley. "Privatization, City Residency, and Black–White Earnings Differentials: Evidence from the Public Transit Sector." *Review of Industrial Organization* 21 (2002): 251–70.

Peoples, James and Wayne K. Talley. "Black–White Earnings Differentials: Privatization versus Deregulation." *American Economic Review* 91 (2001): 164–68.

Poole, Robert W. Jr., and Philip E. Fixler Jr. "Privatization of Public-Sector Services in Practice: Experience and Potential." *Journal of Policy Analysis and Management* 6 (1987): 612–25.

Savas, E. S. "Privatization and State and Local Government." In *Restructuring State and Local Services: Ideas, Proposal, and Experiences,* ed. Arnold Raphaelson, 91–100. Westport, CT: Praeger, 1998.

Scaler, Elliot. *You Don't Always Get What You Pay For: The Economics of Privatization.* Ithaca, NY: Cornell University Press, 2000.

Snyder, Christopher M., Robert P. Trost, and R. Derek Trunkey. "Reducing Government Spending with Privatization Competitions: A Study of the Department of Defense Experience." *Review of Economics and Statistics* 83 (2001): 108–17.

Talley, Wayne K. "The Indirect Cost-Saving Hypothesis of Privatisation: A Public Transport Labour Earnings Test." *Journal of Transport Economics and Policy* 32 (1998): 351–64.

Teal, Roger F. "Public Transit Service Contracting: A Status Report." *Transportation Quarterly* 42 (1988): 207–22.

Chapter 7

New Estimates of Discrimination against Men with Disabilities
The Role of Customer Interaction in the Product Market

Marjorie L. Baldwin

Introduction

In his seminal theory of discrimination, Gary Becker (1957) postulates that discrimination in the labor market can arise from three sources: employers, coworkers, or customers. Whatever the source, the motivation for discrimination is assumed to be individual prejudice against a minority group, manifested by a willingness to incur costs to avoid that group. Becker's theory develops all three potential sources of discrimination, but empirical studies of discrimination typically assume employers are the source. Moreover, most empirical studies provide no direct tests of the assumptions that prejudice motivates discrimination, or that employers are the source.

Persons with disabilities are a minority group with unique characteristics that make it possible to test aspects of Becker's theory. The group is extremely heterogeneous, with natural subgroups defined by different health impairments that are subject to different degrees of prejudice and discrimination in the labor market. Quantitative rankings of the intensity of prejudice toward different impairments are available from attitude studies conducted over the last three decades (e.g., Albrecht, Walker, and Levy, 1982; Royal and Roberts 1987; Tringo, 1970; Westbrook, Legge, and Pennay, 1993; Yuker, 1987) and studies of disability-related discrimination have tested the correspondence between the prejudice rankings and measures of wage discrimination for different impairment groups (Baldwin and

Johnson, 1994; Hendricks, Schrio-Geist, and Broadbent, 1997; Johnson and Lambrinos, 1987; Salkever and Domino, 2000). The studies find weak positive correlations between intensity of prejudice and estimated discriminatory wage differentials, which is consistent with the assumption that prejudice motivates discrimination. Still, the full potential for studies of disability-related discrimination to test Becker's theory has not been explored.

This chapter provides new estimates of discrimination against men with disabilities using the 1996 Survey of Income and Program Participation (SIPP). The two objectives are, first, to compare the new estimates to those from earlier years to examine changes in the years following passage of the Americans with Disabilities Act of 1990 (ADA) and, second, to examine the role of customers as a source of discrimination against men with disabilities.

Customers hold the same types of prejudices as do employers or coworkers, but have more limited opportunities to identify members of a disfavored group. When gender or racial discrimination is the issue, identification is often fairly easy. With disability-related discrimination, identification is more complex as many disabling conditions are unobservable in casual interactions. The opportunity for customers to indulge their prejudices against persons with disabilities depends on the visibility of the condition and whether the product market entails sufficient interaction between customer and employee to reveal the condition. I use visibility rankings of different health conditions, together with product market characteristics, to test the hypothesis that customers are a source of disability-related discrimination. To my knowledge, this is the first test of customer discrimination against workers with disabilities.

The chapter is organized as follows. The next section defines important terms for a study of disability-related discrimination. The third section provides background on theoretical models of customer discrimination, derives characteristics of the product market conducive to customer discrimination, and summarizes related empirical studies. The fourth section describes the data and defines analysis groups based on rankings of health conditions by prejudice and visibility. The methods used to estimate disability-related discrimination are described in the fifth section. The sixth section presents results and the seventh section concludes.

Defining Disability-Related Discrimination

Labor market discrimination occurs when groups of workers with equal average productivity are paid different average wages or face different opportunities for employment. Wage discrimination is measured as the difference between the mean wages of majority and minority workers that cannot be attributed to differences in the groups' productivity-related characteristics. Discrimination is measured between groups of workers rather than between individuals because individual wages and employment opportunities vary with random factors that cannot be dissociated from discrimination. Comparisons between representative groups of majority and minority workers eliminate the effect of random influences so that the effect of discrimination can be isolated, provided that differences in average productivity are controlled adequately. This is a particular challenge in studies of disability-related discrimination because the presence of a disability typically is associated with functional limitations that reduce a worker's productivity in some types of jobs.

An analysis of disability-related discrimination, therefore, requires that the researcher distinguish between the terms *impairment, functional limitation,* and *disability* so that the effect of a health condition on specific job functions (e.g., limitations on handling, lifting, walking) can be distinguished from the more global concept of work disability. Work disability can then be treated as an outcome that is influenced by the nature and severity of functional limitations as well as other characteristics, such as the nature of the work environment. The distinction is fundamental to separating the effects of health-related limitations on productivity from the effects of discrimination.

Definitions that satisfy these requirements were developed by Nagi (1969) and modified by the World Health Organization (1980, 2001). According to Nagi's definitions: an impairment is a "physiological or anatomical loss or other abnormality"; a functional limitation is a restriction of sensory, mental, or physical capacities; and a disability is a restriction on the ability to perform normal daily activities, such as working or attending school, caused by the functional limitations associated with an impairment.

Consider, for example, a worker with epilepsy. Epilepsy is an impairment that causes functional limitations, namely, the inability to walk and perform physical tasks during severe seizures. If seizures are not controlled through medication, and restrict the worker's ability to perform his usual job, the worker is disabled. If seizures are controlled, which is fairly typical, and never interfere appreciably with the worker's job performance, the worker is not disabled.

According to the definition of *discrimination*, wage differentials associated with functional limitations that reduce work capacity are not discriminatory. The challenge is to control for differences in functional limitations between disabled and nondisabled workers so that the effects of discrimination can be isolated. If this challenge can be met,

the heterogeneity of the disabled population provides a unique opportunity to test alternate theories of discrimination in the labor market.
In particular, different health impairments are subject to different levels of stigma, allowing one to test the relationship between discrimination and prejudice, and different impairments have different levels of
visibility, allowing one to test the importance of customers as a source
of disability-related discrimination.

Theories and Evidence of Customer Discrimination

THEORETICAL MODEL

Becker assumes that discrimination is a manifestation of prejudice
against members of a minority group. That is, discrimination stems from
the desire of prejudiced employers, coworkers, or customers to maintain
physical separation from minority workers.[1] In the customer variant of
the model, a firm's output is characterized by attributes, including price,
quality, reliability, speed of service, and the minority status of service personnel. Majority and minority workers are assumed to be perfect substitutes in producing all other attributes of the firm's output, but customers
view the output produced or sold by minority workers as having lower
value and thus demand a lower price.

Becker demonstrates that customer prejudice, or "tastes for discrimination," reduces the wages of minority workers relative to the majority group. Following Becker's model, assume that disabled (D) and
nondisabled (ND) workers are perfect substitutes in production but that
customers prefer not to associate with disabled workers. Let P_D, P_{ND} represent the price of output sold by disabled and nondisabled workers, and
W_D, W_{ND} represent their wage rates. Disabled and nondisabled workers
are equally productive in all noncustomer-related attributes of the production process, so m units of (disabled or nondisabled) labor are required to produce one unit of output for sale. Prejudiced customers,
preferring not to associate with disabled workers, act as if the price of
output sold by disabled workers is $P_D(1+d)$ where d, the discrimination
coefficient, measures the strength of customer tastes for discrimination
against workers with disabilities. (For simplicity, all customers have the
same d, an assumption later relaxed.)

The model predicts that disabled workers interact with customers only
when customers are compensated for their prejudice, and employers do

not lose profits. Customers are indifferent between transactions with disabled or nondisabled workers when:

$$P_D(1 + d) = P_{ND}. \tag{7.1}$$

Profit-maximizing employers are indifferent between hiring disabled and nondisabled workers when the increase in profit generated by hiring additional workers is equal for the two groups, that is:

$$P_D - mW_D = P_{ND} - mW_{ND}. \tag{7.2}$$

Market equilibrium occurs when both equations (7.1) and (7.2) are satisfied, making the relative wage differential between disabled and nondisabled workers

$$\frac{W_{ND} - W_D}{W_D} = \left(\frac{P_D}{mW_D}\right) d.^2 \tag{7.3}$$

Whenever d is positive, wage differentials exist between the disabled and nondisabled.

If the intensity of prejudice against disabled workers varies among customers, the relative wage differential depends on the proportion of disabled and nondisabled workers in the market and the tastes for discrimination of a customer who is just willing to engage in transactions with disabled workers at the given price differential. Customers with stronger prejudices avoid transactions with disabled workers because the price differential is not sufficient to compensate their tastes for discrimination. If the proportion of disabled workers in the market increases, they must attract more prejudiced customers to interact with them, so the equilibrium price differential between output sold by disabled and nondisabled workers increases, as does the relative wage differential.

In other variants of Becker's theory, employers or coworkers are the sources of labor market discrimination. One of the main predictions of the employer discrimination model is that discriminating employers sacrifice profits by hiring an inefficient combination of labor inputs. The discriminatory equilibrium is not sustainable over time unless all employers are prejudiced and entry is blocked. Otherwise, nonprejudiced employers can enter the market, earn higher profits, and drive prejudiced employers out of business. Empirical studies have not shown general declines in discrimination over time in the absence of antidiscrimination legislation, so this is one of the main criticisms of the model.

Interestingly, in the prejudiced-customer variant of Becker's theory, an employer's discriminatory behavior is profit-maximizing and not expected to diminish over time, unless customer tastes for discrimination decline. Although this makes the customer variant attractive theoretically, not all markets are conducive to customer discrimination. The following section describes conditions under which customer discrimination is more likely to occur.

CHARACTERISTICS OF MARKETS CONDUCIVE TO CUSTOMER DISCRIMINATION

The relative importance of customer discrimination as a source of labor market discrimination is likely to vary with characteristics of both the minority group and the product market. Disabilities that are more easily identifiable are more susceptible to customer discrimination than those that are less easy to identify. Product markets that require direct interaction between employees and customers are most susceptible to customer discrimination and the importance of customer discrimination is likely to vary with the duration and nature of interaction required. Prejudiced customers may be highly averse, for example, to interactions involving physical contact with members of a disfavored group, but may tolerate interactions that follow proscribed social mores. Prejudiced individuals who accept members of a minority group into their homes as housekeepers, gardeners, or caregivers for children are good examples.

In an extension of Becker's theory, Kahn (1991) develops a general equilibrium model of customer discrimination and derives market conditions under which customer discrimination can be expected to persist even in competitive labor markets. The model is based on a two-sector economy: one sector (e.g., sales, services) involves customer interaction, the other (e.g., clerical, manufacturing) does not. According to Kahn's model, the probability of wage differentials associated with customer discrimination is an increasing function of (1) the relative size of the minority workforce, (2) the fraction of income spent on the sector that requires customer interaction, and (3) the relative elasticity of output with respect to labor inputs in the two sectors. Each criterion reflects the relative ease with which minority workers can escape customer discrimination by crowding into the sector with limited customer interaction. Kahn estimates that if minority workers comprise less than 30 percent of the (nonfarm) labor force, customer discrimination need not lead to discriminatory wage differentials. The implication is that customer discrimination is unlikely to be an important factor in determining the wages of nonwhites or Hispanics (or workers with disabilities) but may be important in explaining the gender wage gap.

There are, however, several caveats. If minority workers have a comparative advantage in the sector subject to customer discrimination, the other sector is less attractive as a means of escape. Minorities with limited English skills, for example, may be compelled to work in the services sector instead of escaping customer discrimination in clerical jobs with less customer interaction. In situations like this, discriminatory wage differentials associated with customer discrimination can persist even when the minority group is a small fraction of the labor force.

The caveat may well apply to workers with disabilities, whose functional limitations may restrict job opportunities in some sectors of the labor market more than others. Workers with physical limitations, for example, may be forced to seek jobs in the service sector, with greater customer interaction, because their limitations restrict entry into manufacturing jobs with less interaction. Similarly, workers with epilepsy or other seizure-related disorders may be restricted from jobs in the transportation or construction industries where they might escape customer interaction. Of course, the limitations that exclude entry into some jobs also limit productivity in others, so part of the low wages of workers with disabilities is explained by functional limitations. These differences must be controlled in the wage equations to obtain unbiased estimates of discrimination.

Although not in Kahn's model, the visibility of a minority group limits the potential for discrimination as customers can only discriminate against persons whose minority status is easily identified. Employee interaction with customers is more sporadic than interaction with employers or coworkers, so customers have fewer opportunities to identify members of a disfavored group. Women and African Americans are easily identified in face-to-face interactions, and women are easily identified in verbal interactions on the telephone, but the visibility of a disabled worker is less straightforward. One can imagine a continuum of disabilities where some are easily identified in face-to-face interactions (paraplegia, deformities, amputations, blindness); others are easily identified in verbal interactions (speech or hearing disorders); and some are not easily identified in the typical employee–customer relationship (epilepsy, heart conditions, arthritis). This heterogeneity provides a unique opportunity to test the importance of customer prejudice as a source of discriminatory wage differentials between disabled and nondisabled workers. The approach differs from most previous empirical studies of customer-related discrimination, which I have summarized in the following section.

EMPIRICAL STUDIES OF CUSTOMER DISCRIMINATION

A number of studies have analyzed customer discrimination in the market for professional sports, with mixed results. Sports markets are particularly conducive to discrimination studies because it is relatively easy to obtain good measures of worker productivity in the published performance statistics on individual players. Stone and Warren (1999), for example, look for evidence of customer discrimination in the prices of trading cards for National Basketball Association (NBA) players. Controlling for age and physical condition of the card, number of cards produced, and career productivity and rookie status of the player, the authors find no evidence of a racial differential in the price of cards.

Kanazawa and Funk (2001), on the other hand, find evidence of customer discrimination against African American players in the NBA. They estimate the impact of customer discrimination on salaries by analyzing the correlation between number of television viewers and the racial composition of teams. Controlling for other variables that affect television viewership, the results show that teams with more white players have higher ratings than teams with fewer white players. Relative to a black player, an additional white player increases advertising revenues by approximately 17 percent of the mean NBA salary. The different productivity between black and white players largely accounts for the racial salary differential in the NBA.

Bodvarsson and Partridge (2001) extend Becker's theory to develop a model that simultaneously distinguishes between employer, customer, and coworker discrimination. Customer discrimination enters the model through the firm's production function, employer discrimination through the firm's cost function, and coworker discrimination through workers' reservation wage functions. A unique feature of the model is that it incorporates the possibility of discrimination in two directions, that is, members of the minority group may exhibit tastes for discrimination against the majority. The model is tested with data from the 1985–1986 and 1990–1991 NBA seasons. Controlling for differences in player productivity and playing time, characteristics of the metropolitan statistical area, and team winning percentage, the authors find evidence consistent with black fans discriminating against white players.

In one of the few studies of customer-related discrimination unrelated to sports models, Holzer and Ihlanfeldt (1998) estimate the effects of customer discrimination against blacks and Hispanics using data from a survey of employers in four major metropolitan areas.[3] The authors distinguish between occupations that require direct customer contact (sales and services) and those that do not. The results show that the hiring of blacks and Hispanics increases as the percent of a firm's customers who are black or Hispanic increases, and the differences in hiring are significantly larger in jobs that involve customer contact. The evidence is consistent with both majority customers discriminating against workers from the minority group, and minority customers discriminating against workers from the majority. Customer ethnicity has stronger effects on hiring of minorities into white-collar and service occupations than into blue-collar jobs.

The present study follows Holzer and Ihlanfeldt (1998) by distinguishing between occupations that require direct customer contact and those that do not, but extends the literature on customer discrimination in two important ways. First, to my knowledge, this is the first empirical test of the hypothesis that customers are a source of discrimination against workers with disabilities. Second, the study exploits the unique heterogeneity of the disabled population to compare discriminatory wage differentials between minority workers whose impairments are visible to customers and those whose impairments are not.

Defining the Analysis Groups

DATA

The data come from Wave V of the 1996 panel of the SIPP. Interviews for Wave V were conducted between August 1997 and November 1997 and refer to a four-month reference period immediately preceding the interview month. The Topical Module that accompanies Wave V includes questions on health and disability, including thirty-two measures of functional limitations.[4] One or more of twenty-nine impairments are identified as the cause of the limitations. In this study, persons with disabilities are defined as those who report that a health condition "makes it difficult to remain employed or to find a job"; or "limits the kind or amount of work they can do around the house"; or "causes difficulty with certain activities" (such as climbing, standing, walking, seeing, hearing); or causes them to be in "poor health."

The sample is restricted to working-age men who are not receiving transfer payments conditioned on limited wage income, whose hourly wage could be computed, and whose wage or salary income could be subject to discrimination. Excluded are the armed forces, the self-employed, and those younger than sixteen or older than sixty-five. Also excluded are men who received income from social security disability or retirement programs, or Temporary Aid to Needy Families assistance, or who received unemployment or private disability income throughout the reference period. Finally, a small fraction of salaried workers who reported more than one job are excluded because the wage rate for their primary job cannot be calculated. The final samples include 15,472 nondisabled men, of whom 13,723 were employed during the reference period, and 937 men with disabilities, of whom 557 were employed.

Estimates of disability-related discrimination in 1996 are compared to similar results from Baldwin and Johnson (2000) to evaluate the impact of the ADA on the labor market for men with disabilities. Data for the earlier study come from Wave III of the 1990 SIPP. Implementation of the ADA was staggered over a two-year period from 1992 to 1994, so the results from 1990 and 1996 provide comparisons of disability-related discrimination from periods just before and after implementation of the act.

RANKINGS OF IMPAIRMENTS BY PREJUDICE AND VISIBILITY

The existence of negative attitudes toward persons with disabilities is documented in numerous studies (Royal and Roberts, 1987; Tringo, 1970; Westbrook, Legge, and Pennay, 1993; Yuker, 1987). Typically, the studies use social distance scales to rank different health conditions by the degree of prejudice they elicit. The rankings are surprisingly robust over the last thirty years, despite the increased public awareness of disability issues that surrounded passage of the ADA. Consistently, the strongest prejudice is exhibited toward persons with mental or emotional conditions, or substance abuse problems. Negative attitudes toward persons with these conditions are similar to those exhibited toward ex-convicts.

This study uses the rankings of health impairments developed by Royal and Roberts (1987) and Westbrook, Legge, and Pennay (1993) to classify impairments into groups by (1) the degree of prejudice elicited toward an impairment, and (2) the visibility of an impairment. The Royal and Roberts study was selected because it provides rankings for both prejudice and visibility scales. The authors interviewed 151 students, grades 3 through college, to assess their attitudes toward disabling health conditions in terms of four constructs: acceptability, familiarity, severity, and visibility. The acceptability ranking is the basis for classifying impairments into groups subject to more prejudice (MP) and less prejudice (LP) to correspond to previous studies of disability-related discrimination using the SIPP (Baldwin and Johnson, 1994, 2000). The visibility ranking is used to classify impairments into groups that are more visible (MV) and less visible (LV).[5] The results of Westbrook, Legge, and Pennay's (1993) study supplement the prejudice rankings for certain impairments that appear in the SIPP data but not on the Royal and Roberts (1987) scale.[6]

One drawback to the two attitudes studies is that they are taken from samples that are not representative of the persons likely to engage in customer discrimination in the United States. Ideally one would prefer to use rankings based on the responses of employers or persons of working age who are more representative of the general U.S. population than are the selected samples. The prejudice rankings are, however, so robust across studies that one obtains virtually identical classifications using any of the attitudes scales (Westbrook, Legge, and Penny, 1993; Yuker, 1987), so the bias introduced by the respondent pools is likely to be small or nonexistent. Further, Royal and Roberts (1987) is, to my knowledge, the only study to provide visibility rankings of impairments.

The rankings of impairments on the SIPP data by prejudice and visibility are reported in appendix table A1 (available from the editors). The rankings reflect two adjustments to the visibility scale, namely, for 'speech disorder' and 'deafness or serious trouble hearing.' Both impairments are ranked less visible on the visibility scale, where visibility is determined solely on the basis of visual cues. Customer interactions typically involve both verbal and visual communication, however, and speech or hearing disorders are relatively easy to identify by talking to an individual. Thus, these impairments are moved to the more visible category, where more visible impairments are those that can be identified relatively easily through normal customer interactions with an employee.

In general, health conditions that are subject to more prejudice are also more visible. Only five conditions change positions in the two sets of rankings: cancer, epilepsy, AIDS, and alcohol or drug problems are subject to relatively strong prejudice, but ranked less visible; stiffness or deformity of extremities is subject to relatively weak prejudice but ranked more visible. These conditions represent eighty-four cases, or 15 percent of the sample of men with disabilities. The following section describes how estimates of discrimination are derived based on prejudice (the LP and MP groups) and visibility (the LV and MV groups).

Methods

CONTROLLING FOR THE EFFECTS OF FUNCTIONAL LIMITATIONS ON PRODUCTIVITY

The econometric technique used to estimate discriminatory wage differentials decomposes observed wage differentials into a part explained by differences in the productivity-related characteristics of the disabled and nondisabled groups, and a residual, or unexplained, part attributed to discrimination. Failure to control for the productivity-limiting effects of health conditions, therefore, introduces an upward bias in the estimates of disability-related discrimination. Many national survey databases that have been used to study gender- or race-related discrimination do not include adequate controls for the functional limitations associated with disability. An advantage of the SIPP is that it provides information on a wide array of physical, sensory, and cognitive limitations. For each of thirty-two functions, the data indicate whether the respondent has no difficulty performing the function, has some difficulty performing the function, or is unable to perform the function without help.

I use principal components analysis to combine the individual limitations variables into summary scores that are incorporated in the wage and employment functions (Baldwin and Johnson, 1994, 1995, 2000; Johnson and Lambrinos, 1987). This approach reduces multicollinearity among the limitations variables, without imposing subjective judgments of the investigator in determining how the variables should be combined. Principal components analysis allows the data to determine how heavily each variable is weighted on the different summary scores.[7]

Applying principal components analysis to the 1996 SIPP data yields three summary scores, or factors, with weightings of the limitations variables shown in appendix table A2 (available from the editors). The results are intuitively appealing. The variables loaded most heavily on the first factor indicate a respondent's ability to get around inside and outside the house, take a shower or bath, prepare meals, do light housework, and so forth, so factor 1 can be interpreted as a measure of limitations on activities of daily living. Variables loaded most heavily on the second factor indicate the ability to lift and carry an item as heavy as 10 or 25 pounds, climb a flight of stairs, walk a quarter mile, and so forth, so factor 2 can be interpreted as a measure of strength and mobility. Variables loaded most heavily on the third factor indicate the ability to keep track of money and bills, cope with everyday stress, hear a normal conversation, have one's speech understood, and so forth, so factor 3 can be interpreted as a measure of cognitive and communication limitations. The three composite factors are continuous, increasing measures of functional limitations that are included in the wage equations to measure disability-related productivity losses.

There are two primary disadvantages of the principal components approach. First, it is difficult to attach meaningful interpretations to the coefficients of the composite scores that are used instead of direct measures of functional limitations in the models. It is not possible, therefore, to make inferences regarding the average wage loss associated with particular types of limitations, such as the inability to lift heavy objects. Second, Baldwin and Johnson (2000) demonstrate that some information is lost when multiple measures of functional limitations are reduced to composite factors. As a result, differences in functional limitations explain a smaller part of the wage differential, and estimates of discrimination are larger, in models that use the factor approach than in models that include the functional limitations as binary variables.

DEFINING CUSTOMER INTERACTION IN THE PRODUCT MARKET

The key variable identifying workers more likely to be subject to customer discrimination, that is, workers whose jobs require substantial amounts of direct interaction with customers, is constructed by matching occupational data from the SIPP with job requirements from an online database, the Occupational Information Network (O*Net 4.0). O*Net is an online directory of occupations that provides detailed information on worker characteristics, occupation characteristics, worker requirements, occupation requirements, and experience requirements. Occupations are classified by eight-digit O*Net–SOC (Standard Occupational Classification) codes. Searches can be conducted on O*Net for keywords describing job characteristics. Each search returns a ranked listing of occupations by the percent relevance in the O*Net occupational title, alternative titles, job description, and work content statements. A relevance score (0 to 100 percent) indicates the importance of the keyword in each occupational description as measured by its frequency of occurrence relative to descriptions of other occupations.

O*Net is used to identify occupations requiring direct customer interaction. Searches using the keywords customer, patient, client, and patron yield 381 matches for customer, 126 matches for patient, 227 matches for client, and 41 matches for patron. Relevance scores range from 2 to 100 percent Occupations with relevance scores of 10 percent or more are defined as customer-related jobs and matched manually to SIPP occupation codes (three-digit 1990 Census Bureau Occupational Classification Codes).[8]

Overall, 83 percent of occupations identified as customer related on the O*Net database are matched to the SIPP codes.[9] All matched occupations on the SIPP are identified as occupations that require substantial customer interaction according to the O*Net job requirements. A binary variable, "customer" is constructed that equals one if a worker is employed in a matched occupation (high customer interaction) and zero otherwise. The customer variable is included in the decompositions based on visibility rankings to test the hypotheses related to customers as a source of disability-related discrimination. The following section describes the decomposition technique.

ESTIMATING WAGE DISCRIMINATION

Most recent empirical studies of labor market discrimination use variations of the Oaxaca (1973) decomposition.[10] In what follows, the decomposition technique is presented for the case where workers with disabilities are stratified into two groups subject to more or less prejudice (MP or LP groups); a similar decomposition is estimated for disabled workers with more or less visible disabilities (MV or LV groups).

Log-linear wage equations of the form

$$\ln W_i = \beta X_i + c\lambda_i + \varepsilon_i \tag{7.4}$$

are estimated separately for nondisabled workers (ND), and for disabled workers (D) with impairments subject to less prejudice (LP) and more prejudice (MP). The dependent variable is the natural log of the hourly wage rate of the ith worker; X_i is a vector of variables representing worker productivity and labor market characteristics; and ε_i is a mean-zero, random disturbance term.[11] The sample selection variable, λ_i, is included to correct for the bias that results because wages are not observed for nonworkers, so the equation provides unbiased estimates of the offer wage structure.[12] Productivity is represented by years of education, the three factors measuring functional limitations, and four measures of work experience.[13] Labor market variables include union membership, race, and two occupational categories (professional or manager and laborer).

Correcting for sample selection allows the investigator to estimate the difference in offer wages between majority and minority workers. The decomposition technique separates the offer wage differential into a part explained by differences in their productivity-related characteristics and an unexplained part attributed to discrimination. Substituting means and coefficient estimates from the wage equations for ND and LP men into the decomposition formula, we obtain:

$$\overline{\ln W_{ND}} - \overline{\ln W_{LP}} - (\hat{c}_{ND}\bar{\lambda}_{ND} - \hat{c}_{LP}\bar{\lambda}_{LP}) = \tag{7.5}$$
$$(\bar{X}_{ND} - \bar{X}_{LP})[d\hat{\beta}_{ND} + (I-d)\hat{\beta}_{LP}] +$$
$$[\bar{X}_{ND}(I-d) + \bar{X}_{LP}d)(\hat{\beta}_{ND} - \hat{\beta}_{LP})$$

with a similar decomposition comparing the ND and MP groups. The left side of equation (7.5) represents the difference between mean offer wages for disabled and nondisabled workers. The first term on the right represents the difference in offer wages attributable to differences in average productivity, as represented by means of the variables in the wage equation; the second term represents the unexplained part of the wage differential attributed to discrimination and residual effects.

There are several important limitations to the decomposition approach. First, the unexplained part of the wage differential is a residual that includes the effects of productivity differences that have not been measured by the control variables. These differences are not properly considered discriminatory but the second term cannot be further decomposed (Jones, 1983). Second, the decomposition requires the investigator to make an assumption regarding the wage schedule that would prevail in the absence of discrimination. The vector d, with elements valued from 0 to 1, represents the relationship of the nondiscriminatory wage structure to observed wages. I assume the nondiscriminatory wage structure is that observed for nondisabled men ($d = 1$) because workers with disabilities are a small fraction of the employed labor force, but the choice of values for d is controversial.[14]

The specification described above is virtually identical to that used by Baldwin and Johnson (2000) using the 1990 SIPP. The only important difference is that the 1996 data include an expanded set of functional limitations variables with better controls for cognitive limitations. Thus, the results presented below can be compared to the 1990 results to identify changes in the labor market experiences of men with disabilities before and after implementation of the ADA, the first objective of the chapter.

To address the second objective, identifying the importance of customer discrimination in determining the wages of workers with disabilities, two additional models are estimated. In model 1, the decompositions described above are re-estimated comparing non-disabled men to men with disabilities that are MV or LV. In model 2, a customer interaction variable is added to the wage equations, and the decomposition formula isolates the effect of customer discrimination in the unexplained part of the wage differential.

Specifically, the estimates for model 2 are derived from log-linear wage equations,

$$\ln W_i = \beta X_i + \gamma C_i + c\lambda_i + \varepsilon_i, \tag{7.6}$$

estimated separately for ND workers and for workers with LV and MV disabilities. In equation (7.6), C is the binary variable identifying workers in jobs that require customer interaction, and γ represents the marginal returns to customer-related jobs. The offer wage differential is decomposed into three parts:

$$\overline{\ln W_{ND}} - \overline{\ln W_{LV}} - (\hat{c}_{ND}\overline{\lambda}_{ND} - \hat{c}_{LV}\overline{\lambda}_{LV}) = \tag{7.7}$$
$$[(\overline{X}'_{ND} - \overline{X}'_{LV})[d\hat{\beta}'_{ND} + (I-d)\hat{\beta}'_{LV}) + (\overline{C}_{ND} - \overline{C}_{LV})$$
$$(d\hat{\gamma}_{ND} + (I-d)\hat{\gamma}_{LV})] + [(\overline{C}_{ND}(I-d) + \overline{C}_{LV}d)(\hat{\gamma}_{LV} - \hat{\gamma}_{ND})]$$
$$+ [(\overline{X}'_{ND}(I-d) + \overline{X}'_{LV}d)(\hat{\beta}'_{ND} - \hat{\beta}'_{LV})].$$

As before, the left-hand side represents the offer wage differential between ND and LV men. The first term on the right is the explained part of the offer wage differential, including the part attributed to differences in the proportions of disabled and nondisabled workers in customer-related jobs $\overline{C}$. The second term is the part of the unexplained differential attributed to differences in the returns to customer-related jobs, as measured by differences in the estimated coefficients of the customer interaction variable $\hat{\gamma}$. The third term is the part of the unexplained differential attributed to differences in the estimated coefficients of the remaining variables in the model $\hat{\beta}$.

Note that customer interaction contributes to the offer wage differential in two ways. Differences in the *proportions* of workers in customer-related jobs contribute to the explained part of the differential, while differences in the *returns* to customer-related jobs contribute to the unexplained part. Differences in the proportions of disabled and nondisabled workers in customer-related jobs are presumed to reflect worker preferences. If, instead, they reflect employment discrimination, estimates of customer-related discrimination from the decomposition are biased downward. This is not unique to the customer interaction variable; differences in experience, occupation, and other variables in the wage equations may reflect discrimination rather than worker choice.

Keeping this limitation in mind, the decompositions from model 2 test the following implications of the customer discrimination model: (1) Men with more visible disabilities are less likely to be in customer-related jobs; (2) Men with more visible disabilities employed in customer-related jobs incur significant wage penalties; and (3) Customer interaction explains more of the wage differential for men with more visible disabilities than for men with less visible disabilities.

Estimates of Wage Discrimination

RESULTS BASED ON PREJUDICE RANKINGS

Table 7.1 presents mean wages and employment rates for nondisabled men, and men with disabilities subject to more or less prejudice. Results for 1996 are compared to results from an earlier study using similar methods and data from the 1990 SIPP (Baldwin and Johnson, 2000).

Table 7.1 Mean Wages and Employment Rates by Disability Status: Stratified by Prejudice Rankings

| | 1990 | | | 1996 | | |
| | Non-disabled Men (N=11,708) | Men with Disabilities | | Non-disabled Men (N=15,472) | Men with Disabilities | |
		LP (N=662)	MP (N=240)		LP (N=725)	MP (N=212)
Proportion Employed	.89	.71	.58	.89 (.31)	.65 (.48)	.47 (.50)
Mean Wage	$13.35	$11.13	$10.90	$17.44 (24.23)	$14.79 (23.26)	$11.59 (7.76)

Source: Baldwin and Johnson (2000); 1996 SIPP, Wave V.
Note: Standard deviations in parentheses.

Consistent with other studies of the post-ADA period (Bound and Waidman, 2000; DeLeire, 2000), the result portray a picture of stagnant or deteriorating labor market outcomes for men with disabilities during the 1990s, particularly for men with impairments subject to more prejudice. The employment rate for nondisabled men is 89 percent in both 1990 and 1996, but the employment rate for men with disabilities subject to less prejudice declines by 6 percentage points (from 71 percent to 65 percent) and for men with disabilities subject to more prejudice by 11 percentage points (from 58 percent to 47 percent) over the same period.[15] The mean wage ratio for LP men verus nondisabled men increases slightly between 1990 and 1996 (from 83 percent to 85 percent), but the wage ratio for MP men declines dramatically (from 82 percent to 66 percent).

Table 7.2 presents decompositions of the wage differentials, based on prejudice rankings, for 1990 (Baldwin and Johnson, 2000) and 1996. Observed wage differentials are the difference in mean log wages corrected for selection bias. The resulting difference in offer wages is decomposed into an explained part due to productivity-related characteristics, and an unexplained part due to discrimination and residual effects.

For both LP and MP groups, the explained part of the wage differential increases between 1990 and 1996, indicating a widening gap in the productivity-related characteristics of disabled and nondisabled men, while the unexplained part of the differential decreases, suggesting a decline in discrimination. Consider the results for men in the LP group. Between 1990 and 1996, the explained part of the wage differential increases from 1.6 to 2.3 percent of the nondisabled offer wage. The increase is largely attributed to an increasing gap in the educational level of disabled and nondisabled men, and to increasing occupational segregation of men with disabilities. The unexplained part of the wage differential, however, declines from 16.5 to 1.3 percent of the nondisabled offer wage and, as a result, the overall offer wage differential declines dramatically.

Similar trends can be observed in the results for men in the MP group. The explained part of the wage differential increases from 3.4 to 11.7 percent of the nondisabled offer wage, again because of widening gaps between mean educational levels and occupational distributions of nondisabled and disabled men. The unexplained wage differential declines from 23.7 to 17.7 percent of the nondisabled offer wage, but here the decline in estimated discrimination is not sufficient to offset the increase in the explained wage differential, so the overall offer wage differential increases between 1990 and 1996. The results for disability-related wage discrimination are consistent with Hotchkiss (2003), who also found declining unexplained wage differentials in the 1990s.

Table 7.2   Decompositions of Wage Differentials between Disabled and Nondisabled Men: Stratified by Prejudice Rankings

	1990		1996	
	Disabled LP	Disabled MP	Disabled LP	Disabled MP
Wage Differential	$2.22	$2.45	$2.65	$5.85
Difference in Log Wages	0.153	0.228	0.179	0.335
Difference in Offer Wages	0.181	0.271	0.037	0.294
Components of the Explained Differential				
Functional Limitations	0.029	0.027	0.005	0.011
Education	0.026	0.031	0.036	0.068
Race	−0.006	−0.003	0.002	−0.000
Union	0.001	0.001	−0.001	0.009
Experience	−0.049	−0.034	−0.041	−0.010
Occupation	0.015	0.013	0.023	0.039
Total Explained Differential	0.016	0.034	0.023	0.117
Unexplained Differential	0.165	0.237	0.013	0.177

Source: Baldwin and Johnson (2000); 1996 SIPP, Wave V.

The comparisons between 1990 and 1996 suggest both good and bad news regarding changes in labor market outcomes for men with disabilities in the post-ADA period. There is evidence of declining disability-related wage discrimination for both the LP and MP groups. This has improved the relative offer wage position of men with disabilities subject to less prejudice, and enabled men with disabilities subject to more prejudice to retain roughly equivalent relative offer wages in 1990 and 1996, despite a widening education gap between disabled and nondisabled men. Nevertheless, the widening education gap, increasing occupational segregation, and declining relative employment rates for men with disabilities are disturbing trends. One possibility is that wage discrimination has declined in response to antidiscrimination legislation, but prejudices are now more likely to be expressed in hiring decisions and job assignments.[16]

The decompositions indicate that men with disabilities subject to more prejudice experience greater disability-related wage discrimination than do men with disabilities subject to less prejudice. In 1996, the unexplained wage differential, attributed to discrimination and residual effects, is 35 percent of the offer wage differential (0.013/0.037) for ND/LP men, compared to 60 percent (.177/.294) for ND/MP men. The unexplained wage differential is only 1.3 percent of the nondisabled offer wage for LP men, but 17.7 percent for MP men. Thus, the decompositions based on prejudice rankings are consistent with the assumption that prejudice motivates disability-related discrimination.[17] In the following section, similar decompositions are presented for men with disabilities stratified by visibility rankings to examine whether customer discrimination contributes to disability-related wage differentials.

RESULTS BASED ON VISIBILITY RANKINGS

Table 7.3 presents wage and employment statistics from the 1996 data stratified by visibility rankings. No comparable data exists for 1990. The results show no important differences in employment rates for men with less visible versus more visible disabilities, but mean wages are lower for the MV group. The disabled–nondisabled wage ratio is 83 percent for men in the LV group compared to 75 percent for men in the MV group.

The decompositions based on visibility rankings are in table 7.4. The visibility rankings differ from the prejudice rankings in that cancer, epilepsy, AIDS, and substance use disorders, ranked in the most disadvantaged more prejudice group, move to the less disadvantaged less visible category, while stiffness or deformity of extremities moves from the less prejudice to more visible category (appendix table A1).

Focusing on model 1, which is identical to the models reported above for disabled men stratified by prejudice rankings, the results suggest that men with more visible impairments have poorer wage outcomes, and are subject to greater discrimination in the labor market, than men with less visible impairments. Mean wages for men in the LV group are 83 percent of the mean wage for nondisabled men. Correcting for sample selection bias, the offer wage differential is only 1.8 percent of the nondisabled offer wage and the unexplained, or discriminatory, component of the differential is negative, indicating no evidence of wage discrimination against men with less visible disabilities. In contrast, the mean wage for the MV group is only 75 percent of the mean wage for nondisabled men, and the offer wage differential is 31.4 percent of the

Table 7.3   Mean Wages and Employment Rates by Disability Status: Stratified by Visibility Rankings

	Nondisabled Men (N=15,472)	Men with Disabilities	
		LV (N=758)	MV (N=179)
Proportion Employed	.89	.60	.62
	(.31)	(.49)	(.49)
Mean Wage	$17.44	$14.52	$13.15
	(24.23)	(23.68)	(7.97)
Proportion of Employed in Customer Interaction Jobs	.39 (.49)	.38 (.48)	.31 (.46)
Mean Wage in Customer Interaction Jobs	$20.83 (35.27)	$16.48 (34.54)	$14.55 (10.60)

Source: 1996 SIPP, Wave V.
Note: Standard deviations in parentheses.

nondisabled offer wage. The unexplained component is more than 30 percent of the nondisabled offer wage and accounts for 95 percent (0.306/0.314) of the offer wage differential. Not only does the evidence suggest that the MV group encounters more discrimination than the LV group, but the MV group also experiences more discrimination than the MP group identified by the prejudice rankings (table 7.2). There is, however, considerable overlap between the MV and MP groups (differentiated by only eighty-four cases), so one must be cautious in drawing conclusions about the relative importance of visibility.

THE ROLE OF CUSTOMER DISCRIMINATION IN THE PRODUCT MARKET

Table 7.3 reports descriptive statistics for workers employed in jobs that require substantial customer interaction. Men with more visible disabilities are less likely to be employed in customer-related jobs (31 percent) than are nondisabled men (39 percent) or men with less visible disabilities (38 percent). For all groups of men, wages in customer interaction jobs are higher than the mean wage for all jobs, but men with disabilities, and particularly men with visible disabilities, enjoy smaller wage premiums for customer interaction than do nondisabled men (19 percent for nondisabled men, 13 percent for LV men, 11 percent for MV men). Both the occupational segregation of men with disabilities away from customer-related jobs, and the smaller wage premiums for men with disabilities in those jobs, contribute to disability-related wage differentials. Table 7.4 (model 2) shows how controlling for customer interaction affects the decomposition results.

Table 7.4   Decompositions of Wage Differentials between Disabled and Nondisabled Men: Stratified by Visibility Rankings

	Model 1		Model 2	
	Disabled LV	Disabled MV	Disabled LV	Disabled MV
Wage Differential	$2.92	$4.29	$2.92	$4.29
Difference in Log Wages	0.211	0.186	0.211	0.186
Difference in Offer Wages	0.018	0.314	0.020	0.320
Components of the Explained Differential				
Functional limitations	0.012	−0.018	0.010	−0.021
Education	0.039	0.050	0.039	0.050
Race	0.003	−0.006	0.003	−0.006
Union	0.001	0.001	0.001	0.001
Experience	−0.036	−0.033	−0.037	−0.033
Occupation	0.028	0.013	0.028	0.012
Customer-related jobs	—	—	0.001	0.004
Total Explained Differential	*0.047*	*0.008*	*0.044*	*0.007*
Returns to Customer-Related Jobs	—	—	0.027	0.035
Other Unexplained	—	—	−0.051	0.278
Total Unexplained Differential	*−0.029*	*0.306*	*−0.024*	*0.313*

Source: 1996 SIPP, Wave V.

The results are consistent with the hypothesis that customers discriminate against men with disabilities. Differential returns to customer-related jobs contribute to the unexplained, or discriminatory, components of the wage differential for both LV and MV groups, but the effect is greater for men with more visible disabilities. The effect of differential returns to customer-related jobs is 2.7 percent of the nondisabled offer wage for the LV group, compared to 3.5 percent for the MV group. The wage differential associated with customer interaction is, however, small relative to other sources of discrimination against the MV group, only 10 percent of the unexplained differential.

Differences in the proportions of disabled and nondisabled men employed in customer-related jobs (documented in table 7.3) also contribute to disability-related wage differentials but these differences are counted with the explained part of the wage differential. In fact, it is unclear if differential employment in customer-related jobs reflects the choices and preferences of workers with disabilities or their customers. In the former case, wage differentials associated with worker preferences are not discriminatory. In the latter case, wage differentials associated with customer preferences reflect discrimination, and the estimates of differential returns to customer-related jobs understate the true effect of customer discrimination in the labor market.

Who are the workers with more visible disabilities in jobs that require customer interaction? The most common health conditions are stiffness or deformity of the extremities (47 percent), blindness or vision problems (17 percent), or deafness or serious trouble hearing (11 percent). They are overwhelmingly white (98 percent), and have higher levels of education, on average, than other men with disabilities. Job titles include pharmacist, lawyer, nursery worker, bus driver, and sales representative, among others. The sample is small (n = 33) so one should be cautious, but it appears that qualities attached to greater rewards in the labor market (e.g., race, education) help compensate for the disadvantage associated with a visible health impairment in gaining entrée to customer interaction jobs.

In sum, the evidence is consistent with the hypothesis that customers are a source of disability-related discrimination in the labor market. Men with disabilities in general, and men with visible disabilities in particular, are less likely to be employed in jobs involving customer interaction, and earn lower wage premiums in those jobs, than do nondisabled men. Differential returns to customer-related jobs contribute to the unexplained wage differentials between nondisabled and disabled men, and the effect is greater when it is easier for customers to identify a disabled employee.

Discussion

This work exploits the heterogeneity of the disabled population to examine the source of discrimination in the labor market. The evidence fits Becker's theory that customer prejudice is a cause of discrimination. Men with impairments subject to more prejudice experience poorer labor market outcomes and greater discrimination than men with impairments subject to less prejudice. Men with more visible impairments have poorer outcomes and are more subject to customer discrimination.

Comparisons of the results from 1990 and 1996 are unsettling. Although there is evidence of declining wage discrimination against men with disabilities in the six years following passage of the ADA, the results also depict eroding employment opportunities. Relative employment rates for men with disabilities decline in the post-ADA period, and occupational segregation increases. The results suggest that the ADA has not delivered on the promise of increasing employment opportunities for workers with disabilities, a conclusion consistent with evidence from the dispensation of disability-related discrimination charges filed with the Equal Employment Opportunity Commission. Moss et al. (1999) report that over 60 percent of ADA-related charges filed through March 1998 are allegations of illegal discharge (52 percent) or discrimination in hiring (9 percent), yet less than 2 percent of closed cases result in job reinstatements or new jobs for workers with disabilities. To the extent that employers perceive a low risk of penalties for employment discrimination against workers with disabilities, we may be observing a post-ADA era in which discrimination in hiring, job terminations, and occupational assignments replace wage discrimination as less costly alternatives to express tastes for discrimination against workers with disabilities.

Another possible explanation for increasing occupational segregation of workers with disabilities is the ADA mandate to provide reasonable accommodations to otherwise qualified workers with disabilities. Changes in occupational distributions could be explained by differences in the costs of providing accommodations in different occupations, or by economies of scale in the provision of accommodations in some occupations more than others. Empirical evidence on the costs of accommodations suggests that most impose little or no direct cost on employers, but the indirect costs are not typically studied and may be considerable.

To my knowledge, this is the first study to exploit differences in the visibility of minority groups to test the hypothesis that customers are a source of discrimination in the labor market. Decompositions based on visibility rankings are consistent with the hypothesis that customers are a source of disability-related discrimination. Men with disabilities are less likely to be employed in customer-related jobs, and those who are do not enjoy the wage premium that nondisabled workers receive for customer interaction. Customer interaction plays a more important role in explaining wage differentials for men with more visible disabilities than for men with less visible disabilities.

The present study demonstrates that using both the unique features of a minority group and particular characteristics of the product market can yield new insights into how discrimination operates. Continuing this line of investigation will not only increase our understanding of the mechanisms underlying discrimination in the labor market, but also link empirical investigations of discrimination more closely to their theoretical foundations.

Notes

The author expresses gratitude to Barry T. Hirsch for references to O*Net, and to William G. Johnson, Edward J. Schumacher, and Lester Zeager for helpful comments. Any remaining errors are my own.

1. Arrow (1973) extends the concept of separation to include social distance as well.

2. Becker calls this expression for the relative wage differential the "market discrimination coefficient." The market discrimination coefficient is the product of the individual discrimination coefficient, d, and the ratio of output price to the costs of one unit of production by disabled workers.

3. The data come from a survey administered to 800 employers in Atlanta, Boston, Detroit, and Los Angeles between June 1992 and May 1994.

4. Some variables, such as work experience and nonwage incomes, are constructed from Topical Modules accompanying other Waves.

5. The acceptability ranking is derived from responses to the question, "How much would you like to have this person as a friend?" Students are asked to rank impairments on a scale of (1) least acceptable to (5) most acceptable. The visibility ranking is derived from responses to the question, "How easily could you tell that people have (Disability Name) just by looking at them?" Students rank impairments on a scale from (1) not at all visible to (5) very visible (Royal and Roberts, 1987, 124).

6. The authors ask respondents to "consider what level of acceptance is most usually found for each disability," and rank disabilities according to the following response scale: (1) no acceptance (people would prefer a person with this disability to be kept in an institution or out of sight); (2) low acceptance (persons would try to avoid a person with this disability); (3) moderate acceptance (a person with this disability would be acceptable as a fellow worker); (4) high acceptance (a person with

this disability would be acceptable as a friend); (5) and full acceptance (people would accept a person with this disability marrying into their family) (Westbrook, Legge, and Pennay, 1993, 617). Respondents include 665 health practitioners from six ethnic communities in Australia.

7. An alternate approach to controlling for the effect of functional limitations on workplace productivity is to include each of the limitations as a control variable in the models. The responses for different functional limitation variables are, however, highly correlated because impairments often produce multiple limitations. Arthritic degeneration of the joints, for example, is likely to limit several functions related to mobility (e.g., climbing, lifting, walking), while a mental or emotional disorder is likely to limit multiple cognitive functions (e.g., keeping track of money or bills, getting along with other people, coping with everyday stress). The use of a dummy variable for each limitation in a wage equation typically produces results in which none of the individual limitation variables are statistically significant. In addition, some less common limitations do not occur in some samples, reducing the regression models to less than full rank for those samples.

8. O*Net provides a crosswalk between O*Net–SOC codes and other classification systems, but the crosswalk does not include three-digit Census Bureau codes.

9. More than 25 percent of the unmatched occupations are in gaming; these occupations cannot be identified separately from other recreation-related occupations on the SIPP codes. However, most of the recreation-related jobs on the SIPP are classified as customer related through matches to other O*Net codes, so the gaming occupations are correctly classified. Most of the other O*Net occupations that fail to match are because the occupation is more narrowly defined on O*Net than on the SIPP (e.g., legal secretary fails to match because SIPP identifies the broader category "secretary"). These occupations may be misclassified if the broader SIPP category is not considered a customer-related job.

10. The advantage of the decomposition technique is that it allows the entire wage structure to differ between majority and minority groups. Thus, the method detects discrimination that appears as differential returns to the productivity-related characteristics of the two groups, controlling for differences in their mean productivity.

11. The wage rate is defined as the reported wage for hourly workers, total wage income divided by total hours worked in the four-month reference period for salaried workers.

12. The sample selection variable (Heckman, 1980) is constructed from coefficient estimates of an employment function estimated for the full sample of workers and nonworkers. The system is identified by including age, marital status, and nonwage incomes only in the employment function. Marital status and nonwage incomes are expected to influence workers' reservation wages but have little or no effect on employers' offer wages. Age often serves as a proxy for work experience in offer wage functions, but the SIPP includes good measures of general and job-specific work experience, so age is also excluded

from the wage equation. In theory, all variables in the wage equation should also be included in the employment function, however, some of the variables in the wage equation—namely, occupation, union membership, and work experience—are not observed for nonworkers. This may severely limit the selectivity bias correction in the models, but a more restrictive wage equation is likely to overestimate discrimination.

13. Four measures of work experience are included in the model: Specific experience measures years worked for the current employer, general experience measures years worked for other employers, and missing experience measures years in which a person was of working age but neither employed nor in school. Specific experience is also included as a square term to control for declining investments in job-specific training over time.

14. The nondiscriminatory wage structure for minority workers is unobservable but is assumed bounded by the observed wage structures for the majority and minority groups. Most studies of discrimination set $d = 1$ (the nondiscriminatory wage structure is the wage structure of the majority group), $d = 0$ (the nondiscriminatory wage structure is the wage structure of the minority group), or $d = 0.5$ (Reimers, 1983). Cotton (1988) argues that the weights should represent the proportions of majority and minority workers in the employed labor force. My choice of $d = 1.0$ approximates Cotton's rule because the samples of disabled workers are no more than 5 percent of the total sample in any regression. An alternate weighting scheme suggested by Neumark (1988) obtains the nondiscriminatory wage structure from a pooled regression for the full sample. Oaxaca and Ransom (1988) argue that the pooled regression approach is less attractive in models that include controls for sample selection bias because the estimated parameters from the pooled sample are not a linear function of the estimated parameters from the separate regressions.

15. Hotchkiss (2003) argues that the observed declines in employment rates in the post-ADA period are generated by decreases in labor force participation among the disabled. She reports that unconditional employment rates for disabled workers (corrected for selection bias) have increased steadily since 1992.

16. DeLeire (2001) uses SIPP data to analyze changes in disability-related wage discrimination over an earlier time period: 1984 to 1993. The results are not easily compared to the results reported here because he does not use a standard decomposition technique to estimate the unexplained wage differential, and because he stratifies the disabled group differently. Specifically, men with health impairments are divided into two groups: those who report impairment-related work limitations, and those who report their impairment does not limit their productivity. DeLeire assumes the wage differential for the latter group is entirely attributed to discrimination, and uses it to identify the explained and unexplained wage differentials for the former group. He finds no decrease in discrimination against disabled workers between 1984 and 1993.

17. Comparisons between the MP/LP results are dependent on the assumptions that productivity differences between the two groups are controlled adequately, or that unmeasured productivity differences are uncorrelated with

the MP/LP distinction. One particular concern where these assumptions may not be satisfied is cognitive limitations. Cognitive limitations are more typically associated with mental disorders than physical disorders, but there are few measures of cognitive limitations on the SIPP. If the limitations variables do not measure cognitive limitations adequately, the estimates of discrimination may be biased upward, with greater impact on the MP results.

References

Albrecht, Gary L., Vivian G. Walker, and Judith A. Levy. "Social Distance from the Stigmatized: A Test of Two Theories." *Social Science and Medicine* 16 (1982): 1319–28.

Arrow, Kenneth J. "The Theory of Discrimination." In *Discrimination in Labor Markets,* ed. Orley Ashenfelter and Albert Rees, 3–33. Princeton, NJ: Princeton University Press, 1973.

Baldwin, Marjorie L., and William G. Johnson. "Labor Market Discrimination against Men with Disabilities in the Year of the A.D.A." *Southern Economic Journal* 66 (2000): 548–66.

———. "Labor Market Discrimination against Women with Disabilities." *Industrial Relations* 34 (1995): 555–77.

———. "Labor Market Discrimination against Men with Disabilities." *Journal of Human Resources* 29 (1994): 1–19.

Becker, Gary. *The Economics of Discrimination.* Chicago: University of Chicago Press, 1957.

Bodvarsson, Örn B., and Mark D. Partridge. "A Supply and Demand Model of Co-Worker, Employer and Customer Discrimination." *Labour Economics* 8 (2001): 389–416.

Bound, John, and Timothy Waidman. "Accounting for Recent Declines in Employment Rates among the Working-Age Disabled." *Journal of Human Resources* 37 (2002): 231–50.

Cotton, Jeremiah. "On the Decomposition of Wage Differentials." *Review of Economics and Statistics* 70 (1988): 236–43.

DeLeire, Thomas. "Changes in Wage Discrimination against People with Disabilities: 1984–1993." *Journal of Human Resources* 36 (2001): 144–58.

———. "The Wage and Employment Effects of the Americans with Disabilities Act." *Journal of Human Resources* 35 (2000): 693–715.

Heckman, James J. "Sample Selection Bias as a Specification Error with an Application to the Estimation of Labor Supply Functions." In *Female Labor Supply,* ed. J. P. Smith, 206–48. Princeton, NJ: Princeton University Press, 1980.

Hendricks, Wallace, ChrisAnn Schrio-Geist, and Emir Broadbent. "Labor Market Outcomes for Persons with Long-Term Disabilities and College Educations." *Industrial Relations* 36 (1997): 46–60.

Holzer, Harry J., and Keith R. Ihlanfeldt. "Customer Discrimination and Employment Outcomes for Minority Workers." *Quarterly Journal of Economics* 113 (1998): 835–67.

Hotchkiss, Julie. *The Labor Market Experiences of Workers with Disabilities: The ADA and Beyond.* Kalamazoo, MI: W.E Upjohn Institute, 2003.

Johnson, William G., and James Lambrinos. "The Effect of Prejudice on the Wages of Disabled Workers." *Policy Studies Journal* 15 (1987): 571–90.

Jones, F. L. "On Decomposing the Wage Gap: A Critical Comment on Blinder's Method." *Journal of Human Resources* 28 (1983): 126–30.

Kahn, Lawrence M. "Customer Discrimination and Affirmative Action." *Economic Inquiry* 29 (1991): 555–71.

Kanazawa, Mark T., and Jonas P. Funk. "Racial Discrimination in Professional Basketball: Evidence from Nielsen Ratings." *Economic Inquiry* 39 (2001): 599–608.

Moss, Kathryn, Michael Ullman, Barbara E. Starrett, Scott Burris, and Matthew C. Johnsen. "Outcomes of Employment Discrimination Charges Filed under the Americans with Disabilities Act." *Psychiatric Services* 50 (1999): 1028–35.

Nagi, Saad Z. *Disability and Rehabilitation.* Columbus: Ohio State University, 1969.

Neumark, David. "Employers' Discriminatory Behavior and the Estimation of Wage Discrimination." *Journal of Human Resources* 23 (1988): 279–95.

Oaxaca, Ronald L. "Male–Female Wage Differentials in Urban Labor Markets." *International Economic Review* 14 (1973): 693–709.

Oaxaca, Ronald L., and Michael R. Ransom. "Searching for the Effect of Unionism on the Wages of Union and Nonunion Workers." *Journal of Labor Research* 9 (1988): 139–48.

O*Net 4.0. National O*Net Consortium. U.S. Department of Labor, Employment and Training Administration. http://online.onetcenter.org/.

Reimers, Cordelia. "Labor Market Discrimination against Hispanic and Black Men." *Review of Economics and Statistics* 65 (1983): 570–79.

Royal, George P., and Michael C. Roberts. "Students' Perceptions of and Attitudes toward Disabilities: A Comparison of Twenty Conditions." *Journal of Clinical Child Psychology* 16 (1987): 122–32.

Salkever, David S., and Marisa E. Domino. "Within-Group Structural Tests of Labor-Market Discrimination: A Study of Persons with Serious Disabilities." In *The Economics of Disability: Research in Human Capital and Development*, vol. 13, ed. Alan Sorkin, 33–50. Stamford, CT: JAI Press, 2000.

Stone, Eric W., and Ronald S. Warren Jr. "Customer Discrimination in Professional Basketball: Evidence from the Trading-Card Market." *Applied Economics* 31 (1999): 679–85.

Tringo John L. "The Hierarchy of Preference toward Disability Groups." *Journal of Special Education* 4 (1970): 295–306.

Westbrook, Mary T., Varoe Legge, and Mark Pennay. "Attitudes towards Disabilities in a Multicultural Society." *Social Science and Medicine* 36 (1993): 615–24.

World Health Organization. *International Classification of Functioning, Disability, and Health.* Geneva: World Health Organization, 2001.

———. *International Classification of Impairments, Disabilities, and Handicaps.* Geneva: World Health Organization, 1980.

Yuker, Harold E. "The Disability Hierarchies: Comparative Reactions to Various Types of Physical and Mental Disabilities." Unpublished manuscript, Hofstra University, 1987.

Chapter 8

Regulatory Reform and
Racial Employment Patterns

Kaye Husbands Fealing and James H. Peoples

Introduction

Economic regulation of transportation and public utilities helped create an environment allowing labor to share industry rents with owners.[1] The Wharton research series The Racial Policies of American Industry indicates that prior to the enactment of equal employment opportunity guidelines targeting the transportation sector, blacks were highly unlikely to share industry rents. Empirical research reveals that even with the passage of equal employment opportunity policies, some of these industries failed to employ blacks in high-paying occupations or in lucrative industry sectors (Heywood and Peoples, 1994; Husbands, 1998). Thus, even though telecommunications firms and airlines faced governmental pressure to employ minorities in high-skilled, high-paying occupations, compared to whites, blacks remained less likely to be employed in those occupations. One possible reason for the continued racial employment disparity is economic regulation that blocked entry and sheltered transportation and telecommunications industries from vibrant competition (Becker, 1957).

Deregulation that fostered competition made it more costly for firms to continue exercising discriminatory preferences. Previous research shows that following deregulation there was a significant increase in the share of jobs going to black workers in the more lucrative trucking sectors and in higher-paying railroad industry occupations (Husbands, 1998). Moreover, black workers maintained their preregulation employment shares in high-paying telecommunications and airline occupations following deregulation. Studies utilizing multivariate techniques confirm increased black employment following deregulation in trucking and airlines (Agesa, 2001; Heywood and Peoples, 1994). However, these techniques have not been used to examine employment patterns for other network industries. In addition, with the exception of trucking, past research does not compare racial employment patterns in deregulated network industries with that of other industries in the service sector. Making the sectoral comparison is critical to determining whether racial employment patterns in deregulated network industries are unique or part of a broader trend.

This chapter contributes to the analysis of regulatory reform (changes in market structure) and employment discrimination by using probit estimations to examine deregulation's effect on racial employment. Racial employment findings for trucking, rail, airlines, telecommunications, and utilities are then compared to employment estimates for the remainder of the service sector.

Competition and Employment Discrimination

Gary Becker (1957) formalized the hypothesis that is the foundation of this study.[2] His model suggests that increased market competition following deregulation will have the unintended effect of reducing employment discrimination. When regulation hinders competition between firms in the product market, discriminatory employers have greater latitude to exercise their preferences. For example, they might choose to hire white workers instead of black workers, or men instead of women. In a competitive product market, however, the cost of discrimination places discriminatory employers at a competitive disadvantage.

In practice, many employers may operate in markets that exhibit noncompetitive behavior. In the absence of competition, government legislation such as nondiscrimination laws can create a disincentive to engaging in discriminatory hiring practices. The choice of whether the market or government should correct market inefficiencies—such as employment discrimination—is a critical economic and policy issue. Examining network industries provides the unique opportunity to address this issue, since such industries have experienced both government policies encouraging stepped-up competition and antidiscrimination legislation.

Prior to regulatory reform, rate and entry regulation might have allowed employers at network industries to exercise discriminatory preferences. Evidence reported in the Wharton series on The Racial Policies of American Industry shows that immediately preceding the 1960s civil rights legislation in the United States, black workers in network industries were nearly exclusively employed in low-wage occupations. For instance, very few black truck drivers were in the lucrative long-haul segment of the trucking industry. Even among nondriver occupations, blacks were mainly employed as laborers and service workers (Leone, 1970). Blacks were also disproportionately employed as laborers and service workers in the airline, rail, and energy sectors during the pre–civil rights era.[3] In contrast, black telecommunications workers were mainly employed as telephone operators prior to the civil rights movement. While this clerical occupation paid more than laborers and service jobs, blacks in the telecommunications industry were not well represented in high-wage occupations. Only 2.8 percent of black workers were officials and managers and only 1.6 percent of black workers were categorized as professionals in the telecommunications industry (Wallace, 1976).

During the 1960s and 1970s, federal initiatives addressed racial employment disparities in network industries. Table 8.1 summarizes these initiatives. President John F. Kennedy's 1961 Executive Order 10925 targeted rail, airlines, and trucking.[4] In 1963, the trucking industry also faced Executive Order 11114, which extended the former order to include trucking companies with contracts below $10,000. Government equal employment policies directed at energy utilities focused on government-sponsored manpower development and training programs. These programs were financed through the voluntary Job Opportunities in the Business Sector (JOBS) initiative of 1968 (Anderson, 1970). Employment guidelines stipulated by the 1973 AT&T consent decree formalized goals and rules for improving minority hiring and upward mobility at AT&T.

Equal employment policies varied in success for the five network industries examined in this study. The pattern is consistent with the argument that large dominant firms are most likely to alleviate tendencies toward discrimination under government persuasion, since they are secure enough to take such steps and they have the most to lose (Shepherd, 1969). Thus, among the five industries examined in this study, the most significant employment gains by minorities occurred in telecommunications. Six years following the 1973 consent decree, minority employment in professional and managerial occupations rose from 3.7 to 9.9 percent and from 4.0 to 9.2 percent, respectively (Peoples and Robinson, 1996). Minority employment gains in white-collar occupations also happened in the oligopolistic rail and airline industries, but not to the extent in telecommunications. Less impressive minority employment gains occurred at energy utilities and these gains varied by region. Major utility employment gains for blacks occurred in urban locations, where blacks represented more than 10 percent of the labor force (Anderson, 1970).

Table 8.1 EEOC Legislation for Network Industries

Industries	Year	Legislation	Brief Details	Initial Effects
Rail	1961	Executive Order No. 10925	Contractors should "take affirmative action" to ensure that applicants are hired and treated during employment without regard to their race, creed, color, or national origin.	Slow but steady upward mobility of blacks in the railroad industry. Carriers with government contracts a key factor.
Airlines				Steady improvement in the proportion of black workers in a few white-collar occupations in the airlines industry—mainly sales and office clerical occupations. (*continued*)

Table 8.1 (*continued*)

Industries	Year	Legislation	Brief Details	Initial Effects
Trucking	1963	Executive Order No. 11114	Government could investigate a company's employment practices as long as a bill of lading was issued.	Little movement of black truckers from the low-wage cartage sector to the high-wage long-haul sector. New hires on carriers with government contracts up measurably.
Utilities	1968	Voluntary JOBS Program	Government support for financing vocational training, counseling, and health services.	Minority employment gains varied by region; major gains for blacks occurred in urban locations.
Telecom	1973	Consent Decree— AT&T, EEOC, DoJ, DoL	Within five years of the decree, the race-gender profile of AT&T's workforce should mirror that of the local labor pool.	Measurable gains by blacks in high-wage positions such as managers and administration in the telecom industry.

Government-enforced equal employment opportunity policies were least successful in the trucking industry. Union seniority rules posed a major barrier to black employment in the lucrative long-haul segment of this industry. Drivers in the low-wage local cartage sector faced high transfer costs owing to lost seniority. Blacks concentrated in local cartage were unwilling to give up all of their seniority to transfer to the long-haul sector.

In summary, federal equal employment opportunity policies provided an impetus for minority employment gains in network industries. However, racial employment disparities persisted after these policies were instituted—most notably in trucking. Becker's model suggests that pro-competitive government policies might also help to correct employment discrimination. Compared to the other four network industries, the postderegulation trucking industry exhibits the most competitive characteristics. For example, relatively low barriers to entry in this industry give workers greater choices of employers. In addition, the relatively low training costs make it easier to acquire the skills of a truck driver.

Deregulation and Racial Employment Patterns

U.S. network industries share a common economic policy history, although economic outcomes varied by industry. By 1935 rail, trucking, airlines, telecommunications, and energy utilities all faced federal regulation of rates and market structure.[5] Beginning in the mid-1970s deregulation eased these restrictions, with varied competitive results.

Table 8.2 summarizes the events that precipitated major changes in the government's role in regulating network industries and the resulting changes in market structure in those sectors. A pro-competitive outcome is expected to facilitate convergence in occupational probabilities for black and white workers, while persistent market concentration is expected to fortify firms against pressure to hire workers in various occupations irrespective of race. These expectations are given in the last column of table 8.2.

Prior to deregulation, railroads experienced losses or much smaller rates of return than did other nonfinancial U.S. corporations (Grimm and Winston, 2000). Although Congress passed the 1976 Railroad Revitalization and Regulatory Reform (4R) Act in an attempt to liberalize operations and pricing, it was the Staggers Act in 1980 that gave railroads the freedom to negotiate their own rates. Following deregulation, mergers and consolidation of services prevailed in the railroad sector, with tight controls on labor costs. Financial gains were not immediate, however the 1990s brought average annual returns on equity more than triple that during the 1970s. Thus, regulatory reform is expected to have a moderate effect on racial

Table 8.2 Deregulation and Divestiture in Network Industries

Industries	Year	Legislation	Effects	Expectation on Racial Employment Convergence
Rail	1976; 1980	4R Act; Staggers Act	Mergers and consolidation of services with tight controls on labor costs.	Some effect.
Airlines	1978; 1994	Airline Deregulation Act; Airline Improvement Act	Entry then exit and consolidation of carriers. Modest increase in the number of competitors at the route level. Hub-spoke distribution system introduced.	Little to no effect.
Trucking	1980; 1994	Motor Carrier Act; Airline Improvement Act	Stepped-up competition, with the number of certified motor carriers doubling during the initial six years after regulatory reform. Wage premiums cut in half.	Most effected.
Utilities	1992; 1996	Energy Policy Act; FERC Orders 888 and 889	Mergers and consolidation of dozens of electric utilities or gas and electric utilities.	Little effect.
Telecom	1982–84; 1996	Consent Decree; Telecom Act	AT&T divests of key operations. Large regional monopolies and a few long-distance oligopolies.	Little or no effect.

employment disparities in this sector, primarily because of the increased cost controls and the competitive pressure of the merger mechanism.

Market rivalry intensified markedly in the for-hire trucking sector with the initiation of economic deregulation in 1978. Two years later, Congress formally eased entry restrictions and allowed carriers greater freedom to set rates with the Motor Carrier Act of 1980 (MCA-1980). The effects of stepped-up competition ensued almost immediately with Moore (1986) reporting that the rate of return on transportation investment for major carriers fell from 24.0 percent in 1978 to 14.5 by 1979.[6] These returns remained near the 1979 level throughout the early 1980s.

Despite increased interstate competition in the for-hire trucking sector, intrastate regulation of these carriers remained the norm in many states until passage of the 1994 Airline Improvement Act (AIA) (Taylor, 1994). Peoples (2003) reports that the AIA stimulated a significant increase in the number of trucking carriers and that despite rising fuel prices, trucking rates did not increase following the removal of state rate regulation. Thus, deregulation of the trucking sector is expected to yield the most significant employment effects relative to the other network industries in this study.

In the years leading up to the Airline Deregulation Act of 1978, carriers had record profits (Borenstein, 1992). Entry of low-fare carriers immediately followed passage of the act and severe economic losses followed (Morrison and Winston, 2000). Airlines implemented more efficient logistical routing systems with the purpose of improving operating efficiency. These systems led to increased market shares for major air carriers and the shakeout of many entrants and a few incumbent carriers. Along some routes, however, price competition was periodically fierce. Market conditions following deregulation imply that managers at airlines would have less ability to exercise discriminatory employment preferences. However, low labor supply elasticities limit the convergence of black–white employment shares for some high-wage occupations in the airline industry.

In 1982 Judge Green issued the consent decree requiring American Telephone and Telegraph (AT&T) to divest its local operating companies and its equipment division by January 1, 1984.[7] Following divestiture AT&T maintained a majority of the long-distance market, although its market share fell from 90 percent in 1984 to 55 percent in 1994. Crandall and Hausman (2000) report that the Herfindahl Index in the long-distance telephony sector was 2,640 in 1998, well below the 8,000 recorded in 1984.[8] Taylor and Taylor (1993) report that between 1984 and 1991, long-distance rates fell by 50 percent in real terms, in large part because of cost reductions—lower fees paid by long-distance companies to the local Bell Operating Companies (BOCs). The 1996 Telecommunications Act was designed to promote competition in the local exchange markets. While this act did lower barriers to regional competition, the BOCs still maintain regional monopolies.[9] Since monopoly power prevailed in the telecommunications sector following divestiture, little change is expected in the racial composition of occupations in that industry.

The Energy Policy Act of 1992 was intended to foster competition in the wholesale market for electricity, while maintaining the "traditional" structure of the electricity sector. Under this act, the Federal Energy Regulatory Commission (FERC) opened transmission grids previously controlled by individual utilities to nonutility power producers. A wave of mergers followed, as companies sought cost savings. Joskow (2000) reports that between 1995 and 1999, more than two dozen mergers were initiated between electric utilities or gas and electric utilities. In 1996 FERC issued Orders 888 and 889 that encourage further competition in wholesale and retail electricity. These policies help create an environment that encourages price competition. As firms in this sector focus on cost savings, the opportunity cost of employment discrimination is not expected to be exempt.

In summary, pro-competitive regulatory reform in network industries has had its most significant effect on market structure in the trucking sector. Nonetheless, other deregulated network industries now place greater emphasis on production efficiency and low costs following structural reforms. The new environment could influence racial employment disparities, especially if the lack of competition prior to deregulation allowed the inefficiency of racial employment discrimination. The convergence of racial employment shares is also dependent on prevailing labor supply elasticities.

Data and Empirical Approach

The 1973–1981 May Current Population Survey (CPS) files and 228 monthly CPS–Outgoing Rotation Group (CPS-ORG) files for January 1983 through December 2001 are utilized to assemble data on employment patterns for individual workers.[10] These sources report worker characteristics, current earnings, regional and local residency, and industry and occupation of employment. The sample is limited to private sector workers sixteen years old or older. The resulting population is large enough to examine racial employment patterns in network industries by regulatory regimes. However, the sample of blacks in network industries is too small to gain accurate annual measures of racial employment patterns.

Descriptive statistics by industry and regulatory regime are presented in tables 8.3 through 8.8. With the exception of utility workers, blacks are more likely than whites to have a college education after regulatory reform. This contrasts with the lower probability that blacks have a college education prior to deregulation.[11] This trend suggests that regulatory reform might be associated with increased employment of blacks in highly skilled occupations. Yet, tables 8.3 through 8.8 suggest that relative occupational gains for blacks only occur in trucking and rail.

Specifically, table 8.3 indicates that white truck drivers dominate unionized workers in the for-hire sector prior to regulatory reform but that following reform, black and white for-hire truck drivers are as likely to be union members. This suggests that blacks faced lower barriers to employment in the lucrative long-haul segment of the for-hire market. Yet, the eroding union membership disparity does not bring higher earnings for black for-hire truck drivers. Instead, the prederegulation earnings advantage for whites declines following deregulation as unions faced greater pressure to moderate wage gains (Hirsch, 1988; Rose, 1987). Indeed, table 8.3 reveals a substantial erosion of the white earnings premiums following deregulation of for-hire trucking.

Declining racial employment disparities following deregulation is apparently limited to truck drivers. Table 8.4 shows that the occupational distribution for blacks and whites employed in any occupation within the for-hire trucking sector does not change appreciably following deregulation. Compared to blacks, whites are more likely to be employed as managers and they are less likely to be employed as laborers. Both racial groups are equally likely to be employed as transportation operatives.

In the rail sector, deregulation is associated with an appreciable black employment shift from laborer to transportation operative and a shift from craft to transportation operative for white workers (see table 8.5). Becker's hypothesis on competition and employment discrimination may be supported by the results in table 8.5: rail transportation operatives earn more than laborers and craft jobs are at least as lucrative as rail transportation operative jobs.[12] The earnings data reveal a substantial prederegulation white earnings advantage and that advantage does not change significantly following deregulation. The sustained white earning premium may be because white workers attained dominant employment status among transportation operatives prior to deregulation.

Table 8.6 reports on airline workers and shows that blacks were more likely to be employed in low-paying service jobs prior to deregulation while whites were more likely to be employed in high-wage technician jobs. Deregulation does not change this racial pattern. Yet, table 8.6 shows that blacks have been nearly as successful as whites finding employment in high-paying, managerial, professional and craft jobs prior to and following deregulation. The prederegulation employment of blacks in these occupations can be in part attributed to the implementation of Equal Employment Opportunity Commission guidelines in the late 1960s.

Table 8.3 Mean Profile of For-Hire Truck Drivers in the Motor Carrier Industry

Variable	Pre-MCA (1973–1979)		Post-MCA (1980–1994)		Post-AIA (1995–2001)	
	White	Black	White	Black	White	Black
Female (%)	1.60	0.47	3.39	3.00	8.77	7.06
Married (%)	86.59	85.64	74.66	66.80	72.08	59.70
Age	38.28	37.74	39.00	38.98	41.31	39.76
Completed College (%)	12.27	13.87	19.88	22.16	19.76	24.07
Received High School Diploma (%)	46.06	43.06	55.11	52.41	46.21	44.67
Full Time (%)	92.38	90.43	92.46	91.05	94.04	94.02
Weekly Earnings (1983 $)	522.81	384.99	398.53	354.85	395.33	360.83
Weekly Hours Worked	48.95	42.60	48.29	44.04	48.50	44.23
Union Member (%)	58.38	51.19	30.13	28.05	22.90	23.68
Resides in						
Northeast (%)	19.02	18.66	19.66	17.94	14.97	12.63
Midwest % (%)	33.69	9.56	30.61	12.85	41.13	29.15
South (%)	28.34	59.80	28.97	62.27	26.47	52.93
West (%)	18.93	11.96	20.74	6.91	17.41	5.25
Number of Observations	2,297	209	5,232	1,633	7,257	1,005

Table 8.4 Mean Profile for All Workers in the For-Hire Sector in the Motor Carrier Industry

Variable	Pre-MCA (1973–1979)		Post-MCA (1980–1994)		Post-AIA (1995–2001)	
	White	Black	White	Black	White	Black
Female (%)	10.14	5.20	14.89	10.62	17.26	13.50
Married (%)	80.00	75.41	69.41	58.03	67.18	50.84
Age	37.21	36.36	37.43	36.79	39.64	37.37
Completed College (%)	20.09	17.95	27.63	28.00	23.21	26.71
Received High School Diploma (%)	45.86	40.60	50.41	47.52	41.78	40.33
Full Time (%)	88.88	83.42	87.27	83.13	89.05	84.87
Weekly Earnings (1983 $)	470.89	354.23	371.98	314.36	372.77	320.77
Weekly Hours Worked	45.22	40.14	44.30	40.71	44.72	41.04
Union Member (%)	46.73	46.68	25.29	25.94	19.45	24.31
Occupations						
Manager (%)	6.02	1.10	7.00	2.24	8.42	3.72
Professional (%)	0.87	0.00	0.43	0.18	0.96	0.36
Sales (%)	0.35	0.00	1.90	0.47	1.62	0.48
Technician (%)	0.49	0.00	0.51	0.29	0.68	0.48

(continued)

Table 8.4 (*continued*)

Variable	Pre-MCA (1973–1979)		Post-MCA (1980–1994)		Post-AIA (1995–2001)	
	White	Black	White	Black	White	Black
Clerical (%)	14.17	9.11	15.27	11.79	14.17	12.42
Craft (%)	9.09	7.73	6.89	3.08	4.90	2.40
Nontransportation Operatives (%)	1.11	3.03	0.95	1.43	0.85	1.50
Transportation Operatives (%)	57.41	57.73	56.0	60.00	58.20	60.32
Laborer (%)	9.97	18.78	10.37	19.22	9.69	17.35
Farmer(%)	0.00	0.00	0.05	0.07	0.02	0.06
Service(%)	0.49	2.48	0.50	0.11	0.44	0.90
Resides in						
Northeast (%)	20.71	20.72	20.59	18.70	16.16	12.90
Midwest (%)	33.16	11.32	30.33	13.85	40.74	30.19
South (%)	27.16	57.45	28.79	59.57	25.69	50.42
West (%)	19.94	10.49	20.27	7.87	17.39	6.48
Number of Observations	4,001	362	7,199	2,721	12,468	1,666

Table 8.5   Mean Profile of Railroad Workers

Variable	Pre-Stagger's Act (1973–1979)		Post-Stagger's Act (1980–1994)	
	White	Black	White	Black
Female (%)	6.10	9.30	8.00	17.04
Married (%)	82.90	75.00	79.35	65.16
Age	41.60	39.96	42.19	41.11
Completed College (%)	24.12	22.67	31.00	35.21
Received High School Diploma (%)	52.73	36.04	50.70	43.35
Full Time (%)	98.00	96.50	97.55	96.74
Weekly Earnings (1983 $)	513.00	405.02	511.33	414.77
Weekly Hours Worked	42.87	40.28	43.83	41.12
Union Member (%)	81.27	83.13	78.58	77.10
Occupations				
Manager (%)	14.37	5.80	11.18	6.50
Professional (%)	3.33	1.20	2.20	2.00
Sales (%)	0.09	0.00	0.50	0.25
Technician (%)	0.38	0.00	0.87	0.87
Clerical (%)	15.35	14.53	12.30	15.03
Craft (%)	33.14	19.18	22.64	20.17
Nontransportation Operatives (%)	4.60	2.90	4.77	5.38
Transportation Operatives (%)	16.46	15.69	36.79	25.56
Laborer (%)	9.40	29.07	7.06	17.41
Farmer(%)	0.00	0.00	0.01	0.12
Service(%)	1.49	11.63	1.50	6.39
Resides in				
Northeast (%)	17.58	12.79	13.70	14.78
Midwest (%)	35.45	21.51	36.71	26.94
South (%)	26.17	61.62	25.24	51.37
West (%)	20.78	4.07	24.32	6.89
Number of Observations	2,338	172	8,620	798

Table 8.6 Mean Profile of Airline Workers

Variable	Prederegulation (1973–1978)		Postderegulation (1979–2001)	
	White	Black	White	Black
Female (%)	26.65	35.92	32.61	40.41
Married (%)	73.11	66.02	63.44	48.46
Age	36.64	34.85	37.63	36.78
Completed College (%)	50.43	45.63	46.35	46.32
Received High School Diploma (%)	40.41	33.98	30.84	31.99
Full Time (%)	88.06	91.26	85.83	86.80
Weekly Earnings (1983 $)	509.59	396.73	442.26	329.89
Weekly Hours Worked	39.06	38.88	39.52	38.71
Union Member (%)	43.75	46.60	36.31	37.37
Occupations				
Manager (%)	5.96	3.88	9.98	5.84
Professional (%)	4.21	1.94	2.97	1.88
Sales (%)	0.16	0.00	0.73	1.00
Technician (%)	11.13	0.00	13.38	2.51
Clerical (%)	34.52	33.98	30.65	35.44
Craft (%)	21.40	16.50	18.65	13.70
Nontransportation Operatives (%)	4.05	0.97	1.23	0.94
Transportation Operatives (%)	1.83	2.91	1.64	2.70
Laborer (%)	4.29	9.71	6.38	11.31
Farmer (%)	0.00	0.00	0.12	0.00
Service (%)	12.17	29.12	14.20	24.63
Resides in				
Northeast (%)	22.59	28.15	17.35	19.35
Midwest (%)	19.57	17.47	22.78	17.85
South (%)	31.42	33.98	31.62	45.44
West (%)	26.41	20.39	28.24	17.34
Number of Observations	1,257	103	14,815	1,591

able 8.7 Mean Profile of Telecommunications Workers

Variable	Predivestiture (1973–1986)		Postdivestiture (1987–1994)		Post-Telecom Act (1995–2001)	
	White	Black	White	Black	White	Black
Female (%)	45.52	71.62	44.05	68.68	41.11	59.03
Married (%)	73.77	60.39	71.86	58.69	65.62	46.63
Age	37.32	32.27	39.23	36.31	40.08	37.78
Completed College (%)	36.90	39.90	43.07	50.59	35.87	41.23
Received High School Diploma (%)	56.51	50.83	48.43	40.12	32.44	29.70
Full Time (%)	96.97	96.81	97.50	97.40	96.65	96.27
Weekly Earnings (1983 $)	450.33	363.25	483.74	402.52	494.13	386.94
Weekly Hours Worked	39.96	39.10	40.58	39.67	41.81	40.11
Union Member (%)	54.00	64.65	46.39	59.87	33.87	42.14
Occupations						
Manager (%)	10.10	4.70	13.59	8.40	19.82	13.85
Professional (%)	8.12	4.24	9.06	5.35	10.73	7.17
Sales %	2.22	2.27	4.48	5.27	7.60	7.72
Technician %	2.62	1.97	4.67	3.30	5.44	3.67
Clerical %	39.17	62.36	33.40	53.89	27.57	46.13

(continued)

TTable 8.7 (*continued*)

Variable	Predivestiture (1973–1986)		Postdivestiture (1987–1994)		Post-Telecom Act (1995–2001)	
	White	Black	White	Black	White	Black
Nontransportation Operatives %	0.37	0.75	0.70	1.02	0.56	0.68
Transportation Operatives %	0.45	1.21	0.45	0.23	0.29	0.27
Laborer %	0.53	0.60	0.75	0.86	0.57	0.95
Farmer%	0.00	0.00	0.02	0.00	0.03	0.00
Service%	0.66	2.88	0.67	2.50	0.53	1.13
Resides in						
Northeast %	23.41	24.58	27.71	26.20	23.84	20.11
Midwest %	23.90	20.94	22.47	19.66	28.50	26.06
South %	28.29	39.60	28.97	42.64	27.91	43.14
West %	24.37	14.87	20.84	11.48	19.73	10.67
Number of Observations	6,145	659	9,328	1,271	14,102	2,202

The results for telecommunications workers are presented in table 8.7. They reveal that regulatory reform is associated with a significant occupational shift for black workers. Blacks are less likely to be employed as clerical workers following divestiture in 1984 and following passage of the 1996 Telecommunications Act. Blacks are also more likely to be employed as managers, professionals, and sales workers following regulatory reform. Whites employed in the telecommunications industry experienced the same change in their occupational distribution. The major racial differences in the occupational distribution are twofold: there is a disproportionate share of blacks employed as clerical workers despite the employment shift from these jobs and there is a disproportionate share of whites employed as craft workers. Still, the shift from clerical to managerial, professional, and sales jobs depicts a move toward better-paying jobs for blacks in this industry.

For power utilities deregulation is not associated with any marked change in the occupational distribution for whites or blacks (see table 8.8). Blacks are disproportionately employed as clerical workers, while whites are more likely to be employed in better-paying craft jobs. Blacks are much less likely to be managers both before and after regulatory change.

In summary, the descriptive statistics reveal a substantial decline in racial occupational disparity only for for-hire truck drivers and rail workers. Yet, caution is needed when interpreting these findings since they do not control for differences in worker characteristics. For example, the statistics in tables 8.3 through 8.8 indicate that compared to whites, blacks employed in network industries are more likely to be female and to reside in the southern United States. Thus, clerical jobs are generally female dominated and receive relatively low pay compared to craft, professional, and managerial positions. The disproportionate share of blacks residing in the South may limit access to professional jobs. Therefore, multivariate techniques are needed to test if measurable worker characteristics help explain the mean employment patterns.

The following occupational status equations were estimated to address the bias that results from profiles differing among black and white workers in network industries:

$$\Pr(\mathit{high\ wage\ job}=1)_j = \Phi\{\beta_0+\beta_1X_j + \beta_2\mathit{Black}_j \qquad (8.1)$$
$$+ \beta_3\mathit{Dereg}_j + \beta_4(\mathit{Black*Dereg})_j + \mu_j\}$$

$$\Pr(\mathit{low\ wage\ job}=1)_j = \Phi\{\beta_0+\beta_1X_j + \beta_2\mathit{Black}_j \qquad (8.2)$$
$$+ \beta_3\mathit{Dereg}_j + \beta_4(\mathit{Black*Dereg})_j + \mu_j\}$$

Table 8.8 Mean Profile of Utility Workers

Variable	Pre-Energy Policy Act (1973–1991)		Post-Energy Policy Act (1991–2001)	
	White	Black	White	Black
Female (%)	20.02	31.12	21.84	37.20
Married (%)	79.71	66.24	78.22	58.14
Age	39.42	35.74	40.07	37.82
Completed College (%)	42.00	42.80	48.33	48.06
Received High School School Diploma (%)	45.36	41.76	40.87	41.08
Full Time (%)	98.25	98.48	98.00	100.00
Weekly Earnings (1983 $)	490.45	379.13	502.64	378.34
Weekly Hours Worked	40.71	40.30	41.30	40.49
Union Member (%)	36.22	41.09	34.55	45.73
Occupations				
Manager (%)	11.07	5.44	14.24	3.10
Professional (%)	10.83	5.04	10.91	6.20
Sales (%)	1.30	1.04	1.79	3.10
Technician (%)	4.47	3.68	5.25	6.20
Clerical (%)	22.54	33.68	20.10	35.65
Craft (%)	38.49	28.48	37.01	28.68
Nontransportation Operatives (%)	3.45	4.00	3.12	4.65
Transportation Operatives (%)	1.45	4.00	1.19	1.55
Laborer (%)	3.70	7.68	3.86	6.20
Farmer(%)	0.21	0.32	0.39	0.00
Service(%)	2.23	6.40	2.06	4.65
Resides in				
Northeast (%)	21.67	14.56	24.83	20.15
Midwest (%)	26.36	21.28	34.50	24.80
South (%)	32.01	55.84	30.09	50.38
West (%)	19.95	8.32	20.57	4.65
Number of Observations	15,014	1,250	1,502	129

Here Φ is a normal probability, and j indexes individual workers. The dependent variable *high wage job* equals 1 if the worker is employed in a high-wage occupation and 0 if the worker is employed in a low- or moderate-wage job.[13] The dependent variable *low wage job* equals 1 if the worker is employed in a low-wage occupation and if the worker is employed in a high- or moderate-wage job.[14] The matrix X consists of individual worker information including age and hours worked per week, as well as dummy variables identifying marital status, union status, sex, U.S. region of residence, educational attainment, and full-time employment status.[15] In addition the annual national unemployment rate is included as an occupation determinant to control for time-variant distortions such as changes in the business cycle. The variable *Black* is a dummy variable equaling 1 if the individual is black and 0 if the individual is white. The variable *Dereg* is a dummy variable depicting the postderegulation observation period.[16] The final variable in the occupational status equations is the interaction of the *Black* and *Dereg* dummy variables.

Racial Employment Results

This study's hypothesis and the descriptive statistics suggest that product market competition influenced racial employment disparities mainly for union truck drivers in the for-hire trucking sector. In table 8.9, Panel-1 reports the predicted mean union status probabilities for for-hire drivers, adjusting for worker characteristics. The specification of the union status equation used to derive these predicted means resembles equations (8.1) and (8.2) except that the binary variable equals 1 if the driver is a union member and the explanatory variables for this equation do not include occupation dummy variables.[17] The findings in Panel-1 reveal a declining probability of blacks and whites belonging to a union occurring mainly following the MCA-1980 and prior to the 1994 AIA. Following the MCA-1980 blacks are equally likely as whites to belong to a union, and following the 1994 AIA blacks are slightly more likely to belong to a union. Such findings provide support of Becker's hypothesis that increased competition lowers racial disparities and they are consistent with earlier findings by Heywood and Peoples (1994).

Table 8.9 also presents predicted union status probabilities for the private carriage sector. These examine whether the for-hire union status results are unique or are part of an overall industry trend. The findings in Panel-2 indicate that black drivers were more likely to be a union member than white drivers in the private carriage sector prior to regulatory reform. This union status disparity does not change significantly following regulatory reform. When compared to the for-hire findings, these private carriage

Table 8.9   Predicted Union Status Probability of For-Hire Truck
Drivers and Private Carriage Truck Drivers (Converted from Probit
Estimations of Union Status Equation)

Panel-1:   For-Hire Truck Drivers

	Pre-1980 MCA	Post-1980 MCA	Post-1994 AIA
Union Member Probability			
White	58.71	28.10**	25.78**
Black	51.60	29.22**	28.77**

Panel-2:   Private Carriage Truck Drivers

	Pre-1980 MCA	Post-1980 MCA	Post-1994 AIA
Union Member Probability			
White	28.43	15.62**	10.93**
Black	34.09	20.33**	16.50**

**Employment probability is statistically significantly different from prederegulation employment probability at the 1 percent level.

results suggest that the trend toward a more equal probability of union employment following deregulation is unique to the for-hire sector.

Predicted occupational probabilities for the five network industries, when adjusting for worker characteristics, are presented in table 8.10. The results in table 8.10 follow from estimating equations (8.1) and (8.2) to compute occupational probabilities.[18] The findings suggest that, compared to whites, blacks are significantly more likely to be employed in low-wage occupations rather than high-wage occupations prior to regulatory reform, regardless of industry. The predereregulation racial employment disadvantage of blacks erodes in rail, trucking, and telecommunications following the passage of the Staggers Act, the AIA, and the 1996 Telecommunications Act, respectively.

Panel-1A of table 8.10 shows that the erosion of the racial disparity for low-wage jobs in the for-hire trucking sector is the result of a slight decline in the probability that blacks are employed in these jobs and of a slight increase in the probability that whites are employed in these jobs following the passage of the AIA in 1994. There is an increase in the chance of blacks being in high-wage jobs (from a very small base) but no real change in the white probability.

Table 8.10 Predicted Employment Probabilities of Workers in Deregulated Network Industries (Converted from Probit Estimations of Employment Equation)

Panel-1A: For-Hire Trucking

	Pre-1980 MCA	Post-1980 MCA	Post-1994 AIA
Low-Wage Employment Probability			
White	6.06	7.64	8.08
Black	12.10	12.51	10.93
High-Wage Employment Probability			
White	6.30	5.48	6.68
Black	1.32	1.83	3.44

Panel-2A: Rail

	Pre-Staggers	Post-Staggers
Low-Wage Employment Probability		
White	4.18	4.46
Black	18.62	11.70*
High-Wage Employment Probability		
White	16.11	10.56**
Black	6.20	6.81

Panel-3A: Airlines

	Pre-Airline Dereg. Act	Post-Airline Dereg. Act
Low-Wage Employment Probability		
White	7.35	7.64
Black	12.30	13.65
High-Wage Employment Probability		
White	19.49	22.06*
Black	6.43	10.56*

(*continued*)

Table 8.10   (*continued*)

Panel-4A: Telecommunications

	Pre-divestiture	Post-divestiture	Post-Telecomm. Act
Low-Wage Employment Probability			
White	2.17	2.17	0.91
Black	4.85	3.59	1.58*
High Wage Employment Probability			
White	22.06	25.46**	22.36
Black	15.15	21.48**	17.62

Panel-5A: Energy Utilities

	Pre-EPA	Post-EPA
Low-Wage Employment Probability		
White	21.19	20.61
Black	32.64	31.92
High-Wage Employment Probability		
White	62.17	60.64
Black	47.61	50.00

*Employment probability is statistically significantly different from preregulation employment probability at the 10 percent level.
**Employment probability is statistically significantly different from preregulation employment probability at the 1 percent level.

    Railroad employment findings are reported in Panel-2A of table 8.10 and indicate that the erosion of the racial employment disparity for low-wage jobs is due to a declining probability that blacks are employed in these jobs. In contrast, the probability that whites are employed in these jobs does not change much over regulatory regimes. Conversely, the erosion of the racial employment disparity for high-wage rail jobs is due to a declining probability that whites are employed in these jobs, while the probability that blacks are employed in these jobs does not change much over regulatory regimes.

Panel-3A presents the racial employment results for airlines, revealing a mixed pattern. The probability of employment in low-wage occupations remains roughly constant for both races. Both races experience a gain in the probability of employment in high-wage jobs following regulatory reform with the gain modestly larger for blacks.

The telecommunications results presented in Panel-4A reveal that the post–Telecommunications Act erosion of racial employment disparity for low-wage jobs is largely due to the declining probability of black employment. It should be noted that neither race is very likely to be employed as low-wage workers. The postdivestiture erosion of racial employment disparity for high-wage jobs in this industry mainly results from the increased probability of black employment. However, high wage employment probabilities for black and white workers fall to predivestiture levels following passage of the 1996 Telecommunications Act.

The findings in Panel-5A report the racial occupational patterns for utility workers and suggest no change in the racial employment disparity for low-wage jobs. The post-EPA erosion of racial employment disparity for high-wage jobs flows from a slight reduction in the probability of white employment and a slight increase in the probability of black employment. The findings also reveal a nontrivial percentage of blacks employed in high-wage jobs prior to regulatory reform. While equal employment opportunity legislation might have contributed to the successful employment of blacks in high-wage occupations, the abundance of high-wage jobs in this industry has also contributed to black employment in lucrative utility industry jobs.

The findings in several industries indicate postregulatory reform gains by blacks. The evidence on union truck drivers in for-hire trucking and on all occupations in rail provides the strongest support. Declining disparities in these industries might, however, be part of a larger service sector shift toward a more equitable racial distribution of jobs. Within Becker's theoretical framework, the inherent competitiveness of the service sector provides an environment that discourages employment discrimination. Predicted occupational probabilities for the nonnetwork service sector derived from estimating equations (8.1) and (8.2) are presented in table 8.11. The findings suggest that blacks are more likely to be employed in low-wage rather than high-wage occupations prior to the respective regulatory reforms. Hence, racial employment disparities were not unique to the five network industries prior to regulatory reform. In contrast to the results for network industries, the estimated coefficients on the race-deregulation interaction terms indicate that racial employment disparities eroded significantly for the service sector following the regulatory reform dates associated with each industry.

Table 8.11 Predicted Employment Probabilities of Nonnetwork Workers in Service Sector Industries

Panel-1B: Using Dates Associated with For-hire Trucking

	Pre-1980 MCA	Post-1980 MCA	Post-1994 AIA
Low-Wage Employment Probability			
White	31.21	26.11**	22.66**
Black	62.55	48.40**	41.29**
High-Wage Employment Probability			
White	31.92	39.47**	42.07**
Black	13.35	23.27**	27.09**

Panel-2B: Using Dates Associated with Rail

	Pre-Staggers	Post-Staggers
Low-Wage Employment Probability		
White	31.21	24.20**
Black	62.93	45.22**
High-Wage Employment Probability		
White	31.98	39.47**
Black	12.71	24.20**

Panel-3B: Using Dates Associated with Airlines

	Pre-Airline Dereg. Act	Post-Airline Dereg. Act
Low-Wage Employment Probability		
White	3.59	3.29
Black	5.37	4.18
High-Wage Employment Probability		
White	31.92	40.13**
Black	12.51	24.20**

(*continued*)

Table 8.11   Predicted Employment Probabilities of Nonnetwork Workers in Service Sector Industries (*continued*)

Panel-4B: Using Dates Associated with Telecommunications

	Pre-divestiture	Post-divestiture	Post-Telecomm. Act
Low-Wage Employment Probability			
White	28.43	24.20**	20.90**
Black	55.57	43.25**	39.36**
High-Wage Employment Probability			
White	31.92	40.13**	43.25**
Black	13.35	23.89**	27.76**

Panel-5B: Using Dates Associated with Energy Utilities

	Pre-EPA	Post-EPA
Low-Wage Employment Probability		
White	46.02	42.07**
Black	64.06	56.28**
High-Wage Employment Probability		
White	36.69	38.97*
Black	17.36	23.89*

*Employment probability is statistically significantly different from prederegulation employment probability at the 10 percent level.
**Employment probability is statistically significantly different from prederegulation employment probability at the 1 percent level.

The findings in table 8.11 show that the erosion of racial employment disparity for low-wage jobs in the nonnetwork service sector is attributable to a larger decline for blacks than for whites in the probability of employment. The service sector results using the airline industry dates for regulatory reform and occupational definitions provide a notable exception. Indeed, neither race experienced any marked change in low-wage employment probabilities when using the airline dates. Furthermore, neither racial group is heavily employed in the type of jobs that receive low pay in the airline industry. When compared to the network findings in table 8.10, the racial employment disparity erosion in nonnetwork service industries generally surpasses that found for network industries. The notable exception is the significant erosion of racial employment differences for low-wage jobs in the rail industry.

The erosion of racial employment disparity for high-wage jobs in the service sector follows from a larger increase for blacks than for whites in the probability of employment in these occupations. The declining high-wage disparity is only of a magnitude of 3 to 5 percentage points. Nonetheless, blacks and whites employed in nonnetwork service sectors experienced a nontrivial employment gain in high-wage occupations for the observation period following regulatory reform in network industries. Such upward mobility did not occur within all five network industries examined in this study.

Conclusion

Major regulatory changes toward network industries started in the late 1970s, as transportation, telecommunications, and public utilities faced an easing of rate and entry regulation. The rationale for regulatory reform was that competitive market forces would promote efficient pricing and productive efficiency. The shift to competitive market pricing could also have the unintended effect of eroding racial employment disparities. Economic theory suggests that better employment opportunities for qualified blacks might arise because employers who exercise their discriminatory preferences are placed at a greater disadvantage in competitive markets.

This study examines racial employment patterns in five deregulated network industries. The findings on union drivers in trucking strongly support Becker's hypothesis. Occupational employment results suggest that only rail and trucking show racial employment disparity erosion following regulatory reform. Yet for rail the erosion of the employment disparity in high-wage jobs is due to the declining percentage of whites employed in these occupations. The findings on union drivers are unique to the deregulated for-hire sector, whereas only the findings for low-wage rail workers match the racial disparity erosion results reported for other U.S. service sectors.

The empirical results of this study indicate that pro-competitive policies are most influential when the industry has low barriers to entry and when the major occupation has an elastic labor supply curve. Indeed, black and white truck drivers are now just as likely to belong to a union. However, union premiums for truck drivers are lower than they were prior to deregulation. In industries such as airline, telecommunications, and public utilities where workers do not face an elastic labor supply curve and where pro-competitive economic policies have not yielded their intended outcome, implementation of rules regarding fair employment practices remains important for occupational employment gains by blacks.

Notes

1. The extent of monopoly rent varies by industry with major carriers in the inherently competitive trucking industry earning above normal profits before deregulation, while railroad carriers routinely faced losses.

2. In addition to Becker's model on product market rivalry limitations, other mechanisms have been shown to enable managers to exercise discriminatory preferences: imperfection in the agency relationship between owners and managers (Williamson, 1963); large coordination costs that create imperfections in the takeover mechanism (Grossman and Hart, 1980; Walkling and Long, 1984); and diminished information on optimal market performance (Heywood, 1986).

3. See Risher (1971), Northrup, Theiblot, and Chernish (1971), and Anderson (1970) for pre–civil rights employment patterns in rail, airline and energy sectors, respectively.

4. See Leone (1990), page 94.

5. In the railroad industry, noncompetitive pricing prompted regulation with the passage of the 1887 Interstate Commerce Commission Act. By 1935, the ICC extended its power by regulating the for-hire sector of the trucking industry, which provides local and long-haul service to shippers. That same year, the Federal Power Act and the Public Utility Holding Company Act shaped the regulatory environment of the electricity sector. A year earlier, the Federal Communications Commission (FCC) assumed regulatory control over the telecommunications industry and in 1938 the Civil Aeronautics Board gained regulatory authority over passenger airlines.

6. Using financial date covering 1973–1978, Moore reports average rate of returns for major trucking companies ranging from a low of 19.5 in 1975 to a high of 25.7 in 1973.

7. Southern Pacific Railroad International (SPRINT) and Microwave Communications Incorporated (MCI) challenged the government-sanctioned monopoly over telephony in the U.S. in the early 1970s. This challenge initiated the FCC investigation in 1974 that lead to the break-up of AT&T. Before divestiture and as potential entrants waited to gain full access to the market, AT&T's rates remained high relative to marginal costs.

8. The Herfindahl Index (HI) is the sum of squared market shares. An HI greater than 1,800 typically indicates an oligopolistic market structure.

9. The real challenge to local and long-distance rates will come from the wireless sector, where rates persistently decline.

10. The 1982 survey is excluded, since the union membership question was not asked.

11. In the utility sector blacks and whites are equally likely to have a college education across regulatory regimes.

12. Rail transportation operative occupations are relatively lucrative primarily because these occupations include the high-skill jobs of locomotive conductors and engineers.

13. The dependent variable is union status when examining racial employment differences in the for-hire trucking industry.

14. Managers, professional and technicians are the high wage occupations for rail, trucking, airlines, and telecommunications. Managers, professional and craft workers are the high wage occupations for energy utility services. Service workers, laborers and nontransportation operatives are the low wage occupations for rail. Farmers, laborers, non-transportation and transportation operatives are the low wage occupations for airlines. Farmers, laborers, nontransportation operatives and service workers are the low wage occupations for telecommunications. Clerical, farmers and service workers are the low wage occupations for energy utility services. Lastly, service workers, farmers, laborers, and nontransportation operatives are the low wage occupations for trucking.

15. Two dummy variables capture the effect of educational attainment on occupation employment. Workers who have not attained a high school diploma are the benchmark comparison group. A dummy listed as *diploma* denotes those workers receiving at most a high school diploma and a dummy listed as *college* denotes those workers who have attained a college degree.

16. The earnings specification for the trucking and telecommunications sample include two deregulation dummies to account for the two major deregulation policies in these industries. For example *Dereg1* is a dummy equaling one for post-1980 MCA or for the post-1984 telecommunications divestiture period. The dummy D*ereg2* equals one for the post-1994 AIA or the post-1996 Telecommunications Act.

17. The complete union status estimation results are available from the authors on request.

18. The complete occupational status estimation results are available from the authors on request.

References

Agesa, Jacqueline. "Deregulation and the Racial Composition of Airlines." *Journal of Policy Analysis and Management* 20 (2001): 223–37.

Anderson, Bernard E. *The Negro in the Public Utility Industries.* Report No. 10 in the series The Racial Policies of American Industry. Industrial Research Unit, Department of Industry, Wharton School of Finance and Commerce, University of Pennsylvania, Philadelphia, 1970.

Becker, Gary. *The Economics of Discrimination.* Chicago: University of Chicago Press, 1957.

Borenstein, Severin. "The Evolution of U.S. Airline Competition." *Journal of Economic Perspectives* 6 (1992): 45–73.

Crandall, Robert W., and Jerry A. Hausman. "Competition in U.S. Telecommunications Services: Effects of the 1996 Legislation." In *Deregulation of Network Industries: What's Next,* ed. Sam Peltzman and Clifford Winston, 73–112. Washington, DC: AEI–Brookings Joint Center for Regulatory Studies, 2000.

Grimm, Curtis, and Clifford Winston. "Competition in the Deregulated Railroad Industry: Sources, Effects, and Policy Issues." In *Deregulation of Network*

Industries: What's Next, ed. Sam Peltzman and Clifford Winston, 41–72. Washington, DC: AEI–Brookings Joint Center for Regulatory Studies, 2000.

Grossman, Sanford, and Oliver Hart. "Takeover Bids, the Free-rider Problem and the Theory of the Corporation." *Bell Journal of Economics* 10 (1980): 42–64.

Heywood, John S. "Labor Quality and the Concentration-Earnings Hypothesis." *Review of Economics and Statistics* 68 (1986): 343–48.

Heywood, John S., and James Peoples. "Deregulation and the Prevalence of Black Truck Drivers." *Journal of Law and Economics* 47 (1994): 133–55.

Hirsch, Barry. "Trucking Regulation, Unionization and Labor Earnings: 1973–1985." *Journal of Human Resources* 23 (1988): 296–319.

Husbands, Kaye. "Commentary on Regulated Industries and Measures of Earnings Discrimination." In *Regulatory Reform and Labor Markets*, ed. James Peoples, 325–62. Boston: Kluwer Academic Publishers, 1998.

Joskow, Paul L. "Deregulation and Regulatory Reform in the U.S. Electric Power Sector." In *Deregulation of Network Industries: What's Next*, ed. Sam Peltzman and Clifford Winston, 113–88. Washington, DC: AEI–Brookings Joint Center for Regulatory Studies, 2000.

Leone, Richard D. *The Negro in the Trucking Industry.* Report No. 15 in the series The Racial Policies of American Industry. Industrial Research Unit, Department of Industry, Wharton School of Finance and Commerce, University of Pennsylvania, Philadelphia, 1970.

Moore, Thomas G. "Rail and Trucking Deregulation." In *Regulatory Reform: What Actually Happened*, ed. Leonard Weiss and Michael Klass, 14–39. Boston: Little Brown and Company, 1986.

Morrison, Steven A., and Clifford Winston. "The Remaining Role for Government Policy in the Deregulated Airline Industry." In *Deregulation of Network Industries: What's Next*, ed. Sam Peltzman and Clifford Winston, 1–40. Washington, DC: AEI–Brookings Joint Center for Regulatory Studies, 2000.

Northrup, Herbert R., Armand J. Theiblot Jr., and William N. Chernish. *The Negro in the Air Transport Industry.* Report No. 23 in the series The Racial Policies of American Industry. Industrial Research Unit, Department of Industry, Wharton School of Finance and Commerce, University of Pennsylvania, Philadelphia, 1971.

Peoples, James. "Trucking Regulation and Industry Performance." University of Wisconsin–Milwaukee Working Paper, 2003.

Peoples, James, and Rhonda Robinson (1996), "Market Structure and Racial and Gender Discrimination: Evidence from the Telecommunications Industry." *American Journal of Economics and Sociology* 55 (1996): 309–25.

Risher, Howard W. Jr. *The Negro in the Railroad Industry.* Report No. 16 in the series The Racial Policies of American Industry. Industrial Research Unit, Department of Industry, Wharton School of Finance and Commerce, University of Pennsylvania, Philadelphia, 1971.

Rose, Nancy. "Labor Rent-Sharing and Regulation: Evidence from the Trucking Industry." *Journal of Political Economy* 95 (1987): 1146–78.

Sheperd, William, G. "Market Power and Racial Discrimination in White-Collar Employment." *Antitrust Bulletin* 14 (1969): 141–61.

Taylor, John, C. "Regulation of Trucking by the States." *Regulation* 17 (1994): 23–35.

Taylor, William E., and Lester D. Taylor. "Postdivestiture Long-Distance Competition in the United States." *American Economic Review* 83 (1993): 185–90.

Walkling, Ralph, and Michael Long. "Agency Theory, Managerial Welfare and Takeover Bid Resistance." *Rand Journal of Economics* 14 (1984): 185–68.

Wallace, Phyllis. *Equal Employment Opportunity and the AT&T Case,* Cambridge, MA: MIT Press, 1976.

Williamson, Oliver. "Managerial Discretion and Business Behavior." *American Economic Review* 53 (1963): 1032–57.

Chapter 9

Market Structure, Payment Methods, and Racial Earnings Differences

John S. Heywood and Patrick L. O'Halloran

Introduction

While both earnings differences and payment methods have generated a vast amount of literature, the two subjects rarely interact. Moreover, these two subjects have only very rarely been tied to the product market. This chapter argues that the racial earnings difference should be smaller among those receiving output-based pay such as piece rates and commissions. When discriminating in earnings, the intensity of racial preferences must be greater when an owner or manager confronts a standardized measure of productivity than when effort is subjectively evaluated and those evaluations are used to set earnings. More importantly, use of a standardized measure of productivity makes the practice of discrimination more transparent and this improved information increases the probability of detection. The increased probability of detection raises the expected cost of discrimination and should be associated with a reduction in its extent. Finally, we suggest that increased product market competition is associated with greater use of output-based pay and so reduced racial earnings differentials.

Using the National Longitudinal Survey of Youth 1979 (NLSY79), we show that among those paid piece rates or commissions there is no evidence of a racial earnings difference even as a significant racial difference is confirmed for those paid time rates. Confirming this pattern the earnings premium associated with piece rates and commissions is greater for nonwhites than whites. In a mirror image the racial earnings gap among those receiving individual bonus payments, payments largely based on managerial evaluations, is larger than that for those receiving traditional time rates. These results hold after controlling for many firm and individual characteristics such as human capital, industry, occupation, plant size, and family status. Additionally, these basic patterns persist even after accounting for sample selection into payment method and for individual fixed effects.

The chapter is organized as follows. The next section makes use of the existing literature to put the argument in context. The third section presents a brief axiomatic model illustrating how more "objective" based pay schemes such as piece rates and commissions can lower racial earnings differentials. The fourth section describes the data and presents descriptive statistics. The results of the initial empirical estimations are presented in the fifth section. Estimations that control for sample selections and fixed effects are provided in the sixth section, and the seventh section proffers a conclusion and policy recommendations.

Framing the Issue

Discrimination in the labor market is typically attributed to personal prejudice either on the part of employers, employees, or customers. In the traditional employer prejudice framework, discrimination is costly to firms, putting them at a cost disadvantage relative to nondiscriminating firms (Becker, 1957). According to this view the extent of discrimination reflects the intensity of prejudice, on the one hand, and the cost of discrimination on the other hand. Those establishments operating in more competitive product markets have smaller rents and should be less able to afford discrimination, the cost of discrimination is higher. Many researchers have confirmed this hypothesis, showing that both earnings and employment differentials are narrower in more competitive product markets (see Ashenfelter and Hannan, 1986; Hellerstein, Neumark, and Troske, 2002; Heywood, 1998; Heywood and Peoples, 1994; Peoples, 1994).

Largely unspecified in this work has been the process through which product market competition lowers racial differences in the labor market. We emphasize that competitive pressures provide firms an impetus to adopt payment schemes that more closely link workers' pay to their performance in an effort to minimize costs and increase labor productivity. Indeed, the increased use of output-based pay by firms in markets with competitive product structure has been confirmed by previous research (see Burgess and Metcalfe, 2000; Drago and Heywood, 1995; Heywood and Jirjahn 2002). This relationship is seen as part of a general phenomenon in which product market competition limits the extent of discretion in wage setting (Bertrand and Mellainathan, 1999) and in which increased competition limits the ability of firms to enter into long-term implicit agreements with workers (Bertrand, 1999). As a result, firms in highly competitive markets enter into shorter-term employment relations and make heavy reliance of short-term incentives such as piece rates (Goldin, 1986). These payment schemes generate objective evidence on worker productivity that require a greater intensity of prejudice to produce the same racial earnings differential, all else equal. Moreover, the objective evidence on worker productivity makes racial discrimination more easily observed, increasing the probability of its detection by authorities and the courts.

Imagine two polar cases as identified by Baker, Gibbons, and Murphy (1988). In the first case, the output of individual workers cannot be easily identified because of incomplete monitoring or because worker productivity is fundamentally interdependent, so-called team production (Alchian and Demsetz, 1972). In this case supervisors evaluate workers by judging their "effort" or input (Lazear, 1986). This process allows the preferences of the supervisor to be easily translated into differences in evaluations and, ultimately, into differences in earnings. While this translation may be restricted by bureaucratic rules (Prendergast and Topel, 1996) or by concern over reputation (Baker, Gibbons, and Murphy, 1994), it is unlikely to be eliminated.[1] Elvira and Town (2001) confirm that supervisors' performance evaluations are influenced by the race of their subordinates by showing that a white supervisor of both white and nonwhite subordinates typically gives the white a better rating than the nonwhite even after controlling for demographic variables and productivity (as measured by the researcher). As a result two workers who have the same productivity may have an earnings difference that reflects race but have supervisory evaluations that support the difference.

In the second case, individual workers are paid by the piece, a payment scheme made possible by the absence of team production. At the end of each evaluation period, the supervisor has a list of workers, their individual outputs, and a preestablished wage increment to be paid for each unit of output. Here it is much harder for racial preferences to be translated into differential earnings. In short, the basic barrier of objective fairness is more immediate and the intensity of preference must be that much greater. Added to any cognitive barrier of the supervisor is the critical notion of external transparency. Those judging the earnings structure from outside, including the courts, are much more likely to be persuaded by racial or gender earnings discrepancies between workers with identical measured productivity than about earnings discrepancies between workers that reflect different supervisor evaluations. Thus, the improved information on productivity associated with output-based performance pay increases the expected cost to the firm of discrimination by increasing the probability of detection and of paying the associated penalties.

Output-based pay may not completely eliminate the realm for racial or gender preferences. Every piece counted must meet a quality standard, one that may allow supervisors scope for judgment. Yet, the reduced scope for judgment and the productivity measures associated with individual output-based pay increase the cost of allowing prejudice to become differential treatment by race.[2]

This hypothesis has received some sporadic support during the previous three decades. Using individual data, Jirhan and Stephan (2004) found that gender wage differentials in Germany were smaller among those paid piece rates than those paid hourly wages. They recognize that due to differences in expected tenure and labor force attachment, women are much more likely to be paid piece rates and are subject to greater positive selection than men. Yet, the narrower German gender differential persists among piece rate workers even after controlling for tenure and the presence of young children. Gunderson (1975) used Canadian establishment data by occupation showing that the average male–female wage difference within occupations across firms was smaller when the firms made use of incentive pay systems such as piece rates and commissions. In the United States, broad measures of the extent of performance pay within an industry interact with individual measures of earnings such that racial differentials are smaller in those industries making greater use of performance pay (Belman and Heywood, 1988). The first two studies do not look at racial differentials and the third focuses only on an aggregated industry measure of performance pay when such aggregated measures are well-known to often produce misleading results (Moulton, 1990). Nonetheless, all three studies are loosely supportive.

If the choice of payment method is simply at the discretion of supervisors, those supervisors with greater tastes for discrimination may well avoid output-based methods. This would render the payment method largely endogenous to the desire to discriminate. Yet, payment methods are not at the discretion of managers. Previous research shows that underlying technology largely drives the adoption of output-based pay. They are more prevalent where worker performance is easily measurable and where tasks are relatively easy (Jirjahn and Stephan, 2004). Only in circumstances without substantial team production does output-based pay provide a relatively objective measure of performance with small monitoring costs (Brown, 1990; MacLeod and Parent, 1999). Thus, Parent (2002) found the majority of piece rates in the United States among precision machine operatives, textile operatives, and other operatives and the majority of commissions among sales workers, personal service workers, and a subset of managers and administrators. These patterns reflect, in good part, the underlying technology of production associated with these jobs. Put somewhat differently, in those circumstances in which output-based pay would be optimal, adopting an alternative payment method in order to discriminate is itself an increased cost associated with discrimination.

A Theoretical Model

To explore the effects of payment schemes on measured earnings discrimination and motivate the testing, we present a representative theoretical model.[3] Consider managers who maximize utility over profits and employment of whites:

$$\max U(\Pi, W). \tag{9.1}$$

Utility increases with profits and with employment of whites. The firm's short-run profits are given in the usual manner:

$$\Pi = Pf(W + N) - r_W W - r_N N \tag{9.2}$$

where P is the price of the final product using the inputs of white workers, W, and nonwhite workers, N, and r_W and r_N are the respective wage rates. We assume that the critical issue is the proportion of white and nonwhite workers and take the scale effects to be a second order issue. Thus, we assume fixed employment, $L = W + N$, and assume white and nonwhite workers are equally productive. The labor supply schedules for workers are assumed to have positive slopes:

$$r_W = r_W(W) \text{ and } r_N = r_N(L - W). \tag{9.3}$$

Thus, white wages increase with the employment of whites and nonwhite wages decrease with the employment of whites: $r'_W > 0$ and $r'_N > 0$.

Introducing an explicit cost of discrimination captures the method of pay. This cost is distinct from the implicit cost generated from using an inappropriate ratio of white and nonwhite workers and can be thought of as the cost of adverse public opinion and the expected costs of legal action.[4] This cost is thought of as a proportion, α, of the difference between white and nonwhite wages. The notion is that as the difference between wages increases, the chance of detection and adverse legal decisions and publicity increases. Including this cost parameter and combining equations (9.1)–(9.3) yields the following objective function for managers to maximize with respect to W:

$$U(Pf(L) - r_W(W)*W - r_N(L-W)*(L-W) - (r_W(W) \\ - r_N(L-W))\alpha, W). \tag{9.4}$$

The first order condition to this problem is:

$$U_\Pi\left[-r_W - r'_W(W) + r_N + r'_N(L-W) - \left(r'_W + r'_N\right)\alpha\right] + U_W = 0 \tag{9.5}$$

identifying $\frac{U_W}{U_\Pi} = \delta_W > 0$ as Becker's taste for discrimination, this can be rearranged:

$$-r_W\left[1 + \frac{1}{\eta_W}\right] + r_N\left[1 + \frac{1}{\eta_N}\right] - \left(r'_W + r'_N\right)\alpha + \delta_W = 0 \tag{9.6}$$

where η_N and η_W are the labor supply elasticities for nonwhites and whites, respectively. Note that if the elasticities are the same and managers have no taste for discrimination, $\delta_W = 0$, then the first order condition requires the firm to pay nonwhites and whites equally in order to cost-minimize. This happens only when the firm hires an equal number of nonwhites and whites.[5] Consider the circumstance where the elasticities are equal and constant but $\delta_W >$.[6] The resulting first order condition becomes

$$(-r_W - r_N)\theta + \left(r'_W + r'_N\right)\alpha + \delta_W. \tag{9.7}$$

Here the managers maximize utility, hiring fewer nonwhites and more whites such that the difference in wages times the shared elasticity parameter plus the increasing penalty associated with the wage difference equals the psychic rate of trade-off between profit and fewer nonwhite workers. For this to be a maximum it must be the case that the second derivate of equation (9.5) with respect to N be negative, SOC < 0. The resulting comparative static follows from the derivative of equation (9.5) with respect to α:

$$\frac{\partial N}{\partial \alpha} = U_\Pi\left(r'_W + r'_N\right) + U_{\Pi\Pi}A(r_W - r_N) - U_{W\Pi}A(r_W - r_N)/soc < 0 \tag{9.8}$$

where $A = \left[-r_W - r'_W(W) + r_N + r'_N(L-W) - \left(r'_W + r'_N\right)\alpha\right] = -\delta_W < 0$ from equation (9.5) and is the profit loss from replacing a black worker with a white worker (the price of a unit of discrimination). The first and second terms are unambiguously positive but the sign of the cross-partial in the third term depends on the form of the utility function. Nonetheless, if the discrimination is a normal good, the sum of the second and third sign are together unambiguously positive, making the entire comparative static negative as indicated (Silberberg, 1990, 326). Thus, the racial wage gap varies negatively with the expected detection costs of discrimination. Our presumption is that expected detection increases with output-based payment schemes and, as a consequence, those schemes should be associated with reduced racial wage gaps.

This model differs from that presented in Heywood and O'Halloran (2005). While this model casts discrimination as a utility maximization problem, Heywood and O'Halloran modify work by Barbezat and Hughes (1990), presenting a profit maximization problem in which discrimination is presumed to be profitable but its extent is restrained by the expected costs of being caught by regulatory authorities. Despite this important difference, the fundamental conclusions are similar. We now move to test those conclusions.

Data Description

The data are drawn from the 1996 and 1998 waves of the NLSY79.[7] The sample eliminates governmental employees, the self-employed, those working in agriculture, and those with missing information for any of the selected variables. The resulting sample size across the two years is 6,861 observations. As shown in table 9.1, the average earnings of non-whites are 77.2 percent of the average earnings of whites.

The NLSY79 identifies whether earnings on the respondent's job come from individual performance pay. If the respondent answers yes, the type of performance pay is identified. The three most common types are piece rates, commissions, and bonuses.[8] Nonetheless, as reported in table 9.1, only 2.7 percent of the sample receives piece rates, only 5.3 percent receives commissions, but 15.3 percent receive bonus pay. These percentages are roughly consistent with previous percentages from the 1989–1991 waves of the NLSY79 (Parent, 2002). While piece rates are evenly distributed by race, whites are more likely to receive commissions and bonuses. In the estimations to follow we combine piece rates and commissions into a single category of individual output-based performance pay (following Parent, 1999).

Whites on piece rates or commissions in our sample earn almost 14 percent more than those not on piece rates ($16.96 versus $14.92) but nonwhites on piece rates or commissions earn over 29 percent more than their counterparts not on piece rates or commissions ($14.66 versus

Table 9.1 Descriptive Statistics by Race

Variable	White Mean	Nonwhite Mean	Male Mean	Female Mean
Hourly Wage	$15.07	$11.64	$16.59	$12.21
Piece Rates	2.69%	2.47%	3.28%	2.00%
Commissions	5.69%	3.42%	6.73%	3.76%
Bonuses	15.97%	12.57%	18.54%	12.01%
Tenure (years / 10)	0.523	0.437	0.540	0.474
Potential Experience [[age − grade − 6) / 10]	1.627	1.704	1.636	1.646
AFQT Score	51.839	24.513	47.506	46.129
Highest Grade Achieved	13.386	12.608	13.227	13.260
Small Firm (less than 100 employees)	61.65%	53.46%	62.04%	58.18%
Medium Firm (100 to 499 employees)	20.47%	21.88%	20.02%	21.46%
Large Firm (500 to 999 employees)	5.62%	6.28%	5.68%	5.81%
Largest Firm (over 1,000 employees) (reference)	12.26%	18.38%	12.26%	14.55%
Shift Work (regular day shift)	75.62%	71.36%	75.39%	74.28%
Off Shift Work (evening or night shift)	15.22%	21.24%	15.40%	17.29%
Irregular Shift Work (split shift or hours vary) (reference)	8.14%	7.08%	8.21%	7.66%
Professional, Technical, and Kindred Workers	20.32%	13.21%	17.14%	20.98%
Managers and Administrators, Except Farm	17.65%	9.71%	17.06%	15.29%
Sales Workers	5.25%	3.42%	4.56%	5.28%
Clerical and Unskilled Workers	15.01%	17.90%	5.33%	26.20%
Craftsmen and Kindred Workers	13.51%	7.64%	22.08%	2.35%
Operatives Except Transport	4.62%	8.67%	10.35%	7.87%
Transport Equipment Operatives	8.14%	13.60%	7.16%	1.16%
Laborers, Except Farm (reference)	3.77%	6.28%	8.27%	2.32%
Farmers and Farm Managers	0.36%	0.08%	0.51%	0.09%

(continued)

Table 9.1 (*continued*)

Variable	White Mean	Nonwhite Mean	Male Mean	Female Mean
Farm Laborers and Farm Foremen	0.39%	0.95%	0.66%	0.33%
Service Workers, Excluding Private Household	10.26%	17.98%	6.62%	16.96%
Private Household Workers	0.50%	0.48%	0.03%	0.98%
Agriculture, Forestry, and Fishing	2.18%	2.63%	3.39%	1.07%
Mining	0.84%	0.24%	1.03%	0.42%
Construction (reference)	7.89%	5.41%	13.09%	1.52%
Manufacturing	21.66%	18.77%	26.07%	15.98%
Transportation, Communication, and Other Public Utilities	7.21%	10.34%	10.15%	5.31%
Wholesale and Retail Trade	19.08%	16.63%	16.80%	20.54%
Finance, Insurance, and Real Estate	7.26%	5.97%	5.36%	8.76%
Business and Repair Services	8.37%	10.98%	9.93%	7.72%
Personal Services	3.37%	6.21%	1.85%	6.02%
Entertainment and Recreational Services	1.64%	1.43%	1.63%	1.58%
Professional and Related Services	19.13%	20.53%	9.56%	29.66%
Public Administration	0.34%	0.40%	0.23%	0.48%
Female	48.41%	51.07%	17.54%	19.14%
Married (Nonwhite)	64.94%	41.61%	60.55%	60.77%
Urban Resident	76.37%	85.44%	77.67%	78.42%
Hours of Work	40.56	40.10	44.63	36.14
Union Coverage	12.46%	16.07%	16.40%	9.69%
Number of Children	1.333	1.416	1.182	1.522
Child Under 6 Years of Age	31.32%	21.96%	30.75%	28.41%
Year = 1996 (1, 0 otherwise)	52.98%	51.23%	53.48%	51.80%
Number of Observations	5,604	1,257	3,506	3,355

$11.40). Examined differently, nonwhites earn 76 percent of the average white wage among those not paid by piece rates or commissions but 86 percent of the average white wage among those paid piece rates or commissions. These raw averages are suggestive of lower racial earnings differentials in the face of performance pay.

Furthermore, while those paid bonuses earn more than those who do not, the racial pattern is reversed from that just isolated. Nonwhites earn 81 percent of whites among those not receiving bonuses ($13.95 versus $11.10) but only 73 percent of white earnings among those receiving bonuses ($21.00 versus 15.39). As most individual bonuses are dependent on a subjective supervisory evaluation (Geddes and Heywood, 2003), this raw difference fits the suggestion that the objectivity of the payment scheme influences the racial earnings pattern: the smallest racial difference among those paid piece rates and commissions and the largest among those receiving bonuses with an intermediate difference among those paid time rates.

Following traditional estimates of earnings differentials, a wide variety of demographic and human capital variables will be used as explanatory controls. These include race and gender, marital status, union status, education, tenure with the firm, experience and experience squared, number of children at home in the household, an indicator if a young child is in the household, urban residency, and the average hours per week worked over the previous year. In addition, we include the Armed Forces Qualification Test (AFQT) percentile score. To further control for firm characteristics, four additional categorical variables measure firm size, two shift variables are included and one-digit occupation and industry controls are included as well. As shown in table 9.1, whites are more likely to be professionals, to be married, have fewer children, more education, tenure, and higher AFQT scores. Also, males are more likely to be in craft and operative occupations, have longer tenures, and work in the manufacturing and transportation industries. As a consequence, including the controls should lower the estimated racial earnings gap.

Initial Estimates

This section presents estimates of log earnings equations including the long list of variables detailed above as well as a year dummy to capture the difference between waves. In each case the interesting issue is the exploration of the adjusted earnings gaps analogous to the raw differences presented in the last section. Table 9.2 (see p. 196) presents estimations on four subsamples: for those on piece rates or commissions and those not, as well as for whites and nonwhites. The results of the controls present few surprises, with the majority of coefficients taking the expected sign, size, and significance. The critical variables are presented at the top of the table.

As can be seen the coefficients on the nonwhite dummy take opposite signs in the two different payment scheme estimations. The coefficient is positive but not statistically significant among those paid by piece rates or commissions, suggesting no evidence of a racial earnings gap among these workers. The coefficient is negative and statistically different from zero at any conventional test among those not paid piece rates or commissions. Thus, even after controlling for a very substantial list of explanatory variables, nonwhites earn about 4 percent less than whites among those paid time rates but no difference can be identified among those paid piece rates or commissions.

This pattern is further supported by the differing influence of performance pay across the racial groups. Those receiving piece rates or commissions earn more than their equivalents earning time rates for both racial groups.[9] Yet, the coefficients indicate a substantial difference in the size of that effect. The point estimate indicates a 9.0 percent increase in earnings associated with piece rates and commissions for whites but a nearly half again as large return of 13.1 percent for blacks.

The racial earnings gap estimated across the broad group of occupations may, however, be misleading. In many occupations there is virtually no use of piece rates or commissions. This raises the possibility that the role attributed to payment schemes may be a function of unmeasured differences across occupations. Thus, the occupations with piece rates and commissions could have lower earnings dispersion including lower racial differences and this would be inappropriately attributed to the differential use of payment schemes. This is examined by limiting attention to the occupational categories in which piece rates and commissions are relatively common: operatives, laborers, craft workers, and sales workers. This reduces the sample size but should also provide an additional control as the extent of differences among workers and jobs is now more limited. The set of estimates from table 9.2 are reestimated using the identical specification except that the occupational dummies are now reduced by the excluded occupations. Table 9.3 shows that despite a sample size one-third of the original, the results remain. Indeed, they appear even more convincing. Again, there is no indication of a racial earnings gap among those paid piece rates or commissions and the race coefficient still remains positive. Among those paid time rates, there exists a highly significant earnings difference of more than 8.3 percent. Again, this is confirmed by different returns to piece rates and commissions by race. The return for whites is now only a small fraction of that for nonwhites but remains weakly significant. Piece rates and commissions for nonwhites are associated with a large earnings increase of 18.9 percent.

Table 9.2 Log Wage Equations by Race and Payment Method

	(1) Piece Rates or Commissions	(2) No Piece Rates or Commissions	(3) Whites	(4) Nonwhites
Piece Rates	—	—	0.086 (3.84)**	0.123 (2.47)*
Nonwhite	0.028 (0.50)	−0.038 (2.53)*	—	—
Female	−0.311 (5.15)**	−0.207 (16.08)**	−0.235 (16.45)**	−0.145 (5.22)**
Tenure	0.691 (4.32)**	0.424 (12.68)**	0.421 (11.35)**	0.501 (6.92)**
Tenuresq	−0.031 (3.22)**	−0.015 (7.79)**	−0.015 (7.10)**	−0.018 (4.07)**
Exper	1.281 (2.27)*	−0.163 (1.53)	0.094 (0.75)	−0.352 (1.56)
Expsq	−3.711 (2.23)*	0.578 (1.87)	−0.221 (0.60)	1.206 (1.92)
AFQT SCORE	0.004 (3.18)**	0.003 (12.14)**	0.003 (10.26)**	0.005 (8.19)**
Highest Grade	0.062 (3.34)**	0.049 (11.72)**	0.0520 (10.97)**	0.050 (5.76)**
Small Firm	0.048 (0.42)	−0.134 (8.14)**	−0.137 (7.10)**	−0.095 (2.96)**
Medium Firm	0.179 (1.40)	−0.071 (3.88)**	−0.078 (3.68)**	−0.021 (0.58)
Large Firm	0.041 (0.24)	−0.002 (0.08)	−0.009 (0.30)	0.001 (0.02)

(continued)

Table 9.2 (*continued*)

	(1) Piece Rates or Commissions	(2) No Piece Rates or Commissions	(3) Whites	(4) Nonwhites
Main Shift	0.099 (1.52)	0.047 (2.39)*	0.056 (2.71)**	0.004 (0.08)
Off Shift	0.056 (0.52)	0.008 (0.37)	-0.007 (0.28)	0.055 (1.12)
Married	0.022 (0.30)	.064 (5.11)**	0.055 (3.93)**	0.113 (4.37)**
Union cov	0.104 (1.25)	0.158 (9.70)**	0.168 (9.02)**	0.116 (3.64)**
Urban	0.168 (2.66)**	0.134 (10.26)**	0.134 (9.50)**	0.161 (4.85)**
Hrswk	0.002 (1.00)	-0.001 (2.10)*	0.000 (0.68)	-0.003 (2.75)**
Numchd	0.008 (0.32)	-0.012 (2.31)*	-0.011 (1.78)	-0.020 (2.09)*
Youngkid	0.023 (0.36)	0.079 (5.84)**	0.073 (4.91)**	0.093 (3.02)**
Yr_1996	-0.127 (2.40)*	-0.074 (6.42)**	-0.080 (6.26)**	-0.073 (2.95)**
Occupations	YES	YES	YES	YES
Industries	YES	YES	YES	YES
Constant	-0.245 (0.39)	1.724 (13.39)**	1.506 (10.13)**	1.713 (6.40)**
Observations	540	6,321	5,604	1,257
R-squared	0.40	0.50	0.48	0.51

Note: The absolute values of t-statistics are in parentheses.   *Significant at 5 percent level   **Significant at 1 percent level.

Table 9.3 Log Wage Equation with Sample Limited to Sales, Craft, Laborer, and Operative Occupations

	Nonwhite Coefficients		Piece Rate Coefficients	
	(1) Piece Rates	(2) No Piece Rates	(3) Whites	(4) Non- whites
	0.056	−0.080	0.055	0.173
	(0.55)	(3.60) **	(1.91)	(2.74) **
Observations	327	2,148	1,977	498
R-squared	0.38	0.44	0.38	0.50

Note: The absolute values of t-statistics are in parentheses. Each regression includes the full set of controls as indicated in table 9.2. **significant at 1 percent level.

While the connection between gender and performance pay is complicated (Goldin, 1986), it is valuable to risk the consequences of yet further reducing sample size to examine separate estimates for men and women. Table 9.4 shows the influence of piece rates and commissions by race and gender. The results show that the previous pattern does not seem to be gender specific. For both men and women, the return to being paid piece rates or commissions is greater for nonwhites than for whites. Interestingly, the return for white women is essentially zero, confirming Parent (1999).[10]

Table 9.4 Piece Rate and Commission Coefficients by Race and Gender with the Sample Limited to Sales, Craft, Laborer, and Operative Occupations

	(1) White Men	(2) Nonwhite Men	(3) White Women	(4) Nonwhite Women
Piece Rate	0.082	0.164	−0.047	0.224
	(2.42) *	(2.10) *	(0.87)	(2.34) *
Observations	1,479	359	498	139
R-squared	0.36	0.49	0.43	0.66

Note: The absolute values of t-statistics are in parentheses. Each regression includes the full set of controls as indicated in table 9.2. *significant at 5 percent level.

Table 9.5 Nonwhite Coefficient from a Subsample Limited to
Professional and Managerial Occupations

	(1) Bonus Pay	(2) No Bonus Pay
Nonwhite	−0.121	−0.030
	(2.02) *	(0.84)
Observations	568	1,848
R-squared	0.51	0.32

Notes: The absolute values of t-statistics are in parentheses. Each regression includes the full set of controls as indicated in table 9.2. *significant at 5 percent level.

In comparison to piece rates and commissions, bonuses are thought to be a more subjective form of compensation than hourly or salary compensation; therefore, one would expect to see higher racial wage differentials among those paid bonuses relative to those who strictly receive hourly or salary compensation. Also, as previously mentioned, bonuses tend to be concentrated among professional and managerial occupations. Limiting the sample to those paid bonuses among professional and managerial occupations reveals higher racial wage differentials than those paid hourly or salary. As shown in table 9.5, the race coefficient for the log wage equation changes from −0.12 for those whose pay is partially received in the form of bonuses to −0.03 for those whose pay is strictly either hourly or salary. Therefore, nonwhites appear to receive lower pay if a portion of their pay is in the form of bonuses.

Additional Estimation

This section considers two interrelated estimation difficulties: sample selection and individual fixed effects. At issue is the possibility that the influence attributed to piece rates and commissions is a function of sorting across unmeasured variables correlated with race. Such a possibility might well flow from the theoretical conjectures given above. First, it is well recognized that payment schemes that reward productivity not only elicit additional productivity from existing workers but also tend to attract the inherently more productive. Indeed, Lazear (2000) suggests that 44 percent of the increase in productivity associated with starting a piece rate scheme results from increasing the productivity of existing workers and the remainder is associated with attracting inherently more productive workers. Moreover, if the gap in the reward for productivity between piece rates and time rates is larger for nonwhites, as the theory implies, the extent of sorting may differ between races. In short, piece rates and commissions may attract a relatively more productive group of nonwhites, a productivity not controlled for by the explanatory variables.

Therefore, two estimations that control for fixed effects are run. The estimations are designed to hold constant the productivity of each worker and so control for the anticipated sorting. The first estimation accounts for fixed effects by adding separate indicator variables for each worker. The estimate is then generated on the intraworker variation across the two waves. While small numbers limit the efficiency of the estimation, the basic results remain supportive of the notion that racial discrimination is reduced among those paid piece rates and commissions. Obviously, race does not change so the racial indicator drops out of the estimation, along with all variables constant over time. Nonetheless, the fixed effect estimate allows separate estimates of the return to piece rates by race. As shown in the top panel of table 9.6, the coefficients remain positive but that for whites falls far short of significance. The size of the coefficient for nonwhites is many times larger than that for whites and is statistically significant. The fixed effect estimate indicates a return substantially larger than the comparable estimate that did not control for fixed effects (0.123 without fixed effects and 0.164 with fixed effects). While the results shown are for an unbalanced panel, they are exactly mimicked by the results from a balanced panel of workers observed in both years.[11]

Also examined is a change equation in which the changes in the variables difference out fixed effects associated with those earning piece rates. The coefficient on piece rates is estimated on those who change between time rates and piece rates.[12] The results, as shown in table 9.6, are broadly similar to those already reported. The coefficient on the change in piece rates is positive for both white and nonwhite workers but much larger for nonwhites and significant only for nonwhites. Thus, the fixed effect estimates are broadly supportive of the notion that nonwhites gain more from being paid piece rates and commissions. The effect identified in the cross-sections does not seem to flow from differential ability sorting by race. If anything the estimates suggest that sorting may be more pronounced for whites. As a consequence, the larger gain for nonwhites associated with receiving piece rates and commissions results in reduced racial earnings differentials.

Table 9.6 Piece Rate and Commission Coefficients from Fixed Effects Models and Change Equations

	(1) White	(2) Nonwhite
Fixed Effect Model		
Piece Rate and Commission Coefficient	0.012	0.165
	(0.46)	(2.55) **
Observations	5,604	1,257
R-squared	0.16	0.24
Change Equation		
Δ in Piece Rate or Commissions	0.011	0.164
	(0.41)	(2.53) **
Observations	2,314	510
R-squared	0.09	0.18

Note: The absolute values of t-statistics are in parentheses. The results in the top panel are from the corrected unbalanced panel estimates and include the full set of controls as indicated in table 9.2. The estimates in the second panel include a full set of change variables as described in the text including those associated with the vector of industry and occupational controls. **significant at 1 percent level.

In addition to these attempts to hold constant fixed effects, another alternative is to estimate a sample selection model assuming that the choice of piece rate or hourly wage is not random. If there are excluded determinants of this choice correlated with earnings, it is possible that the coefficients on the critical earnings determinants such as race are biased. Following Heckman (1978) a first stage estimates the probability of being paid piece rates. This estimation is identified by using the two-digit occupational dummies. There is modest evidence that nonwhites are less likely to be paid piece rates. From this estimate the inverse Mills ratio (IMR) is added to the two earnings equations estimated separately by payment method. The IMR is statistically significant in the time payment wage equation but not in the piece rate and commission equation.

Table 9.7 summarizes the critical result on race. It also presents the now familiar pattern that nonwhites do not receive lower earnings when paid by piece rates or commissions. Moreover, it remains the case that nonwhites do receive lower earnings when paid by time. In particular the point estimate for nonwhites in the piece rate and commission equation

Table 9.7	Selection Corrected Estimates

	Piece Rate and Commission	Time Rates
Full Sample		
Nonwhite	0.0364	−0.0400
	(0.499)	(2.624) **
IMR	0.0211	0.3396
	(0.188)	(2.527) **
Chi-squared	504.4**	6325.7**
N	540	6,321
Reelevant Occupations		
Nonwhite	0.0408	−0.0675 **
	(0.417)	(2.923)
IMR	0.1639	0.2338 **
	(1.094)	(3.237)
Chi-squared	271.9**	1672.7**
N	327	2,148

Note: The absolute values of t-statistics are in parentheses. **significant at 1 percent level.

is actually positive but not significant, while that in the time rate equation indicates nonwhites earn 4 percent less. Despite the importance of correcting for sample selection, these estimates are virtually unchanged from those in columns (1) and (2) of table 9.2 that failed to make such a correction.

Conclusion

Firms operating in competitive product markets are more likely to utilize output-based payment methods such as piece rates and commissions. A critical consequence of the increased propensity to utilize output-based payment methods is the reduced racial wage differential. The racial wage differential is reduced for those paid piece rates or commissions and increased for those paid bonuses. This is due to the higher psychic costs managers or supervisors encounter while practicing discrimination in the presence of piece rates or commissions when output can be objectively measured. Therefore, managers or supervisors find it much more difficult to include other criteria such as race in their employee evaluations if part of the pay scheme includes piece rates or commissions, which are more likely to be employed if product markets are competitive. Furthermore, if part of an individual's pay is in the form of bonuses that are typically thought to be more at the supervisors' or managers' discretion, then the costs associated with including other criteria such as race will be lower. Therefore, managers and supervisors may be more inclined to judge employees based on race rather than productivity when evaluating performance.

Although the prevalence of piece rates and commissions are limited, measured racial earnings discrimination among those paid piece rates or commissions is reduced in comparison to those who do not receive any piece rate or commission pay. Also, for those more numerous individuals receiving some compensation based on bonuses, measured racial earnings differentials are larger in comparison to those who do not receive any bonus pay. Therefore, one would expect to see nonwhites attracted to occupations in which piece rates or commissions are heavily utilized and repelled from occupations in which bonuses are common components of total compensation.

Notes

1. Strong independent worker organizations may also restrict the amount of supervisor favoritism. Freeman and Lazear (1995) identify the codetermination associated with European works councils as playing such a role and strong unions in the United States may be similar.

2. Obviously output-based pay may not capture the full productivity of each worker. For example, if workers help one another or undertake productive activity not reflected in the simple number of pieces, the counted number of pieces is misleading. Yet, Drago and Garvey (1998) suggest "helping effort" is reduced in the face of individual-based incentives and, ultimately, the point regarding discrimination is not the accuracy of the piece rate but its influence on racial differentials.

3. This model is an adaptation of the model developed by Kenneth J. Arrow (1973).

4. The internal psychic cost might be viewed as a sort of cognitive dissonance in which the supervisor wishes to discriminate but not be perceived as a discriminator.

5. This condition is a specific realization of the assumption that the firm would hire randomly between blacks and whites thereby matching their proportions in the workforce at large.

6. Thus, the supply schedules would be $r_w = kW^\phi$ and $r_B = kW^\phi$.

7. For related work that also adds the 2000 wave, see Heywood and O'Halloran (2005).

8. Additional categories include stock options, tips, and other performance-related compensations.

9. While earlier studies do not break out the influence of piece rates and commissions by race, those paid by piece rates earn more, all else equal (see Brown, 1992; Ewing, 1996; Parent, 1999; Seiler, 1984). While a portion of this increase is due to sorting of more productive workers into piece rate jobs, a portion is also due to an increase in productivity from existing workers (Lazear, 2000).

10. Parent (1999) finds a positive effect for piece rates among women only when interacting the presence of piece rates with that of dependents. He does not examine racial differences among women.

11. When further limited to the occupational subsample of those in sales, craft, laborer, and operative occupations, the coefficient for nonwhites remains much larger than for whites but both fail to reach significance. In the balanced panel there are only two hundred black workers who are observed in this subsample in both waves.

12. The assumption is that the earnings magnitude of moving from piece rates to time rates is equal but opposite in sign to that from moving from time to piece rates.

References

Alchian, Armen, and Harold Demsetz. "Production, Information and Economic Organization." *American Economic Review* 62 (1972): 777–95.

Arrow, Kenneth J. "The Theory of Discrimination." In *Discrimination in Labor Markets*, ed. Orley Ashenfelter and Albert Rees. Princeton, NJ: Princeton University Press. 1973.

Ashenfelter, Orley, and Timothy Hannan. "Sex Discrimination and Product Market Competition: The Case of the Banking Industry." *Quarterly Journal of Economics* 101 (1986): 149–73

Baker, George, Robert Gibbons, and Kevin Murphy. "Compensation and Incentives: Practice vs. Theory." *Journal of Finance* 18 (1988): 593–616.

———. "Subjective Performance Measures in Optimal Incentive Contracts." *Quarterly Journal of Economics* 109 (1994): 1125–56.

Barbezat, Debra, and James W. Hughes. "Sex Discrimination in the Labor Market: The Role of Statistical Evidence: Comment." *American Economic Review* 90 (1990): 279–86.

Becker, Gary S. 1957. *The Economics of Discrimination*. Chicago: University of Chicago Press.

Belman, Dale, and John S. Heywood. "Incentive Schemes and Racial Wage Discrimination." *Review of Black Political Economy* 17 (1988): 47–56.

Bertrand, Marianne. "From Invisible Handshake to the Invisible Hand? How Import Competition Changes the Employment Relationship." NBER Working Paper 6900, January, 1999.

Bertrand, Marianne, and Sendhil Mullainathan. "Is There Discretion in Wage Setting? A Test Using Takeover Legislation." *Rand Journal of Economics* 30 (1999): 535–54.

Brown, Charles. "Firms' Choice of Method of Pay." *Industrial and Labor Relations Review* 43 (1990): 165–82.

———. "Wage Levels and Methods of Pay." *Rand Journal* 23 (1992): 366–77

Burgess, Simon, and Paul Metcalfe. "Incentive Pay and Product Market Competition." CMPO Working Paper 00/28, 2000.

Drago, Robert, and Gerald Garvey. "Incentives for Helping on the Job: Theory and Evidence." *Journal of Labor Economics* 16 (1998): 1–25.

Drago, Robert, and John S. Heywood. "The Choice of Payment Schemes: Australian Establishment Data." *Industrial Relations* 34 (1995): 507–32.

Elvira, Marta, and Robert Town. "The Effects of Race and Worker Productivity on Performance Evaluations." *Industrial Relations* 40 (2001): 571–90.

Ewing, Bradley T. "Wages and Performance-Based Pay: Evidence from the NLSY." *Economics Letters* 51 (1996): 241–46.

Freeman, Richard, and Edward Lazear. "An Economic Analysis of Works Councils." In *Works Councils: Consultation, Representation and Co-operation in Industrial Relations*, ed. Joel Rogers and Walter Streck, 36–52. Chicago: University of Chicago Press, 1995.

Geddes, Lori, and John S. Heywood. "Gender and Piece Rates, Commissions and Bonuses." *Industrial Relations* 42 (2003): 419–44.

Goldin, Claudia. "Monitoring Costs and Occupational Segregation by Sex: A Historical Analysis." *Journal of Labor Economics* 4 (1986): 1–27.

Gunderson, Morely. "Male–Female Wage Differentials and the Impact of Equal Pay Legislation." *Review of Economics and Statistics* 57 (1975): 462–69.

Heckman, James J. "Sample Selection Bias as a Specification Error." *Econometrica* 47 (1978): 153–62.

Hellerstein, Judith, David Neumark, and Kenneth R. Troske. "Market Forces and Sex Discrimination." *Journal of Human Resources* 37 (2002): 353–80.

Heywood, John S. "Regulated Industries and Measures of Earnings Discrimination." In *Regulatory Reform and Labor Markets*, ed. J. Peoples, 297–324. Norwell, MA: Kluwer, 1998.

Heywood, John S., and Uwe Jirjahn. "Payment Schemes and Gender in Germany." *Industrial and Labor Relations Review* 56 (2002): 44–64.

Heywood, John S., and Patrick L. O'Halloran. "Racial Earnings Differentials and Performance Pay." *Journal of Human Resources* 40 (2005): 435–53.

Heywood, John S., and James Peoples. "Deregulation and the Prevalence of Black Truck Drivers," *Journal of Law and Economics* 37 (1994): 133–55.

Jirjahn, Uwe, and Gesine Stephan. "Gender, Piece Rates and Wages: Evidence from Matched Employer–Employee Data." *Cambridge Journal of Economics* 28 (2004: 683–704.

Lazear, Edward P. "Salaries and Piece Rates." *Journal of Business* 59 (1986): 405–31.

———. "Performance Pay and Productivity." *American Economic Review* 90 (2000): 1346–61.

MacLeod, W. Bentley, and Daniel Parent. "Job Characteristics and the Form of Compensation." In *Research in Labor Economics* 18, ed. S. Polachek, 177–242. Greenwich, CT: JAI Press, 1999.

Moulton, Brent. "An Illustration of a Pitfall in Estimating the Effects of Aggregate Variables on Micro Unit Observations." *Review of Economics and Statistics* 72 (1990): 334–38.

Parent, Daniel. "Methods of Pay and Earnings: A Longitudinal Analysis." *Industrial and Labor Relations Review* 53 (1999): 71–86.

———. "Incentive Pay in the United States: Its Determinants and Its Effects." In *Paying for Performance: An International Comparison*, ed. Michelle Brown and John S. Heywood, 17–51. Armonk, NY: M. E. Sharpe Press, 2002.

Peoples, James. "Monopolistic Market Structure, Unionization and Racial Wage Differentials." *Review of Economics and Statistics* 76 (1994): 207-11.

Prendergast, Cynthia, and Robert Topel. "Favoritism in Organizations." *Journal of Political Economy* 104 (1996): 958–78.

Seiler, Eric. "Piece Rates vs. Time Rates." *Review of Economics and Statistics* 66 (1984): 363–76.

Silberberg, Eugene. *The Structure of Economics: A Mathematical Analysis*, 2nd ed. New York: McGraw-Hill, 1990.

Contributors

Jacqueline Agesa is an associate professor of economics at Marshall University. She received her Ph.D. from the University of Wisconsin–Milwaukee. Her research has been funded by the Ford Foundation and the National Science Foundation. Current research areas include applied industrial organization and issues of gender in developing countries. Her work has appeared in the *American Economic Review* Papers and Proceedings, the *Journal of Development Studies*, the *Journal of Policy Analysis and Management*, the *Southern Economic Journal*, *Social Science Quarterly*, the *Review of Black Political Economy*, and other scholarly outlets.

Marjorie L. Baldwin is a professor in the School of Health Administration and Policy at Arizona State University and director of the Division of Health Administration and Policy in the Mel and Enid Zuckerman Arizona College of Public Health. A health economist, her research focuses on work disability, disability-related discrimination, and the costs and outcomes of work-related injuries. She was a coinvestigator for the Zenith Project, a comprehensive study of the medical care costs of work-related injuries; a principal investigator for a three-state study of managed care's impact on workers' compensation costs; and is currently a principal investigator for the ASU Healthy Back Study, the largest prospective study of work-related back injuries ever conducted in the United States. Her current research focuses on the labor market experiences of persons with serious mental disorders. Professor Baldwin is a member of the National Academy of Social Insurance. She received her Ph.D. from the Maxwell School at Syracuse University.

Clive Belfield is associate director of the National Center for the Study of Privatization in Education at Teachers College, Columbia University, and a faculty member of the Department of Economics at Queens College of the City University of New York. His research interests are in the fields of labor economics and the economics of education. His most recent publications include work on unions and employment growth (*Industrial Relations*, 2004), the economics of curriculum mandates (*Economics of Education Review*, 2004), the role of the family in educational achievement (*UCLA Law Review*, 2002), and the impact of market competition on schooling outcomes (*Review of Educational Research*, 2002).

Kaye Husbands Fealing received her Ph.D. from Harvard University and is the William Brough Professor of Economics at Williams College. Dr. Husbands Fealing's areas of expertise include global competitive strategies, microeconomics, industrial organization, the Pacific Rim, and regulation. As a visiting scholar at MIT's Center for Technology Policy and Industrial Development, she conducted research on NAFTA's effect on the Mexican and Canadian automotive industries, and on strategic alliances between aircraft contractors and their subcontractors. The author of the book *Strategic Adjustment of Price by Japanese and American Automobile Manufacturers*, she has written numerous book chapters. She has consulted or conducted research in the following areas: peak-load pricing models for regulating electricity usage, comparative efficiencies of the Food Stamp and AFDC programs, and efficiency and equity differences between two-part and fixed-rate tariffs. She also served on the board and as president of the National Economic Association.

John S. Heywood is professor of economics and director of the graduate program in human resources and labor relations at the University of Wisconsin–Milwaukee. The author of more than seven dozen articles, his work appears in the *Journal of Political Economy, the Review of Economics and Statistics*, the *Journal of Public Economics*, and the *Journal of Human Resources*. He has held appointments in the United Kingdom, Germany, Australia, and Hong Kong.

Uwe Jirjahn earned his Ph.D. in economics from the University of Hannover and currently teaches economics at the Institute for Quantitative Economics in Hannover Germany. His research interests include labor economics, personnel economics, and industrial organization. He has published his research in the *Scandinavian Journal of Economics, Journal of Economic Behavior and Organization, Industrial and Labor Relations Review,* and the *Cambridge Journal of Economics,* among other journals.

Kristen Monaco is a professor of economics at California State University–Long Beach. Her research focuses on the relationship between market conditions and labor market outcomes, with a particular focus on the trucking industry. Her work has appeared in *Economic Inquiry,* the *Southern Economic Journal,* and *Industrial and Labor Relations Review,* among other journals. Her current major project investigates the labor market conditions of truck drivers at major West Coast ports.

Patrick L. O'Halloran serves as an assistant professor in the Department of Economics and Finance at Monmouth University where he teaches labor economics and economic principles. His research interests include issues of racial discrimination, the determinants of job training, and the labor market for physicians. He is the author of an article in the *Journal of Human Resources* and is currently writing on the relationship between performance pay and promotions within workplaces.

James H. Peoples is professor of economics at the University of Wisconsin–Milwaukee. He is a Ford Foundation Fellow and board member of the National Economics Association. His areas of specialty are applied microeconomics and labor economics. His articles have appeared in the *Journal of Economics Perspectives,* the *Review of Economics and Statistics,* and the *Journal of Regulatory Economics,* as well as other journals. He is the editor of *Regulatory Reform and Labor Markets* and coauthor of *Microeconomic Problems,* with Edwin Mansfield.

Gesine Stephan earned her Ph.D. in economics from the University of Hannover. She is currently head of the Labor Market Policy Research Section at the Institute for Employment Research (Nuremberg, Germany). Her research concentrates on empirical labor economics. Among other journals she has published in *Economics Letters, Labour,* and the *Cambridge Journal of Economics.*

Wayne K. Talley is the Frederick W. Beazley Professor of Economics at Old Dominion University and executive director of the International Maritime, Ports and Logistics Management Institute. An internationally recognized maritime transportation economist, he has published 4 books and over 120 papers. He has held visiting positions at the Marine Policy Center of Woods Hole Oceanographic Institution, the U.S. Department of Transportation, the Interstate Commerce Commission, the National Aeronautics and Space Administration, the Transport Studies Unit at the University of Oxford, the Institute of Transport Studies at the University of Sydney, and the Centre for Transport Policy Analysis at the University of Wollongong, the University of Antwerp, and the Centre for Shipping, Trade and Finance, City University of London. He is editor in chief of *Transportation Research E: Logistics and Transportation Review,* a member of two other editorial boards, and previous general editor of the *Journal of the Transportation Research Forum.* He has served on committees of the Transportation Research Board and U.S. National Research Council and as a member of the Council of the International Association of Maritime Economists.

Xiangdong Wei is a professor of economics, Lingnan University, Hong Kong, an adjunct professor of economics in Lingnan (University) College, Zhongshan University in China, and Honorary Research Fellow in business at the University of Birmingham. He held a previous permanent position at the Royal Holloway College of the University of London and has been a visiting researcher at Indiana University and Purdue University at Indianapolis and the University of Wisconsin–Milwaukee. His research areas are personnel economics, the economics of education, compensating wage differentials, and workplace safety policy and he has a special interest in the Chinese and Hong Kong economy. He has published over a dozen papers in outlets such as the *Journal of Risk and Uncertainty, Economics Letters, British Journal of Industrial Relations, Journal of Comparative Economics, Industrial and Labor Relations Review,* and the *Southern Economic Journal* and has served as a consultant to both the United Kingdom and Hong Kong governments.

Index